P9-BZA-931

friendly Schools PLUS

Whole-School Strategies to Enhance Students' Social Skills and Reduce Bullying in Schools

DONNA **CROSS**
SHANE **THOMPSON**
ERIN **ERCEG**

Solution Tree | Press

a division of
Solution Tree

Republished in the United States by Solution Tree Press

All rights reserved.

555 North Morton Street
Bloomington, IN 47404
800.733.6786 (toll free) / 812.336.7700
FAX: 812.336.7790
email: info@solution-tree.com
solution-tree.com

Visit **go.solution-tree.com/behavior** to download the reproducibles in this book.

Printed in the United States of America

18 17 16 15 14   1 2 3 4 5

Library of Congress Cataloging-in-Publication Data

Cross, Donna, 1960-
  Friendly schools plus evidence for practice : whole-school strategies to enhance students' social skills and reduce bullying in schools / Donna Cross, Shane Thompson, Erin Erceg.
    pages cm.
  Includes bibliographical references.
  ISBN 978-1-936763-18-4 (perfect bound) 1. Bullying in schools--Australia--Prevention. 2. Conflict management--Study and teaching--Australia. I. Thompson, Shane, 1954- II. Erceg, Erin, 1964- III. Title.
  LB3013.34.A8C76 2014
  371.7'820994--dc23
                        2014019695

Solution Tree
Jeffrey C. Jones, CEO
Edmund M. Ackerman, President

Solution Tree Press
President: Douglas M. Rife
Editorial Director: Lesley Bolton
Managing Production Editor: Caroline Weiss
Production Editor: Tara Perkins
Proofreader: Elisabeth Abrams
Cover Designer and Compositor: Rian Anderson
Text Compositor: Rachel Smith

Authors
Professor Donna Cross, Shane Thompson, and Erin Erceg

Contributors
Dr. Natasha Pearce, Associate Professor Stacey Waters, Melanie Epstein, Kate Hadwen, Sarah Falconer, Helen Monks, Dr. Laura Thomas, Amy Barnes, Elizabeth Alderman, Dr. Juli Coffin, Dr. Julian Dooley, Associate Professor Margaret Hall, Dr. Yolanda Trigger, and Samuel Cecins

Published in Australia by Hawker Brownlow Education

Acknowledgments

The Child Health Promotion Research Centre, at Edith Cowan University, Western Australia, would like to thank its current and past staff who have contributed to the development of this resource, either directly or through their involvement in the original research projects.

The Friendly Schools Plus cluster of research used to inform the development of these resources was conducted at Curtin University of Technology between 1999 and 2002 and Edith Cowan University from 2003 to 2012.

We acknowledge and thank the Western Australian Health Promotion Foundation (Healthway) for providing significant funding to support the Friendly Schools research conducted from 1999 to 2012.

Table of Contents

Visit **go.solution-tree.com/behavior** to download the reproducibles in this book.

Introduction

While bullying behavior in schools is widespread and harmful, research conducted at the Child Health Promotion Research Centre (CHPRC) at Edith Cowan University and elsewhere (Baldry & Farrington, 2007; Smith, Schneider, Smith, & Ananiadou, 2004; Vreeman & Carroll, 2007) suggests bullying behavior can be reduced. The CHPRC research team's ongoing research, conducted since 1999 via eleven large empirical studies involving more than 27,000 Australian school-age students, has focused primarily on what schools can do to effectively prevent and reduce bullying behavior.

One of the most effective means to reduce bullying among young people is to enhance their social and emotional understandings and competencies in developmentally appropriate ways throughout their schooling, using a whole-school approach. Friendly Schools Plus addresses the social and emotional learning of young people, both formally through explicit classroom pedagogy and learning strategies and informally through the development of a whole-school culture, organization, and structures that reinforce and uphold these essential understandings, skills, and competencies.

The Friendly Schools Plus initiative is a strengths-based, whole-school participatory process that enables schools to determine their needs and implement current and robust evidence-based policy and practice to enhance students' social and emotional learning and reduce bullying. In particular, *Friendly Schools Plus Evidence for Practice* provides toolkits to assess and augment school staff capacity to recognize, develop, and sustain those components of a whole-school approach that support their students' unique social and emotional learning and foster the prevention of bullying behavior.

Research Supporting Friendly Schools Plus

The Friendly Schools Plus program is based on eleven major research projects conducted since 1999 involving more than 27,000 Australian school-age students from kindergarten to grade 10. This research has focused critically on understanding student bullying behavior and seeking relevant and practical outcomes, while informing Australian and international policy and practices. It is recognized in Australia and internationally as a successful whole-school evidence-based bullying prevention program.

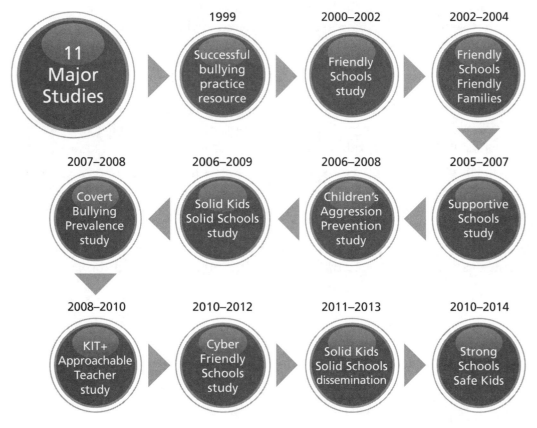

Figure 1: Bullying-related research 1999–2014.

CHPRC research studies have identified ways to strengthen whole-school approaches to reduce all forms of bullying (including cyberbullying) in primary through secondary schools, bullying in Aboriginal contexts, and the prevention of early childhood aggression. These projects have reduced intentional harm from bullying among children and adolescents and raised awareness of the impact that peers, families, schools, and communities can have in preventing bullying behavior.

The Friendly Schools Plus research began in 1999. The first study, a formative review of research, provided a significant summary of evidence-based findings from international bullying-related research, validated by experts from around the world. These findings were synthesized and operationalized into the primary-school-based program, Friendly Schools. The Friendly Schools resource was rigorously tested as part of a randomized control trial (2000–2002) with a cohort of approximately two thousand fourth-grade students and their teachers and parents tracked for three years. Fourth graders were targeted initially, as more Australian children bully and are bullied in the fifth and sixth grades than any other age at school. The Friendly Schools study aimed to ameliorate the increase in bullying behavior at this age. The results from this study were positive (Cross, Monks, Hall, et al., 2011), but further research was needed to understand how to reduce the high levels of bullying in primary school children.

The follow-up three-year study, Friendly Schools Friendly Families (2002–2004), involved a randomized control trial of more than four thousand students, comprising second-, fourth-, and sixth-grade students as well as their teachers and parents. The results showed a significant reduction in bullying among the students who received the intervention (Cross et al., n.d.; Cross et al., 2012).

From 2005 to 2007, the CHPRC's research extended to secondary school students to address the second major increase of bullying behavior that occurred following students' transition from primary to secondary school. This project, Supportive Schools, involved a randomized control trial of a whole-school intervention that provided schools, students, and parents with strategies to help students prevent or deal with the increase in bullying that typically occurs post-transition. Results indicated that this project reduced the mediators associated with bullying among this age group (Cross, Hall, Waters, et al., 2008).

The CHPRC's fourth largest randomized control trial, the Child Aggression Project, began in 2006. This research project followed over two thousand pre-primary school children (and their families) for three years in their schools until they were in second grade. This study was part of a larger international study with the Montreal GRIP Research Unit in Canada, designed to promote supportive school environments and social relationships that limit aggression and disruptive behaviors among children in the early phases of schooling. The results from the Child Aggression Project indicate positive process results and significant interest in these resources from early childhood teachers (Hall, Waters, & Shaw, 2009).

These four large studies recruited insufficient numbers of Aboriginal and Torres Strait Islander children to determine whether mainstream approaches to bullying prevention were effective for these children and adolescents. To address this need, the CHPRC initiated the four-year qualitative Solid Kids, Solid Schools research project in 2006. This research project engaged an Aboriginal steering group and local Yamaji people to help develop and pilot test a variety of resources targeting young people and their teachers, families, and community to reduce the bullying experiences of school-age Aboriginal people. The process data from this research show these resources are well received and used by the Aboriginal community. The Solid Kids, Solid Schools project was extended in 2011 until 2013 to enhance the dissemination and use of this resource in Aboriginal communities.

From 2008 to 2010, the CHPRC conducted a study called Keeping in Touch Plus in conjunction with School Drug Education and Road Aware. This project investigated ways to enhance school teachers' approachability in times of need, as perceived by students. This process evaluation project provided many important insights and strategies to encourage and enable students to seek help in response to a problem they may be experiencing. It also enhanced the capacity of teachers to provide more effective support to these students. These findings were used to improve the support offered by schools when students who are bullied or observe bullying seek adult support.

Since 2007, with the growth of communication technology and the subsequent use of this technology to bully, the CHPRC has received funding to conduct five major formative projects and one summative research project to investigate student cyberbullying. The first of these studies, the Cyberbullying Formative Study, involved focus groups and interviews with several hundred students, parents, and school staff to develop a deeper understanding of the nature and effects of this "new" behavior.

In 2007, the Australian Department of Education, Employment and Workplace Relations funded the Australian Covert Bullying Prevalence Study. This represented the first national prevalence study benchmarking covert bullying in Australia. The study investigated young people's experiences with covert bullying, including the nature and types of covert bullying behaviors used by young people, how often and where these behaviors occur, and risk and protective factors that may inhibit or encourage covert bullying behavior. The study involved triangulation of covert bullying behavior data collected using mixed methods across three separate studies from a total of 20,832 Australian students aged 8–14 from over 200 schools and 456 school staff. Results shed new light on covert bullying, especially cyberbullying among school-age children, identifying effective and sustainable policy and practice (Cross et al., 2009).

In 2008, a follow-up study called the Cyber Leaders Project actively engaged the input of young people to better understand cyberbullying. This study led to the first Australian statewide Student Cyber Leader Summit involving two hundred Western Australian students. This summit has since been replicated with the training of student cyber leaders in Victoria, the Australian capital territory, and South Australia. A further large formative study called the Cyber Friendly Parents Study was funded in 2009 to investigate ways to help parents help their children avoid cyberbullying.

These four formative cyberbullying studies led to the Cyber Friendly Schools Project, the world's first major randomized control trial specifically testing interventions targeting student leaders, teachers, students, and parents to reduce the prevalence of cyberbullying. The cyberbullying strategies included in the Friendly Schools Plus resource are based on promising findings to date from this research. Until the Cyber Friendly Schools Project has concluded, the recommended cyberbullying intervention strategies do not have the same high level of evidence rigor as the previous bullying research conducted by the CHPRC.

Lastly, in 2010 the CHPRC began a five-year study to understand the best ways to enhance the capacity of schools throughout Western Australia to provide quality policy and practice to reduce bullying and other forms of social aggression. This project is called Strong Schools Safe Kids. This research and other new research conducted by the CHPRC will continue to inform the Friendly Schools Plus resources produced by the CHPRC at Edith Cowan University. Go to www.chprc.ecu .edu.au for more information about the CHPRC research.

What Is a Whole-School Approach?

Multicomponent whole-school initiatives involving all members of the school community are more likely to reduce bullying behavior than single-component programs, such as those involving only classroom curriculum (Farrington & Ttofi, 2009).

A whole-school approach, sometimes referred to as a Health-Promoting Schools model, recognizes that all aspects of the school community can promote (or reduce) students' health and well-being and that students' learning and their health are inextricably linked. Given young people spend much of their first seventeen years in a school environment, it is not only the focal point of their academic development but also their social development, where they make friends and develop healthy relationships. Friendly Schools Plus recognizes the importance of a whole-school approach and is organized to provide support to schools, not only through formal classroom teaching and learning, but through all aspects of the whole-school environment. To achieve sustainable behavior change that is integrated, holistic, and strategic, it is necessary to implement a whole-school approach rather than focus only on individual behavior. The essential elements of the Health-Promoting Schools approach include (International Union for Health Promotion and Education [IUHPE], n.d.):

- Healthy school policies
- The schools' physical environment
- The schools' social environment
- Individual health skills and action competencies (through formal teaching and learning)
- Community and family links
- Health services

The multicomponent Friendly Schools Plus program has integrated these components of the Health-Promoting Schools model into a comprehensive whole-school program with an emphasis on:

- Building staff capacity to implement programs to enhance students' relationships and reduce bullying
- Providing policies that shape a respectful, welcoming, and caring school environment
- Building quality relationships between school students and staff
- Maximizing the involvement of family and other members of the community
- Scaffolding students' learning of social and emotional skills, such as self-awareness, self-management, and social awareness
- Enabling students to be advocates for and to encourage positive social interpersonal development behavior online and a targeted behavior offline
- Supporting students who are frequently bullied or helping perpetrators of bullying to change their behavior

Friendly Schools Plus brings together the whole-school community to contribute to the development and ongoing maintenance of the friendly and safe culture of the school.

The Friendly Schools Plus Implementation Model

The Friendly Schools Plus implementation model recognizes that whole-school change is sustained when evidence of good practice aligns with real-world school vision and when practice is supported with sufficient capacity (leadership, organization, competency) to drive an effective implementation process.

Layers of the Model

Evidence for Practice—Whole-School Vision—Sustainability

Whole-school change is sustained when evidence of good practice aligns with real-world school vision and practice.

The evidence for practice to reduce bullying and enhance social and emotional understandings and competencies is provided through the Friendly Schools Plus resources and professional learning. By aligning this current research evidence with the whole-school vision, schools can work toward implementing policies and practices in a coordinated and sustained manner.

Capacity for Implementation—Leadership—Organizational Support—Competencies

Whole-school change is supported with sufficient capacity (leadership, organization, competency).

Chapter 2 will assist schools in building their capacity in the areas of leadership, organizational support, and competencies to support implementation of the Friendly Schools Plus initiative.

The Friendly Schools Plus Process

The Friendly Schools Plus process helps schools review, plan, build capacity, and implement critical evidence-based actions to effectively respond to their strengths and needs in key areas, identified by the research. The following chapters provide more information on the Friendly Schools Plus process.

Schools follow this ongoing process to assess and address these six interrelated key areas:

1. Building capacity
2. Supportive school culture
3. Proactive policies and practices
4. Key understandings and competencies
5. Protective physical environment
6. School–family–community partnerships

Schools are assisted by *Evidence for Practice* to identify evidence-based practices to address their needs and a comprehensive planning tool to guide the planning process toward improvement.

To ensure sustainability of the Friendly Schools Plus initiative, the process must be seen as an ongoing monitoring and review process that supports the implementation of the resources over time.

Friendly Schools Plus Initiative

A multicomponent, evidence-based whole-school initiative involving the whole-school community to build social skills, create supportive environments, and significantly reduce bullying in school communities.

Friendly Schools Plus Resources

- **Planning tool for each key area**
  School teams will conduct their review of current policies and practices, identify their successes and needs, and plan their strategies and actions in each key area. The planning tool is designed for teams to record their planning for future action in each key area.
- *Evidence for Practice* **text and whole-school toolkits**
  A comprehensive book that describes research-based practice approaches that schools can implement to maximize and sustain effective social skill building and bullying prevention strategies.
- **Teacher resource books and teacher toolkits**
  Classroom teacher resource books for students ages four to fourteen and a range of online toolkits to help schools implement the recommended strategies.
- **Website—go.solution-tree.com/behavior**

Steps of the Friendly Schools Plus Process

1. Plan priorities and strategies for school policy and practice.
2. Build collective capability of all staff, through professional learning, to implement whole-school priorities and classroom actions.
3. Use the evidence-based whole-school toolkits from *Evidence for Practice* to respond to identified priorities for positive change.
4. Implement teaching and learning activities from the teacher resource books to develop the social and emotional skills of students, based on their strengths and needs.
5. Review changes in school processes, review teacher practice, and gather evidence of student outcomes to inform future practice.

Getting Started

While the steps for the Friendly Schools Plus whole-school process are numbered, there are multiple entry points for getting started. One school may have made the decision to engage in professional learning to build collective capability to improve whole-school practice. Once this decision has been made, it begins to gather evidence of current practice to inform its actions and priorities. An individual teacher within a school may have purchased and used the teacher resource book in his or her classroom with such positive results that it influences a whole-school initiative. The ultimate goal of the Friendly Schools Plus initiative is to bring together the whole-school community to contribute to the development and ongoing maintenance of the friendly and safe culture of the school.

The Friendly Schools Plus Whole-School Approach Process

The Friendly Schools Plus approach helps schools respond effectively to the social behavior, strengths, and needs of its students while concurrently supporting schools to review, plan, build capacity, and implement critical evidence-based actions to effectively respond to these strengths and needs. This approach is critical for school improvement and long-term planning.

The Friendly Schools Plus process uses a whole-school approach, grounded in quality longitudinal research evidence.

Steps of the Friendly Schools Plus Process

1. Plan priorities and strategies for school policy and practice.
2. Build collective capability of all staff, through professional learning, to implement whole-school priorities and classroom actions.
3. Use the evidence-based whole-school toolkits from *Evidence for Practice* to respond to identified priorities for positive change.
4. Implement teaching and learning activities from the teacher resource books to develop the social and emotional skills of students, based on their strengths and needs.
5. Review changes in school processes, review teacher practice, and gather evidence of student outcomes to inform future practice.

 ## Plan Priorities Using Data

Friendly Schools Plus helps schools plan what specific actions they need to take—by whom and by when—to make the most of strategies they are implementing to enhance social and emotional learning and reduce bullying.

A review of past and current school policies and practices will facilitate discussion for future planning. School staff can knowledgeably and comprehensively determine if the whole-school activities currently provided by the school meet the identified needs of students (and staff) by using the whole-school practice planning tool.

These tools are particularly helpful for:

- Describing the extent and nature of students' social behaviors and actions taken by the school to address these
- Raising staff and other school community members' awareness of these behaviors and the schools' efforts to encourage positive social change
- Determining the school policies and practices that are working well, what can be improved, and what is missing
- Making decisions, setting priorities, and planning for sustainable school action (policies and practices)
- Benchmarking, monitoring, and evaluating changes in school processes and student outcomes

From these findings, a course of action can be planned using the Friendly Schools Plus whole-school practice planning tool to record intended short- and longer-term priorities and strategies, the staff involved, and dates for action and monitoring. This plan will address the needs and gaps identified by the school community and identify ways to build staff capacity to implement the chosen activities. Each school's plan will look different as it is tailored to its local context, such as the behavior of students, what practices are currently in place, and what has previously been implemented.

An important part of the planning process is engaging a team of individuals who are responsible for leading the change process. A template planning tool is included in chapters 2–7, which may assist the school's implementation preparation. As well as the staff who are formally appointed to coordinate this role and who may have dedicated time to carry out the tasks, other school leaders or champions are also important. Staff in these leadership roles are often the first users of the intervention and may require specific capacity support to fulfill their role. Other staff who are involved in the school's planned activities also need to be engaged and prepared with appropriate information, training, and support to convince them of the need and advantage of implementing the proposed change.

 ## Build Collective Capability

Friendly Schools Plus provides professional learning to build collective capability of all staff to implement policy and practice to enhance social and emotional learning and reduce bullying.

In achieving successful change within the school environment, staff should feel part of the decision-making process and be prepared for any proposed changes to their work practices. Professional learning for staff to build their knowledge and skills to prevent, identify, and respond effectively to bullying behavior is essential. However, building their belief that the change will be better than what they were doing before, that they can easily implement the intervention proposed, and that the program is compatible with their role and professional identity only comes with being involved in decision making. Commitment from staff to implement new strategies and make changes to their daily practices will improve if they are provided with capacity that enhances their motivation and increases their competence. Staff who are part of the school's core team responsible for facilitating change will need additional training to build their capacity to support other staff to implement the new practices in their school.

Use Whole-School Toolkits to Respond to Priorities

Friendly Schools Plus provides whole-school practice toolkits to implement changes to policy, the schools' social and physical climate, and links with families and the community to enhance social and emotional learning and reduce bullying.

To help schools build and maintain a more comprehensive whole-school approach, summaries of evidence-based practice and a series of implementation tools are provided to help schools achieve positive change. For example, to enhance the school social environment, evidence is provided to better understand why this component of a whole-school approach is important and how it can be enhanced, and then tools such as newsletter items are provided to help schools implement the changes recommended.

4 Implement Teaching and Learning Activities

Friendly Schools Plus provides explicit multidisciplinary learner-centered teaching and learning resources for students ages four to fourteen to enhance their social and emotional learning and to reduce bullying.

The Friendly Schools Plus teaching and learning resources for four- to fourteen-year-old students use a strengths-based approach that focuses on what creates positive health rather than emphasizing risk factors or causes of poor health (Antonovsky, 1996). It is designed to address three key aspects of students' school experiences shown to be related to improved social and emotional development: (1) promoting positive peer relationships, (2) promoting positive teacher-child relationships, and (3) explicit teaching related to emotions, social knowledge, and social skills. These resources aim to develop students' social and emotional competencies to enable them to recognize and control their emotions, build positive relationships, show consideration for others, make thoughtful and sensible choices, and cope successfully with difficult situations. Outcomes are developed through the following five focus areas:

1. Self-awareness
2. Self-management
3. Social awareness
4. Relationship skills
5. Social decision making

Teachers are encouraged to teach from each of the social and emotional learning focus areas in the order presented, as each builds on the vocabulary, concepts, and skills covered in preceding focus areas.

5 Review Changes in Practices, Processes, and Student Outcomes

Friendly Schools Plus assessment tools can be used to monitor and review the effectiveness of whole-school and classroom-level actions taken to enhance social and emotional learning and reduce bullying.

The Friendly Schools Plus planning toolkits can be used for ongoing monitoring and review or evaluation of school processes and student outcomes. Importantly, as data are collected over subsequent years, behavioral trends can begin to be observed and predicted within the school to enable more responsive school action and school improvement.

Overviews of Strategies for Good Practice and Planning Tools

The strategies and tools outlined in this section are designed to help schools identify and successfully implement whole-school recommendations to enhance students' social skills and reduce bullying in schools. Teams can review, plan, build capacity, and implement the evidence-based strategies in each of the key areas. It is essential to address all key areas in the process to be effective in practice. The identified strategies and initiatives need to be integrated in a coordinated manner, such that action in one key area effects positive change in other areas.

Key Areas

Friendly Schools Plus features six evidence-based practice areas that together build strategies for whole-school action to promote positive social skills and reduce aggression and bullying behaviors among students. The Strategies for Good Practice section is organized around the following six interrelated key areas:

1. Building capacity
2. Supportive school culture
3. Proactive policies and practices
4. Key understandings and competencies
5. Protective physical environment
6. School–family–community partnerships

Actions

The actions are identified from the evidence-based research to be priorities for action within each key area to create supportive environments and significantly reduce bullying in school communities.

Strategies for Good Practice

These are strategies identified in the research to support each of the actions identified in the key areas.

Whole-School Toolkits

Toolkits provide further information to support the strategies for good practice.

> For example:
>
> - Key area—Supportive school culture
> - Actions for building a supportive school culture—Positive peer group influence
> - Strategies for good practice—Peer group actions to reduce bullying (such as positive bystander behaviors) are encouraged and commended at the whole-school level.
> - Whole-school toolkit—See Supportive School Culture toolkit 3.3 for discussion of peer support strategies.

Planning Tool for Each Key Area

School teams will conduct their review of current policies and practices, identify their successes and needs, and plan their strategies and actions in each key area. The planning tool is designed for teams to record their planning for future action in each key area.

Summary of Key Areas

Building Capacity—Chapter 2

Schools that assess and improve capacity support to implement strategies to improve student well-being and reduce bullying should help ensure their actions are effective, sustainable, and systemwide. Sufficient leadership, organizational support, resources, staff professional learning, and strategies that are compatible with school needs are crucial to optimize impact.

Supportive School Culture—Chapter 3

A supportive school culture provides safety, encourages open communication, and supports a sense of connectedness to the school and between staff and students and among students and also protects students from the risks of bullying. The quality of relationships between and among staff, students, and families is vital in fostering a safe, supportive, and engaging school environment. Positive student behavior should be encouraged and acknowledged at the whole-school level.

Proactive Policies and Practices—Chapter 4

Schools with clear and consistent policies and procedures send a strong message to the whole-school community about the school's mission, values, and actions to build a safe and supportive school environment. School policies should be promoted to the whole-school community, particularly at times of higher risk such as orientation and transition. Positive student behavior should be encouraged and rewarded at the whole-school level.

Key Understandings and Competencies—Chapter 5

Schools that enhance staff, students', and families' understandings and skills to enhance students' social development are more likely to enhance students' social development and effectively reduce bullying behaviors. Key common understandings about bullying include the nature, prevalence, and types of bullying as well as information about how bystanders can reduce the prevalence of bullying. Key understandings are supported with skills or competencies needed to prevent, identify, and respond to bullying incidents effectively and consistently.

Protective Physical Environment—Chapter 6

A well-structured physical environment helps promote learning and encourage positive social interactions among students and staff. These structures can be part of the school master plan or created by students. Student art, positive use of space, facilities, equipment, and activities that encourage cooperative behaviors can positively influence student behaviors.

School–Family–Community Partnerships—Chapter 7

Schools that encourage active participation of students' families and community services providers recognize that addressing bullying is the responsibility of the whole-school community. Creating links to relevant health, educational, and community agencies that provide services to students and their families will foster vital support for school action to reduce bullying.

The Planning Tool

A planning tool has been provided at the end of each of the six key area chapters. For the complete version of this tool, visit **go.solution-tree.com/behavior**.

It is recommended that schools use relevant sections of the planning tool to assist with planning in areas they have identified as requiring further action. Schools will have identified which of the six key areas they feel are priorities for initial action. School teams can find the relevant key area chapters to support their decision making in this resource.

The planning tool enables schools to (1) conduct a detailed assessment of their current progress on strategies within each of the six evidence-based practice areas and (2) plan for action based on areas of identified need. Schools may choose to plan for action in an area highlighted in the screening tool as having a low level of activity or may choose to work on any or all of the six areas at any time. All staff, or a select group such as guidance counselors, can complete this tool by rating the progress of each action as *not yet initiated, in planning, preparing staff, partially in place, fully in place,* or *sustained practice.* The collation of these individual ratings provides an overall consensus of the progress the school is making toward its set goals.

Chapters 2–7 each identify the evidence for practice, the actions identified from the evidence-based research to be priorities for action within each key area, and the strategies to support these actions. The planning tool provides school teams with a process to comprehensively review and determine if current whole-school policies and practices are addressing each of the evidence-based actions identified. Within a key area, school teams will be asked to conduct a review of current policies and practices in each action area, identify their successes and needs, and plan their strategies. The planning tool is designed to allow teams to record their planning for future action in each key area.

2.0 PLANNING TOOL: BUILDING CAPACITY FOR ACTION

Statement of Evidence for Building Capacity for Action

Schools that assess and improve capacity support to implement strategies to improve student outcomes such as well-being, counseling, social skills, and reduction in bullying help to ensure their actions are effective, sustainable, and systemwide. Sufficient leadership, organizational support, resources, and strategy compatibility with school needs are crucial to optimize impact.

Review Action 2.1—Committed and Engaged Leadership						
2.1.1 The principal and the leadership team communicate to the whole-school community a clear vision for increasing social skills and reducing bullying as a priority commitment.	Not yet initiated	In planning	Preparing staff	Partially in place	Fully in place	Sustained practice
2.1.2 The principal and the leadership team are actively engaged in leading school action to reduce bullying.	Not yet initiated	In planning	Preparing staff	Partially in place	Fully in place	Sustained practice
2.1.3 The principal and the leadership team enable and encourage all members of the whole-school community (staff, students, families) to actively participate in planning and decision making about school action to reduce bullying through regular, planned monitoring and feedback.	Not yet initiated	In planning	Preparing staff	Partially in place	Fully in place	Sustained practice
2.1.4 The principal and the leadership team develop and promote an effective and clear whole-school policy to reduce bullying.	Not yet initiated	In planning	Preparing staff	Partially in place	Fully in place	Sustained practice
2.1.5 Key staff interested in counseling, led by a coordinator, take responsibility for helping other staff implement school strategies to reduce bullying.	Not yet initiated	In planning	Preparing staff	Partially in place	Fully in place	Sustained practice
2.1.6 The principal and the leadership team engage the support of wider systems to provide leadership, mentoring, and support to the school in their actions to reduce bullying.	Not yet initiated	In planning	Preparing staff	Partially in place	Fully in place	Sustained practice

Plan Action 2.1—Committed and Engaged Leadership						
What needs to be done?	Who is going to do it?	Timeline			What do we need?	Comments and reflections
		Status	Finish	Status		

Figure 2: The planning tool.

Using the Planning Tool

The following figure uses the Building Capacity for Action planning tool as an example to explain the layout of planning tools throughout this resource.

2.0 PLANNING TOOL: Building Capacity for Action

Statement of evidence: *The statement of evidence is provided for each key area. For more detailed information, read the relevant key area chapter in this resource.*

Statement of Evidence for Building Capacity for Action

Schools that assess and improve capacity support to implement strategies, to improve student outcomes such as well-being, counseling, social skills, and reduction in bullying help to ensure their actions are effective, sustainable, and systemwide. Sufficient leadership, organizational support, resources, and strategy compatibility with school needs are crucial to optimize impact.

Review: *The review and plan sections below are conducted for each action within a key area. Each strategy for action is rated according to the criteria in the boxes to the right. This process is designed to stimulate discussion and highlight what is already being done well as well as identify areas for improvement.*

Review Action 2.1—Committed and Engaged Leadership

	Not yet initiated	In planning	Preparing staff	Partially in place	Fully in place	Sustained practice
2.1.1 The principal and the leadership team communicate to the whole-school community a clear <u>vision</u> for increasing social skills and reducing bullying as a priority commitment.						
2.1.2 The principal and the leadership team are <u>actively engaged</u> in leading school action to reduce bullying.						

Plan: *Strategies for action that have been identified for improvement are then addressed in the following planning section. Information about how to address each action can be found in the relevant key area chapters of this resource.*

Plan Action 2.1—Committed and Engaged Leadership

What needs to be done?	Who is going to do it?	Timeline		What do we need?	Comments and reflections
		Status	Finish	Status	

Figure 3: An example of the planning tool.

Evidence Before Action

Social and Emotional Learning

The social, emotional, cognitive, and physical aspects of a person's development are interrelated. Each influences and is influenced by the others. Consequently, it is not uncommon for students who have difficulty managing their emotions and behavior to face great challenges meeting the demands of schooling. This relationship between student behavior and academic problems is not always clear in terms of which comes first, but what is clear is that the presence of one greatly increases the risk of the other. Supporting children's emotional, social, and behavioral development thus enables students to more effectively engage in their learning.

The Friendly Schools Plus resource is designed to address three key aspects of students' school experiences shown to be related to improved social and emotional development: (1) promoting positive peer relationships, (2) promoting positive teacher-child relationships, and (3) explicit teaching related to emotions, social knowledge, and social skills. The resource aims to develop students' social and emotional competencies to enable them to recognize and control their emotions, build positive relationships, show consideration for others, make thoughtful and sensible choices, and cope successfully with difficult situations. These outcomes are developed through the following five key areas in this resource:

1. Self-awareness
2. Self-management
3. Social awareness
4. Relationship skills
5. Social decision making

Bullying can have a significant and negative impact on students' social and emotional development and other learning. An anxious, frightened, and withdrawn student has limited learning potential.

To reduce and ultimately prevent bullying it is important to focus on why most children and young people do not engage in bullying behavior. These individuals tend to display greater social and emotional competence than those who bully others. Children and adolescents who demonstrate social and emotional competence are also more likely to have positive relationships and social capabilities that reduce the likelihood of them being bullied. In addition, in the event that they are victimized or a bystander in a bullying incident, they are more aware of how to manage the bullying situation.

Bullying is more than an event between students who bully and students who are bullied. It is a social relationship involving group values and group standards of behavior, which means it requires consistent action across the school community to achieve positive change.

Students develop personal and social capabilities as they learn to understand themselves and others, and manage their relationships, lives, work, and learning more effectively (Brendgen, Markiewicz, Doyle, & Bukowski, 2001). The capability involves students in a range of practices including recognizing and regulating emotions, developing empathy for and understanding of others, establishing positive relationships, making responsible decisions, working effectively in teams, and handling challenging situations constructively.

Students with well-developed social and emotional skills find it easier to manage themselves, relate to others, develop resilience and a sense of self-worth, resolve conflict, engage in teamwork, and feel positive about themselves and the world around them. The development of personal and social capability is a foundation for learning and for citizenship.

What Is Social and Emotional Learning?

Social and emotional learning is the process of developing and practicing important social and emotional understandings and skills (Lagerspetz, Björkqvist, & Peltonen, 1988). These understandings and skills can be grouped into five key areas (see figure 4).

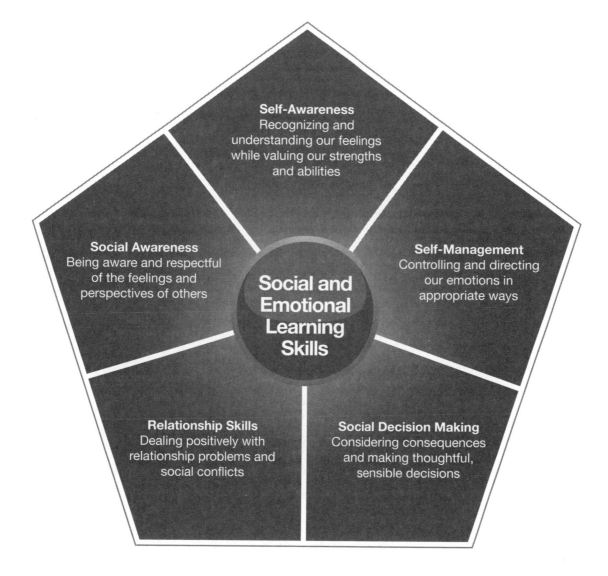

Source: Collaborative for Academic, Social, and Emotional Learning, 2011.

Figure 4: Five social and emotional learning skills.

Self-awareness skills help us recognize and understand our feelings while valuing our strengths and abilities. This involves:

- Being able to identify what we are feeling
- Understanding why we might feel a certain way
- Recognizing and having the confidence to use our strengths and abilities

Self-management skills enable us to control and direct our emotions in appropriate ways. This involves:

- Managing our emotions so they don't stop us from effectively dealing with situations and pursuing our goals
- Striving to achieve our goals despite difficulties

Social awareness skills help us to be aware and respectful of the feelings and perspectives of others. This involves:

- Recognizing what others may be feeling
- Trying to understand a situation from another's point of view
- Accepting and valuing people who are different from ourselves

Relationship skills help us to deal positively with relationship problems and other social conflicts. These skills include:

- Making friends and maintaining healthy relationships
- Dealing effectively with negative social influences and conflicts
- Seeking help if we are not able to solve a social problem ourselves

Social decision-making skills help us consider the consequences of our actions for ourselves and others and make thoughtful, sensible decisions. This involves:

- Understanding how a social situation makes us feel
- Considering the different choices we have and the positive and negative consequences of each of these choices when making a decision
- Making positive choices while considering how these choices may affect ourselves and others (Collaborative for Academic, Social, and Emotional Learning [CASEL], 2003)

Personal and social capability skills are addressed in all learning areas and at every stage of a student's schooling.

When students develop their skills in any one of these elements, it leads to greater overall personal and social capability and also enhances their skills in the other elements (Brendgen et al., 2001). In particular, the more students learn about their own emotions, values, strengths, and capacities, the more they are able to manage their own emotions and behaviors, understand others, and establish and maintain positive relationships.

Benefits of Social and Emotional Learning

Improving social and emotional skills has a positive influence on children and adolescents' attitudes, behaviors, and performance (Lagerspetz et al., 1988). A review of 317 studies involving over 300,000 children and adolescents found that social and emotional learning programs were beneficial for children and young people aged five through eighteen from urban and rural communities with or without behavioral or emotional problems (Crick & Bigbee, 1998). Social and emotional learning improved participants' social and emotional skills, coping skills, and resistance to negative peer pressure; resulted in more positive attitudes toward themselves, others, and their schools; improved social behaviors and cooperation with others; decreased risky, antisocial, and aggressive behaviors; and decreased emotional problems, including anxiety and depression (Crick & Bigbee, 1998).

Other research also suggests that social and emotional learning programs improve health outcomes for young people, including a decreased risk of tobacco, alcohol, and illicit substance use problems; mental health problems and suicide; and sexually transmitted diseases (Lagerspetz et al., 1988).

Social and emotional learning programs can also improve academic success, with students demonstrating improved grades and test scores, more positive attitudes toward school, and better school attendance, as well as heightened trust and respect for teachers, improved management of school-related stress, improved participation in class, and fewer suspensions (Lagerspetz et al., 1988; Smith, Talamelli, Cowie, Naylor, & Chauhan, 2004).

These programs also show evidence of long-term effectiveness, especially if social skills are developed and consolidated across several years (Smith, Talamelli, et al., 2004). Importantly, the positive effects of social and emotional learning can extend beyond the individual with improvements in students' social and emotional skills likely to have a positive influence on their schools, families, and broader communities (Galen & Underwood, 1997).

Social and Emotional Learning in the School Curriculum

To make ethical, constructive choices about personal and social behavior, children and young people need to show understanding about themselves and be able to take the perspective of and empathize with others. Being empathetic means being able to identify with, understand, and care about how another person feels in a certain situation. This is especially important for students to reduce the bullying perpetration and to help those who are victimized.

Many students have not yet had the life experiences to enable them to directly understand or relate to what another person might think, feel, or believe in a certain situation. Students benefit from the explicit teaching and learning activities that interrogate the different perspectives of individuals and groups involved in the social context and the decision-making processes they may apply to different social situations, such as preventing or responding to bullying.

The Friendly Schools Plus resource uses stories and literature, cooperative games, role plays, problem solving, and reflective activities to encourage students to identify and understand their emotions, consider the perspectives of others, negotiate tricky situations, and make well-reasoned decisions (Dooley, Cross, Hearn, & Treyvaud, 2009). This comprehensive resource provides sequential, interactive, and engaging learning activities to explicitly build social and emotional competencies in students that are important for each major developmental stage from primary to secondary school.

Social and Emotional Learning by Developmental Level

The most effective learning programs are those that integrate social learning into the curriculum, specifically targeting and building on social and emotional skills over time, from preschool to high school. While there may be considerable variation in children's and adolescents' social and emotional skills, broad patterns are associated with early and middle childhood as well as early and middle adolescence (Galen & Underwood, 1997; Rigby, 1996).

Early Childhood

From ages four to eight children increasingly begin to use reason to understand the world, consider the needs of others, and take responsibility for their actions. Developing confidence in their abilities and establishing healthy relationships are important during this stage (Crick & Dodge, 1994; Fontaine & Dodge, 2006).

Table 1: Early Childhood Social and Emotional Skills				
Self-Awareness	**Self-Management**	**Social Awareness**	**Relationship Skills**	**Social Decision Making**
Can identify personal: • Likes and dislikes • Needs and wants • Strengths and challenges	Can identify personal: • Emotions • Appropriate classroom behavior Can control impulsive behavior	Can use listening skills to identify feelings of others Can describe: • Ways people are similar and different • Positive qualities in others • Different ways people may experience situations	Can identify: • Ways to work and play well with others • Common problems and conflicts of peers • Approaches to positively deal with conflicts Can demonstrate appropriate social and class behavior	Can explain why aggression toward others is wrong Can identify: • Safe social behaviors • Range of decisions to make at school • Roles in classroom and contribute to these Can make positive decisions with peers

Source: CASEL, 2011.

Middle Childhood

From ages eight to eleven children become increasingly independent but also more aware of social situations and relationships. Feeling like part of a group and receiving social acceptance are particularly important at this time (Crick & Dodge, 1994; Dodge & Coie, 1987).

Table 2: Middle Childhood Social and Emotional Skills				
Self-Awareness	**Self-Management**	**Social Awareness**	**Relationship Skills**	**Social Decision Making**
Can describe: • Personal skills and interests they wish to develop • How family members and others can support positive behavior	Can describe: • Range of emotions and situations that cause them Can demonstrate ways to express emotions in socially acceptable manner Can take steps toward and monitor goal achievement	Can recognize social cues that indicate how others may feel Can describe feelings and views expressed by others Can identify: • Differences and similarities between groups • Contributions of different groups and how to work with these groups	Can describe: • How to make and keep friends • How to work effectively in groups • Causes and consequences of conflicts Can apply constructive approaches to resolving conflicts	Can demonstrate: • Ability to respect rights of self and others • Knowledge of how social norms affect decision making and behavior Can apply the steps of decision making and identify and evaluate consequences Can identify and contribute to roles to help in the community

Source: CASEL, 2011.

Early Adolescence

From ages eleven to thirteen young adolescents have improved self-control and self-reliance. They often have strong concerns about fitting in and physical appearance. Social and emotional skills have become more advanced, with young adolescents better able to analyze consequences and negotiate conflicts and interpersonal problems. Young people are also very concerned about making and keeping friends, including opposite-sex friendships. They also have a greater need for independence from adults, often resisting the influence of parents and teachers and using peers to determine behavioral norms (Crick & Dodge, 1994; Dodge, Lochman, Harnish, Bates, & Pettit, 1997).

Table 3: Early Adolescence Social and Emotional Skills

Self-Awareness	Self-Management	Social Awareness	Relationship Skills	Social Decision Making
Can analyze how: • Personal qualities influence choices and success • Using available supports can improve success	Can analyze factors to enhance or inhibit performance Can apply strategies to manage stress and improve performance Can set a short-term goal and plan to achieve it and analyze success or otherwise	Can predict others' feelings and perspectives Can analyze how personal behavior may affect others Can explain how cultural differences can increase vulnerability to bullying and identify ways to reduce this Can analyze the effects of taking action to oppose bullying	Can analyze ways to build positive relationships with others Can demonstrate cooperation and teamwork to improve group processes Can evaluate strategies for preventing and resolving relationship problems Can identify negative peer influence and determine ways to respond to it	Can evaluate how values such as honesty and respect help to take into account the needs of others when making decisions Can explain the reasons for rules Can evaluate strategies to respond to negative peer influence Can evaluate their contribution to addressing needs in school and in the community

Source: CASEL, 2011.

Middle Adolescence

From ages thirteen to fifteen adolescents increasingly learn to balance freedom and fun with responsibilities, and individuality with peer influence. They value respect from others and independence from adults, and become more concerned with pursuing their own goals (Crick & Dodge, 1994; Vitiello & Stoff, 1997).

Table 4: Middle Adolescence Social and Emotional Skills				
Self-Awareness	**Self-Management**	**Social Awareness**	**Relationship Skills**	**Social Decision Making**
Can analyze how positive adult role models and other supports contribute to success Can set priorities to build strengths and determine areas for improvement	Can analyze how thoughts and emotions affect decision making and responsible behavior Can monitor and find ways to develop more positive attitudes Can analyze and apply strategies to overcome barriers to achieving goals	Can analyze similarities and differences between their own and others' perspectives Can use interpersonal skills to understand others' perspectives and feelings Can examine and respond to negative stereotypes and prejudice Can demonstrate respect for individuals from other social and cultural groups	Can evaluate their contribution to groups in which they are a leader or member Can evaluate the impact of requesting or providing support to others Can analyze actions they can take to help resolve conflicts as an individual or in a group	Can demonstrate taking personal responsibility for ethical decisions Can evaluate how social norms and expectations influence their decision making Can apply decision-making skills to establish responsible social relationships Can evaluate their ability to anticipate the consequences of social decisions Can plan, implement, and evaluate their participation in activities to improve the school and local community

Source: CASEL, 2011.

Each developmental level as described in the tables is associated with the need for increasingly refined social and emotional learning. To meet this need, the Friendly Schools Plus resource gradually increases the complexity of the age-appropriate activities provided for each age group. This allows students to build on and refine their social and emotional skills over time.

Bullying: Evidence Before Action

This chapter presents an overview of the research evidence describing the nature, causes, correlates, and impacts of bullying behaviors, as well as strategies for managing bullying in the classroom. Importantly, this section will help to ensure a consistent and accurate understanding of what is meant by the term *bullying*, its causes, outcomes, and the consequences.

Defining and Measuring Bullying

What Is Bullying?

The definition used by most researchers today is:

> Bullying is a repeated behavior; that may be physical, verbal, and/or psychological; where there is intent to cause fear, distress, or harm to another; that is conducted by a more powerful individual or group; against a less powerful individual or group of individuals who are unable to stop this from happening. (Olweus, 1996)

The key elements of a bullying incident include both a perpetrator's and target's perspective—the perpetrator has more perceived power, he or she repeats the behavior and with intention, while the target feels the bullying is unprovoked or unjustifiable and he or she is not able to stop the behavior from happening. If these elements are not present, using this definition, the behavior would be considered an aggressive act and not an incident of bullying.

When talking with young people about bullying, it is more understandable to describe bullying as a series of descriptive behaviors, rather than one broad term that has many negative connotations, especially when discussing cyberbullying. The behaviors commonly used to describe bullying include being repeatedly:

- Ignored or left out on purpose
- Made fun of or teased in a mean and hurtful way
- Made to feel afraid of getting hurt
- Stared at with mean looks or gestures
- Embarrassed by nasty stories or rumors spread about you
- Forced to do things you don't want to
- Hit, kicked, or pushed around

There has been much discussion about cyberbullying and how it should best be defined. Proposed definitions range from a focus on only behavior to only technology. Following six years of assessing, evaluating, and addressing cyberbullying in schools, the Child Health Promotion Research Centre (CHPRC, 2010) defines cyberbullying as follows:

> Cyberbullying is when a group or an individual use information and communication technologies (ICT) to intentionally harm a person over time, who cannot easily stop this bullying from continuing.

The most important aspect of this definition is that it is not focused on ICT but stipulates that cyberbullying is bullying via ICT. That is, it is about the behavior, not about the technology.

What Is *Not* Bullying?

Given the complex definition of bullying, it is important to also consider what behaviors are not bullying. One example of what is not considered bullying is a fight between two equally matched students. Friendly teasing is also not considered bullying. These examples seem very clear from a perpetrator's perspective but are less so from the perspective of the target or student who is being victimized. Sometimes alleged perpetrators report they were only joking when accused of bullying. The accurate identification of "true" bullying cases is even more complicated when the bullying occurs online or by mobile phone.

Imagine the following: *Tracey is a ninth grader who comes to see you because she is being bullied. She tells you that students in her class are saying nasty things and posting hurtful pictures of her on the Internet. You find out that it was Rachel, another ninth grader. Rachel tells you that she only posted one picture and it was just meant to be a joke.*

If bullying is defined as a repeated act (that is, the definition is from Rachel's perspective), then one act, such as posting an embarrassing picture, may not be considered bullying. However, from the target's perspective (Tracey's), this act may very well be bullying given the picture is available online and can be viewed repeatedly by her and others. To address this definitional challenge, many schools refer to these cyber-related behaviors in their policies, for example, as *cyber aggression* without trying to determine if they are bullying or not, while acknowledging that these behaviors are unacceptable.

Are There Different Types of Bullying Behaviors?

A large variety of behaviors can be used to bully others. For example, bullying can be *physical, verbal, social, relational,* delivered through noncyber (for example, face to face) or cyber means (for example, via phone texting). *Physical bullying* includes behaviors such as hitting, kicking, pushing, tripping, and spitting (Craig, Pepler, & Blais, 2007; Smokowski & Holland, 2005). These overt behaviors (easily seen) are typically more common in boys, and it is relatively easy to identify both the perpetrator and the target (Smokowski & Holland, 2005). *Verbal bullying* involves using words to hurt or humiliate others and includes behaviors such as threats, hurtful teasing, and insults (Craig et al., 2007; Smokowski & Holland, 2005). These behaviors are less easy to detect and likely to be a component of nearly all bullying interactions (Smokowski & Holland, 2005).

Covert bullying refers to behaviors that are hard to see (Cross et al., 2009) and include indirect, relational, and social forms of bullying. The term *indirect aggression* was introduced in the late 1980s to describe aggressive and bullying behaviors that were not easily noticeable and where the perpetrator's identity was largely concealed (Lagerspetz et al., 1988). Indirect aggression could, in fact, include very overt acts that are carried out at times when the likelihood of being discovered is minimal (for example, engaging in property damage at night). In addition, indirect aggression could consist of behaviors enacted through a third party so that there is no direct contact between the perpetrator and the target.

Crick and colleagues conceptualized *relational aggression* as including behaviors that were intended to harm others by damaging relationships or feelings of social acceptance, friendship, or inclusion in peer groups (CASEL, 2011). Thus, relational aggression can comprise many different behaviors, such as playing practical jokes and embarrassing a person, imitating people behind their backs, breaking secrets, being critical, spreading hurtful rumors, sending abusive notes, whispering, or maliciously excluding them (Crick & Bigbee, 1998; Smith, Talamelli, et al., 2004).

Social bullying (or social aggression) refers to a broad behavioral concept encompassing both indirect and relational aggression that includes behaviors intended to damage or harm a person's social status or self-esteem (or both). These behaviors may include verbal rejection, negative facial expressions or body movements, or more indirect forms such as slanderous rumors or social exclusion (Galen & Underwood, 1997).

Of course, *cyberbullying* behaviors are different again given the reliance on ICT as a medium to bully. The measurement of cyberbullying behaviors represents a challenge for researchers, schools, and the community alike because the dynamic environment of the Internet (and mobile phones) means the strategies used to cyberbully others can change. The Australian Covert Bullying Prevalence Study (Cross et al., 2009) revealed some very interesting patterns of cyberbullying behaviors which highlighted, for example, the developmental nature of strategies used to victimize others.

Given the uptake of social networking and the use of social media in later adolescence, it is not surprising that social media is used as one of the most common ways to cyberbully young people (Dooley, Cross, et al., 2009). In contrast, relatively more young children use email than social networking compared to the number of older teenagers who use email versus social networking (Dooley, Cross, et al., 2009). However, this is likely to change as interest in and uptake of social media become more popular. Interestingly, significant differences were found in bullying behaviors between students who were the same age but located in primary versus secondary schools (Dooley, Cross, et al., 2009). This is most likely related to social changes that occur when young people transition from primary to secondary school.

Table 5: Examples of Bullying Behavior		
	Direct	**Indirect**
Physical	• Hitting, slapping, punching • Kicking • Pushing • Spitting, biting • Pinching, scratching • Throwing things	• Getting another person to harm someone
Verbal	• Mean and hurtful name-calling • Hurtful teasing • Demanding money or possessions • Forcing another to do homework or commit offenses such as stealing	• Spreading nasty rumors • Trying to get other students to not like someone
Nonverbal	• Threatening or obscene gestures	• Deliberate exclusion from a group or activity • Removing and hiding or damaging others' belongings
Cyber	• Filming someone without his or her knowledge or permission • Updating someone else's social networking status without his or her permission • Pretending to be someone else on the phone	• Telling someone else the words you want him or her to type as a message • Explaining to someone how to engage in bullying via a website the other person may not be familiar with • Watching someone engaging in cyberbullying and not trying to stop the bullying

Source: Rigby, 1996.

Why Do Most Students *Not* Bully?

Although bullying situations are experienced in most schools at some time, bullying does not occur among all young people all the time. In fact, most students do not bully others. In general, young people who have developed good social and emotional skills, have positive friends, and have supportive environments at home, at school, and in the community are unlikely to bully others.

Nevertheless, some students may use bullying behaviors for a variety of reasons.

Chapter 1

Why Do Some Students Bully?

Children use bullying behaviors for a variety of reasons. These are mainly personal in nature and typically have little to do with the person who is the target of the bullying. Some of the reasons children bully others include:

- To get what they want
- To be popular and admired
- Because they are afraid of being the one left out
- Jealousy of others
- It seems like fun
- Out of boredom
- It has worked for them before
- They enjoy the power
- They see it as their role (for example, leader)
- Their significant role models use bullying behaviors

While these reasons help to explain why children bully others, they don't explain how and why the behavior first starts. Some of the factors associated with the development of bullying in children and young people include:

- Experiencing aggressive behavior at home and elsewhere
- Being harshly, physically punished at home
- Spending time with peers who bully
- Insufficient adult supervision
- Bullying gives them the social rewards they seek
- Bullying others to prevent being bullied
- Getting attention

What Theoretical Evidence Supports an Understanding of Bullying Behavior?

Social Information Processing and Bullying

A number of theoretical models are proposed to describe and explain how young people process social information that drives aggressive and bullying behaviors. To date, the most empirically supported model is proposed by Crick and Dodge (Life Education Committee of Kankakee and Iroquois, 2008a). The social information processing (SIP) model describes five interrelated cognitive processes, or stages, believed to underlie social behaviors.

1. Internal and external stimuli are encoded.
2. Encoded information is interpreted, and attributions of intent and causality are made.
3. A social goal is generated.
4. Responses are generated that will lead to its attainment.
5. The response that is attributed the highest overall value is chosen (Life Education Committee of Kankakee and Iroquois, 2008b).

In terms of aggression research, the stages of attribution (stage 2) and response decision (stage 5) are the most frequently addressed.

The SIP model is used to describe and distinguish between different forms of aggressive behavior. The most common distinction between forms of aggression uses the terms *reactive* and *proactive aggression.* Reactive aggression is impulsive, highly emotionally charged, and most often occurs in response to a frustrating experience. Proactive aggression, on the other hand, is premeditated, controlled, or has the specific intent to harm another (CASEL, 2003; Life Education Committee of Kankakee and Iroquois, 2008c). When this form of aggression is repeated, it is usually considered bullying. Proactively aggressive children attack others to dominate, steal, tease, or coerce (Life Education Committee of Kankakee and Iroquois, 2008d; Olweus, 1996). An important distinction between reactive and proactive aggression is that the latter is usually displayed in the absence of provocation or anger (Bandura, 1973). This type of initiated and intentional aggression has its theoretical roots in social learning (Bandura, 1978; Life Education Committee of Kankakee and Iroquois, 2008c; Patterson, 1982) and is argued to be motivated by a desire for interpersonal dominance or an expectation that aggression is a suitable means of achieving some desired reward (such as money or toys) (Bandura, 1983; Price & Dodge, 1989).

Social Information Processing and Proactive Aggression

Proactive aggression has been linked with a number of positive and negative outcomes, both short- and long-term. The positive qualities of proactive aggression sometimes cause confusion, as it is not always clear why aggression in any form would be considered positive. Proactively aggressive younger children, for example, can be seen as positive leaders with a good sense of humor, high self-esteem qualities, and positive early friendship qualities and popularity (Hawley, 2003; Life Education Committee of Kankakee and Iroquois, 2008c). However, these early positive outcomes soon give way to more functionally and socially negative aspects, and by the age of nine these proactively aggressive children are considered to be the most disruptive and aggressive in their peer group (Life Education Committee of Kankakee and Iroquois, 2008c; Poulin & Boivin, 1999; Price & Dodge, 1989; Prinstein & Cillessen, 2003; Pulkkinen, 1996; Vitaro, Brendgen, & Tremblay, 2002). Among the most concerning long-term correlates of proactive aggression are adult criminality (Camodeca, Goossens, Terwogt, & Schuengel, 2002), bullying in school (Australian Curriculum, Assessment and Reporting Authority, 2012), delinquency and delinquency-related violence, externalizing problems later in life (Pulkkinen, 1996; Vitaro, Gendreau, Tremblay, & Oligny, 1998), and affiliation with delinquent peers (Life Education Committee of Kankakee and Iroquois, 2008d; Poulin & Boivin, 1999). Proactively aggressive children also show specific cognitive biases where they are likely to overestimate positive outcomes for aggression (Connor, Steingard, Cunningham, Melloni, & Anderson, 2004). Connor et al. (2004) suggest that substance-use disorders, a family history of substance abuse, and family violence are specifically associated with proactive aggression.

Proactive aggression is also associated with unique impairments in SIP. Unlike reactive aggression, proactive aggression is associated with the response decision stage of the SIP model (Life Education Committee of Kankakee and Iroquois, 2008d; Schwartz, McFadyen-Ketchum, Dodge, Pettit, & Bates, 1998). As discussed previously, proactive aggression is maintained by processes such as reinforcement that involve being rewarded in some way for aggressive behavior. It is logical to assume that being rewarded for aggressive behavior would lead to positive expectations regarding aggressive behavior. Proactively aggressive children also report more positive intrapersonal consequences for aggressive behavior (as in they reported that being aggressive would make them feel better about themselves) and report a greater belief in their ability to successfully carry out an aggressive act (Vandebosch & Van Cleemput, 2008).

To date, no studies have examined SIP in relation to cyberbullying. Nonetheless, it is likely that the patterns of information processing associated with cyberbullying will be similar to proactive aggression. However, given the media typically used to engage in cyberbullying and that those who engage in cyberbullying behaviors do not necessarily engage in face-to-face bullying, there may be some subtle differences between how social information is processed in these interactions. For example, the expectation of positive outcomes after aggressive behavior may be the same for the person cyberbullying but, importantly, the motivation for this behavior may differ. If, as was suggested by Vandebosch and Van Cleemput (2008), those who bully others are more motivated by revenge, then the explicit goal is to hurt rather than to dominate or to acquire (Havet-Thomassin, Allain, Etcharry-Bouyx, & Le Gail, 2006).

Importantly, due to the nature of the medium in which cyberbullying is enacted, those who bully may not be immediately reinforced for their behavior. For example, if a person engaging in face-to-face bullying behaviors is motivated (and goal-oriented) to inflict harm primarily by using fear, then they will likely be reinforced for this behavior by the body language and facial expression (as well as the verbal response) of their victim. The reinforcement is immediate and tangible. In contrast, a person engaging in cyberbullying who is motivated to socially hurt others may have to wait for a period of time before the impact is apparent, at least until the text message, picture, or other material is distributed among the group. Similarly, the person engaging in cyberbullying behaviors who is motivated to inflict harm using fear has limited external sources of reinforcement and may have to, at least initially, rely on their own reactions to their acts. The reward for engaging in some forms of cyberbullying could be based to a larger extent on the expectations the person engaging in bullying behaviors has for how the target person *will* react versus how the target person *is* reacting, than is the case with face-to-face bullying. This delay between the act—for example, creating a fake website—and the outcome—for example, sharing secrets with the school—would likely result in a heightened sense of expectation and a built-up level of excitement and anticipation for the time when the target person realizes what has been done. Thus, it is feasible that a difference exists between those engaging in cyberbullying behaviors versus face-to-face bullying behaviors, according to the generation of goals and the expectations related to the outcome of an interaction. It may be the case that these differences are only observed in relation to different types of cyberbullying.

There are several other theories that could be used to describe aspects of cognition and behaviors associated with bullying. Rather than conduct an exhaustive review, the following addresses the most empirically tested and influential theoretical models that have relevance to bullying behaviors. To date, relatively little theoretical work has been conducted specifically on bullying (and less on cyberbullying), so most of the theoretical models that follow outline the processes that impact social behaviors and functioning.

Theory of Mind

Theory of mind is generally described as the ability to recognize and make inferences about the feelings, beliefs, or intentions of other people (Channon & Crawford, 2000), and it has been regarded as a crucial component of effective social communication (Happé, Malhi, & Checkley, 2001; Stuss & Anderson, 2004). Nonetheless, to engage in the higher-order cognitive functions required for complex social interactions, it is necessary to first have self-awareness to be able to self-reflect (Mussen, 1983). Thus, to be able to reflect on the functions of other people, it is first necessary to have an internal awareness or understanding of those abilities. These skills usually develop around three to five years of age so that by five years most children recognize that other people can have different beliefs than they do.

This is a little different than Piaget's model (Bandura, 1973), which talks about egocentrism around this age—consistent with the models of moral reasoning and sociomoral reasoning (see following descriptions). Importantly, the awareness that a person has a set of beliefs distinct from my set of beliefs is necessary for me to be able to experience an emotion in response to a situation that I did not directly experience. Therefore, theory of mind must be interpreted as a basic social cognitive skill. Other skills, like empathy, don't develop as well without the existence of the more basic skills. This does not suggest that students who bully others are less able to recognize emotional reactivity in other people but does provide some basis to explain those who continue along the antisocial trajectory into adulthood and show traits described as psychopathic—that is, lacking in empathy.

Social Learning Theory and Bullying

Another theory that has influenced aggression and bullying research is Bandura's social learning theory. Bandura proposed that aggression was the result of learning and, as such, was no different than any other form of learned behavior in that it could be acquired, instigated, and regulated by the same processes (Bandura, 1978; Hoffman, 1960). At the base level, aggression can only be enacted if a person has acquired the requisite skills, for example, a person is not born with the knowledge necessary to shoot a gun but learns how to do this. Bandura argued that a child is not born with aggressive repertoires but can acquire them by observing the actions of others. Through observation, a child can also develop a set of expectations about the likely outcome or response for aggressive behavior. It has long been known that if these aggressive repertoires are used in the home (especially by the child's parents), then there is a much greater likelihood that this style of social interaction will be used by the child (Bandura, 1978).

Bandura also suggests that modern media, through observational processes, has a significant influence on the development and maintenance of aggressive behavior (Bandura, 1978). He suggests media violence desensitizes and habituates children to aggression, especially when it is presented in terms of good triumphing over evil. Other research also suggests there is a strong relationship between self-reported violent behaviors and television-viewing habits and exposure to violence (Singer et al., 1999). Anderson and Dill (2000), in their meta-analytic review, reported a positive relationship between exposure to violent media (specifically violent video games) and aggressive behavior and delinquency. Moreover, Anderson and Bushman (2001) reported that violent video games increase aggressive behavior in both children and young adults.

In terms of the acquisition of aggressive behavior through direct experience, Bandura (1973) noted that it may be possible to acquire a large repertoire of aggressive skills by being directly rewarded for them. Presumably, these behaviors would initially be rewarded in the home and then later by peers. Similarly, many researchers have found that aggressive children are more likely to associate with peers who behave inappropriately (Boivin & Vitaro, 1995; Coie, Terry, Zakriski, & Lochman, 1995; Patterson & Dishion, 1985), which can lead to the maintenance of aggressive behavior (Bandura, 1978). Bandura (1978) suggested that when an aggressor has a positive experience from an aggressive act (for example, when they obtain a desired object through aggressive means), this form of behavior is reinforced and more likely to be used again.

Bandura (1978) suggests reinforcement and punishment are central to the regulation and maintenance of aggressive behavior. If an aggressive child obtained the object of his or her desire (a tangible item or improved or elevated social status) by using aggressive strategies, this behavioral style of interaction will be reinforced both by external influences as well as by the person him- or herself. This form of self-reinforcement would be expected if the aggressor placed a high value on being able to enact aggressive strategies competently. According to Bandura, punishment regulates aggressive behavior by both strengthening or weakening the tendency to be aggressive based on the likelihood this behavior will be punished and the nature, severity, timing, and duration of the negative consequences.

What About Cyberbullying?

It is interesting to ask if we need separate theories to describe or explain cyberbullying. Although cyberbullying is in many ways bullying, the use of technology adds a level of complexity that can impact both the engagement in and experience of these behaviors. It is important to consider if people cyberbully for different reasons than they bully in noncyber ways. Although the literature is sparse, it can be concluded that the motives are varied. The main reasons provided by students for their cyberbullying behavior include:

- Revenge for being bullied in real life (Raskauskas & Stoltz, 2007; Slonje & Smith, 2008)
- A reaction to a previous argument
- A means for the person bullying to display their technological skills
- For fun

Given the motivations, it is highly likely, as suggested by Slonje and Smith (2008), that not having to see the fear in the target's eyes and being less aware of the consequences reduces the potential for empathy and remorse (Due et al., 2005)—factors which would lessen the likelihood of future acts of aggression and bullying. However, these reasons offer only anecdotal evidence and, to date, no studies have thoroughly assessed the motivation that drives cyberbullying and whether it is different than the motivation for face-to-face bullying.

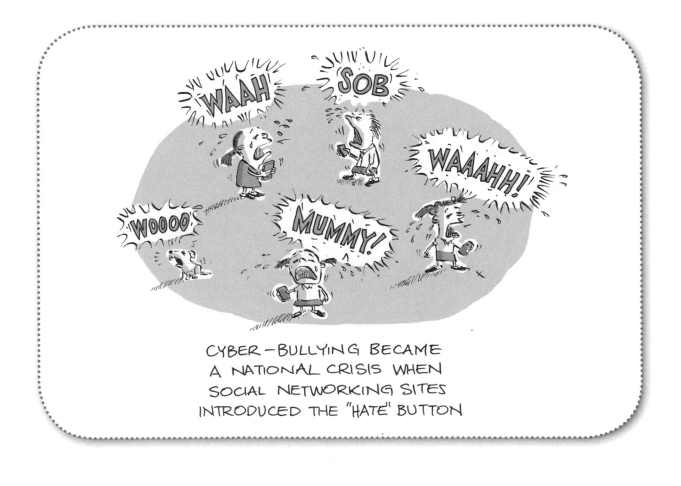

CYBER-BULLYING BECAME
A NATIONAL CRISIS WHEN
SOCIAL NETWORKING SITES
INTRODUCED THE "HATE" BUTTON

How Much of a Problem Is Bullying?

How Common Is Bullying?

A study of bullying prevalence in twenty-eight countries highlighted the significant cultural differences associated with bullying (Craig & Harel, 2004). The highest rates of bullying victimization were observed in Lithuania (41.4 percent of males and 38.2 percent of females) and the lowest in Sweden (6.3 percent of males and 5.1 percent of females). The 2001–2002 Health Behaviour in School-Aged Children cross-national research study found that across the thirty-five participating countries, an average of 11 percent of young people (aged eleven, thirteen, and fifteen) were bullied at least two or three times a month in the previous couple of months, and 11 percent bullied others at this frequency (Cross et al., 2009). In Australia, around one in four fourth- to ninth-grade students are bullied at school every few weeks or more often (27 percent) (Cross et al., 2009). Students in grade 5 across Australia are the most likely to be bullied (32 percent), closely followed by students in eighth grade (29 percent) (Rigby & Smith, 2011). These data are consistent with many previous smaller-scale studies, which have reported prevalence rates of around 25 percent and appear to have remained consistent since the early 1990s (Elias & Weissberg, 2000).

Use of direct physical (for example, punching, kicking) and verbal (such as calling names, yelling) aggression is more common among boys, whereas indirect aggression (such as spreading rumors, exclusion) appears to be more common among girls (Chesney-Lind, Morash, & Irwin, 2007; Crick & Grotpeter, 1995; Fekkes, Pijpers, & Verloove-Vanhorick, 2005; Nansel et al., 2001; Owens, 1996; Owens, Daly, & Slee, 2005; Whitney & Smith, 1993). Rates of aggression between boys and girls have been shown to even out when the different forms that aggression may take (verbal—yelling, teasing, insulting; indirect—secrets, gossip, telling stories, influencing friends) are taken into account in the comparisons (Smith & Slonje, 2010).

The prevalence of cyberbullying remains largely unclear. This is primarily related to the emerging behavior, changing technologies, and difficulties in defining and measuring the problem accurately. Cyberbullying prevalence rates have been reported as high as 25 percent in the United States, Canada, and England and between 5 percent and 15 percent in many European countries (Cross et al., 2009) and Australia (Nansel et al., 2001).

One of the most interesting aspects of the bullying and cyberbullying debate relates to gender differences in the rates of these behaviors. Traditionally, males engage in more bullying behaviors than females (Batsche & Knoff, 1994; Blair, 2003; Forero, McLellan, Rissel, & Bauman, 1999; Kumpulainen, Räsänen, Henttonen, Hämäläinen, & Roine, 2000; Olweus, 1994; Sourander, Helstelä, Helenius, & Piha, 2000). However, Blair reported that females are more likely to communicate using text messaging and email than are males (Williams & Guerra, 2007). This, combined with the more covert (and social) nature of cyberbullying, would make it reasonable to expect that the gender differences demonstrated in face-to-face bullying are, at the least, not as strong in cyberbullying. Indeed, some have reported that males and females were equally likely to report harassing others online (Ybarra & Mitchell, 2004). Similarly, Slonje and Smith (2008) reported no gender differences in the self-reported rates of either engaging in, or being the target of, cyberbullying behaviors (a trend suggesting boys engaged in more acts of cyberbullying than girls was not statistically significant). Although these results do not suggest that females engage in more cyberbullying than males, they do indicate that the gender differences reported in relation to face-to-face bullying are not as strong. Further, girls tend to have more close relationships and friendships and, therefore, may be more willing to exchange intimate details and personal secrets compared to boys who tend to socialize in larger groups and share fewer details.

An important issue related to determining prevalence rates is the measurement method used. Solberg and Olweus (2003) suggested that some of the methodological differences include reporting source (teacher, parent, peer nomination), providing participants with a definition or not, variations in the time period participants are asked to reflect on, different response and rating categories, global versus behavioral items used, and different thresholds used to determine frequency. All of these factors can result in significant differences in the reported prevalence rate, which can have important implications for intervention strategies, extent and intensity of service provision, and perception of the extent to which bullying behaviors are normative in schools.

What Are the Consequences of Bullying?

Being bullied contributes uniquely and directly to mental health problems among young people, and the consequences of bullying can be severe and long lasting (Skapinakis et al., 2011). Recent research evidence has found a wide range of mental health harms associated with being bullied, including suicidal ideation (Eisenberg & Neumark-Sztainer, 2008), eating disorders (Kaltiala-Heino, Rimpelä, Rantanen, & Rimpelä, 2000; Landstedt & Gådin, 2011), deliberate self-harm (Jankauskiene, Kardelis, Sukys, & Kardeliene, 2008), and low self-esteem (Nansel et al., 2001). Being bullied also results in impaired social and emotional adjustment, difficulty making friends, poorer relationships with peers, and increased loneliness (Forero et al., 1999; Kaltiala-Heino et al., 2000; Kochenderfer & Ladd, 1996; Smith, Tallamelli, et al., 2004), increasing the social isolation of those who are bullied.

Students who are bullied and students who bully others are both at a higher risk of experiencing psychosomatic symptoms such as anxiety (Kaltiala-Heino et al., 2000), depression (Hemphill et al., 2011; Roland, 2002), and suicidality (Rivers, Poteat, Noret, & Ashurst, 2009). Bullying can impact negatively on the mental health of not only the perpetrator and the target of bullying, but also those students who witness the bullying (Kumpulainen, 2008). The detrimental consequences of bullying can extend into adulthood, with involvement in bullying being predictive of future psychiatric disorders (Wolke, Woods, Bloomfield, & Karstadt, 2001).

Being bullied is also associated with physical health harms (Frisén & Bjarnelind, 2010) and poorer ratings of health-related quality of life (Srabstein & Piazza, 2008). Students involved in bullying (either as a perpetrator, target, or both) are at a high risk of suffering from injuries, that are accidental, self-inflicted, or inflicted by others (Srabstein & Piazza, 2008). Involvement in bullying has also been linked with higher risk of abusing over-the-counter medications, intentionally harming animals or people, and using weapons that could seriously hurt someone (van der Wal, de Wit, & Hirasing, 2003).

Additionally, students who bully others are at greater risk for other delinquent behaviors (Srabstein & Piazza, 2008), including setting fires, running away, carrying weapons (Hemphill et al., 2011), and using violence (Kaltiala-Heino et al., 2000) as well as increased substance use, alcohol use (Hemphill et al., 2011; Nansel et al., 2001; Srabstein & Piazza, 2008), and binge drinking (Kim, Catalano, Haggerty, & Abbott, 2011). Childhood bullying perpetration can have long-lasting outcomes, and has been linked with higher risk of violence, heavy drinking, and marijuana use at age twenty-one (Farrington & Ttofi, 2011). Recent research has found that bullying others at age fourteen may predict violent convictions, self-reported violence, and low job status in later adolescence and early adulthood. Self-reported bullying may also predict drug use at age twenty-seven through thirty-two and poor life success at age forty-eight (Forero et al., 1999). Of greatest concern is that students who are both bullied and bully others (commonly known as bully/victims) experience all of these ill-health effects to a greater extent than students who are bullied or who bully others (but not involved in both).

Academic harms also result from school bullying, as students who are bullied are more likely to dislike and wish to avoid school (Kochenderfer & Ladd, 1996; Smith, Tallamelli, et al., 2004), and thus have higher rates of absenteeism (Zubrick et al., 1997). In addition, their academic achievement and sense of academic self-efficacy are diminished in comparison to other students (Andreou & Metallidou, 2004; Boulton, 2008; Glew, Fan, Katon, Rivara, & Kernic, 2005). This may be because students who are bullied report more negative consequences for concentration, completion of work, and enjoyment of work in the classroom (Boulton, Trueman, & Murray, 2008; Forero et al., 1999). Finally, students who bully others also tend to dislike school (Glew et al., 2005) and have decreased academic achievement and self-efficacy (Andreou & Metallidou, 2004; Atlas & Pepler, 1998).

What Role Do Bystanders Play in Bullying?

Bullying occurs within a group context with peers present as onlookers in around 85 percent of bullying interactions (Hawkins, Pepler, & Craig, 2001). Bystanders can have active, diverse, and involved roles in the bullying process, from facilitating to inhibiting bullying (Salmivalli, Lappalainen, & Lagerspetz, 1998). It appears that around 20–30 percent of students actively assist or reinforce bullying, and another 26–30 percent of students try to stay outside the bullying situation (Salmivalli, Lappalainen, & Lagerspetz, 1998). Unfortunately, less than 20 percent of students act to stop the bullying and defend the student being bullied (Gini, Pozzoli, Borghi, & Franzoni, 2008).

Research has observed some age and gender differences with regard to the different roles that students may take on as a bystander to bullying. Younger students show more positive attitudes toward students who are bullied (Rigby & Johnson, 2006) and are more likely to intervene to stop the bullying than are older students (Andreou & Metallidou, 2004; Trach, Hymel, Waterhouse, & Neale, 2010). Girls are more likely than boys to try to help the student being bullied or stay outside the bullying situation, whereas boys are more likely than girls to assist or reinforce the bullying (Andreou & Metallidou, 2004; Camodeca & Goossens, 2005; Lodge & Frydenberg, 2005; Goossens, Olthof, & Dekker, 2006; Salmivalli, Lagerspetz, et al., 1998; Salmivalli, Lappalainen, & Lagerspetz, 1998).

Although many students do not agree with bullying, most do not intervene to stop the bullying but instead act in ways that enable and maintain bullying (Craig, Pepler, & Atlas, 2000; O'Connell, Pepler, & Craig, 1999). Possible reasons for students' failure to intervene in a bullying situation and help a person being bullied include their desire for peer acceptance (Burns, Maycock, Cross, & Brown, 2008), uncertainty about what action to take (Hazler, 1996), fear of becoming the next target of the bullying (Craig & Pepler, 1998; Hazler, 1996), lack of knowledge about appropriate strategies to use to intervene (Craig et al., 2000), and assuming that another observer will take action to stop the situation (Darley & Latane, 1968).

Bystanders who are witness to repetitive abuse such as bullying experience considerable distress that can continue into adulthood (Janson & Hazler, 2004). A recent study found that among twelve- to sixteen-year-olds, witnessing bullying was associated with elevated mental health risks that were over and above those mental health risks posed to students directly involved in the bullying, either as targets or perpetrators of the bullying (Rivers et al., 2009). When students do decide to intervene positively to help a student being bullied, this can have very beneficial effects on the outcome of the bullying situation, with observational research finding that bullying stops within ten seconds of peer intervention (Hawkins et al., 2001). Bystander intervention has also been associated with better interpersonal and intrapersonal adjustment of the student who is bullied and less peer-reported victimization one year later (Sainio, Veenstra, Huitsing, & Salmivalli, 2009). When bystanders intervene to stop bullying, these positive actions appear to be strongly endorsed by other students, and students are less likely to assign blame to the student who is bullied (Gini et al., 2008). Conversely, when bystanders join in the bullying or ignore the bullying, these actions are not endorsed by other students, and when bystanders remain passive, other students have a greater tendency to blame the student being bullied (Gini et al., 2008). Further, a recent study found that students who are bullied perceive positive actions from peers as more helpful than positive actions from adults or their own positive actions to address bullying (Davis & Nixon, 2010). Bystanders who try to help a student being bullied also report feeling good about themselves following their attempts to intervene (Lodge & Frydenberg, 2005).

How Can Bystanders Be Mobilized to Reduce Bullying?

Bystanders represent a key population for intervention in bullying, as their behavior may be easier to change than students directly involved in the bullying (Andreou & Metallidou, 2004; Salmivalli, 1999; Salmivalli, Lagerspetz, et al., 1998). Peer support is a strategy used by several antibullying programs; however, it is important that schools emphasize through their policies and ethos that it is the responsibility of all students to reduce bullying, not just those in a peer supporter role. By only bestowing responsibility upon selected students to help or support another student being bullied, a phenomenon called diffusion of responsibility can occur (Darley & Latane, 1968). Students may fail to intervene to help when other bystanders are present because they assume that another student will take action to stop the situation.

Very little research has been completed investigating bystanders to cyberbullying; however, considerably more opportunities exist in cyberspace to demonstrate positive bystander behavior, and this role is even more important for young people as there are few adults in this environment to support students who are bullied. This bystander support is especially important given the potentially increased harmful effects of cyberbullying associated with the unlimited audience (Patchin & Hinduja, 2006; Snider & Borel, 2004). But there is similarly an infinite audience who could also stand up to the bullying and provide support to the student being bullied. More research is needed to identify the effectiveness of bystander intervention strategies that are effective in a cyber context.

What Can Bystanders Do?

The following are tips for students and young people who may witness bullying.

- Ask a teacher or trusted adult for support.
- Let the person doing the bullying know that what he or she is doing is bullying.
- Refuse to join in with his or her bullying, and walk away.
- Support the student who is being bullied.
- Support their friends and protect them from bullying by being there for them (children who are alone are more likely to be the target of bullying).

Chapter 2

Building Capacity

Schools that assess and improve capacity support to implement strategies to improve student well-being and reduce bullying should help ensure their actions are effective, sustainable, and systemwide. Sufficient leadership, organizational support, resources, staff professional learning, and strategies that are with school needs are crucial to optimize impact.

Evidence for Building Capacity

The success of any reform, whether it is a new literacy or counseling strategy, is dependent not only on the strategies or practices but how well they are implemented. Even if the practices are evidence based and found to be effective, that is not sufficient to ensure positive outcomes for students in every school. The "what" (program activities) plus strategies that support the "how" (implementation) increases the chance of positive and sustainable outcomes for students (Frank Porter Graham Child Development Institute, 2011).

For educators, the math is simple (Frank Porter Graham Child Development Institute, 2011).

Figure 5: How to create positive outcomes for students.

Because schools are complex systems, positive change to support effective implementation of a program usually requires a whole-school approach that is delivered effectively to students, staff, and parents. A leading expert on educational change, Michael Fullan (2007), states the three basics of school priority and educational change should be numeracy, literacy, and well-being. While it is well known that healthy students learn better, student well-being is seldom given the same priority as other educational areas. When schools take on programs such as Friendly Schools Plus, they are not only achieving objectives that aim to enhance student well-being but also student learning for numeracy and literacy. Whereas classroom learning activities specifically target student social and emotional skills, which in turn reduce student bullying behaviors, whole-school prevention strategies usually involve broad activities that enhance well-being, safety, and counseling and build a supportive school culture (Cross, Pintabona, Hall, Hamilton, & Erceg, 2004). Secondly, Fullan (2007) states that successful educational change is based on the improvements of relationships. Bullying is a relationship issue, and ways to reduce these behaviors are through improving relationships and social skills, creating a positive culture of support and respect, and engaging students, staff, and parents so they are connected to their school as a community. Building positive relationships among students, between staff and students, and among staff members is crucial not only in achieving change that is supported by everyone but also in achieving a school culture that is positive, inclusive, and does not tolerate bullying behaviors.

Lastly, Fullan argues that the way to successfully engage and motivate the school community to participate in change is through capacity building. He describes capacity building as a powerful, actionable concept that includes a "policy, strategy, or action taken that increases the collective efficacy of a group to improve student learning through new knowledge, enhanced resources, and greater motivation on the part of the people working individually and together." He suggests that the balance between assessment and capacity building has not been achieved, indicating too much emphasis has been placed on standards and assessments and less on action in real contexts. While schools are aware of the need to adopt evidence-based practices that prevent and manage bullying, many are faced with insufficient capacity in terms of resources, teacher training, and systematic support to ensure they are implemented successfully (Cunningham et al., 2009; Cunningham & Henggeler, 2001). Even when a school chooses an evidence-based program like Friendly Schools Plus, they are often not implemented with sufficient fidelity to ensure success (Kallestad & Olweus, 2003; Salmivalli, Kaukiainen, & Voeten, 2005; Stevens, De Bourdeaudhuij, & Van Oost, 2001) and furthermore, not sufficiently sustained to positively influence student and parent outcomes (Durlak & DuPre, 2008; Fekkes, Pijpers, & Verloove-Vanhorick, 2006). Hence recommendations to improve the effectiveness of bullying interventions in schools are largely focused on implementation and sustainability issues (Ferguson, San Miguel, Kilburn, & Sanchez, 2007; Plog, Epstein, Ines, & Porter, 2010).

As discussed in the introduction to this book, the Friendly Schools research project demonstrated promising results in terms of reducing student bullying behaviors (Cross, Monks, Hall, et al., 2011). Process evaluation, however, showed that the intervention was underimplemented with only 30 percent of the recommended whole-school activities implemented, 67 percent of the curriculum activities, and less than a third of parents completing home activities (Cross, Shaw, et al., 2008). Further, a review of the policy implementation process indicated that many schools found it was difficult to fast-track their policy review and development and move on to its implementation and promotion (Cross, Monks, Hall, et al., 2011). Lack of time, energy, and capacity support for school staff was noted as a major barrier to the schools' ability to implement the intervention effectively. The subsequent *Friendly Schools and Families* research project, similar to the *Friendly Schools* project, aimed to reduce student bullying behaviors, but unlike the *Friendly Schools* project it provided schools with mechanisms to build sufficient implementation capacity to increase program effectiveness and promote sustainability (Cross, Shaw, et al., 2008). Findings from the *Friendly Schools, Friendly Families* study showed that over time schools that focus on capacity building strategies as part of overall program delivery demonstrate improved implementation outcomes. In the study, those schools that received high-capacity support demonstrated higher whole-school implementation capacity, higher program implementation levels, and higher levels of parent engagement—a primary outcome of this study compared to schools receiving no capacity support (Pearce, 2010). Parent engagement with the school was significantly higher in those schools that implemented over a three-year period a whole-school intervention that included specific strategies that assessed and built their capacity to engage parents.

Whether it is practices that aim to reduce student bullying or practices that aim to increase student numeracy skills, it is important to understand the process of implementing change across the school. Implementation is defined as "a specified set of activities designed to put into practice an activity or program of known dimensions" (Fixsen, Naoom, Blase, Friedman, & Wallace, 2005). The known dimensions of a bullying program may be new curriculum, new policy, or changes to classroom management. Activities that aim to build the capacity of staff to implement these activities might be professional learning for staff, additional resources such as time for staff to plan for the new activities, and assessment of how compatible the new practices are working within existing structures.

There are many factors that can influence the effectiveness of the implementation process; in fact, more than three hundred variables have been identified (Roberts-Gray, Gingiss, & Boerm, 2007). Alongside the implementation process itself, there are another four domains described by Damschroder et al. (2009) that play an influential role in the implementation of a program.

1. **Intervention characteristics**—Intervention source, evidence of strength and quality, relative advantage over what was done before, adaptability, trialability, complexity, design, quality and packaging, and cost of the intervention

2. **Outer setting**—Extent to which school needs, as well as the barriers and facilitators in meeting those needs, are known and prioritized within the school; degree to which school is networked to external organizations; competitive pressure to implement an intervention; and external policies and incentives

3. **Inner setting**—Structural characteristics such as size, maturity, and social architecture of a school; quality of formal and informal communications within the school; school culture, norms, and values; and implementation climate such as the shared receptivity of involved individuals to an intervention

4. **Characteristics of individuals involved**—Knowledge and beliefs about the intervention; self-efficacy to believe they can execute the course of action to achieve implementation goals; individual stage of change in progressing skills and use of the intervention; individual identification and commitment to their school; and other personal attributes such as values, motivation, capacity, and competence

Chapter 2

School interventions that aim to reduce bullying behaviors require not only successful implementation to be effective but also sufficient capacity to enable this implementation. To build school capacity to implement bullying prevention programs, the following elements are considered key (Smith, Schneider, et al., 2004).

- A committed and engaged principal and leadership team
- Key staff and students who act as knowledge brokers
- Allocated resources such as staff time and evidence-based tools
- System support in terms of policies, procedures, and structures
- Regular staff professional learning
- Compatibility with school community needs
- Collaborative partnerships with parents, agencies, and the wider community

Figure 6: Building school implementation capacity.

Planning for System Support and Resources

When describing the Norwegian school campaigns against bullying behavior, Midthassel and Roland (2008) state the real challenge is not designing an intervention based on research and producing useable resources but instead determining how the intervention interacts with the school system and teachers as the implementers. They highlight the importance of each school's unique context and system such as its priorities, planning, structures, and school community involvement. As with individual or community capacity building, capacity building in schools to improve the implementation of programs to reduce bullying behaviors must consider the context in which the programs are being implemented and how this can affect program outcomes (Smith, Schneider, et al., 2004).

A meta-analysis on the effects of intervention programs on aggressive behaviors found poorly implemented programs produced smaller effects. In particular, programs that were implemented by teachers and were relatively intense were more effective (Wilson, Lipsey, & Derzon, 2003). In a review of promising programs to reduce violence in schools, effective and ineffective program components were identified (Dusenbury, Falco, Laken, Brannigan, & Bosworth, 1997). Adding a violence prevention program to an already overloaded school system where it is not a priority was ineffective. In addition, insufficient organizational and staff capacity to implement strategies presented additional stress for school staff and reduced their motivation and commitment to the intervention (Dusenbury et al., 1997). In an assessment of the relationship between program outcomes and factors that determine success, Smith, Tallamelli, et al. (2004) noted two important criteria, although acknowledged that no "magic" ingredient has been found to date: first, the extent to which the school took ownership of the intervention and pushed it forward across the whole-school community, and second, the length of the study to allow initial strategies to be maintained to address the ongoing nature of bullying (Smith, 2004). Program duration and intensity for students and teachers is one of the main factors associated with a significant decrease in rates of bullying others and being bullied (Australian Communications and Media Authority, 2008).

Actions for Building Capacity

Committed and Engaged Leadership

To increase staff commitment to implement a new reform, strong leadership and a coordinating team of staff are often necessary (Booth, 1997; McBride, Midford, & Cameron, 1999). A principal who is actively engaged and places a high priority on counseling and reducing bullying is more likely to increase the commitment of the staff to the new initiative (Gottfredson & Gottfredson, 2002) and increase the quality of implementation and intervention adherence (Roberts-Gray et al., 2007). Teachers' confidence to address bullying issues is highly dependent on the demonstrated level of practical support from the principal (James et al., 2008). The school team needs to include representatives from across the school community. It is important that the roles of students, teachers, administration staff, parents, and community members in the change process are recognized and consulted if not represented on this team. The school team members act as knowledge brokers whose responsibility lies in communicating knowledge throughout the school community and facilitating change in a coordinated way.

When responding to bullying incidents, an additional structure to the implementation team may be necessary, such as a team involving teachers who know the students, the school nurse, and school counselors. This additional structure may be more effective than relying only on the classroom teacher to liaise and provide support to parents, and redefining roles means that practical ways to intervene when there is an issue are more likely and the school's prevention and response to bullying behavior are standardized (Laukkanen, Shemeikka, Notkola, Koivumaa-Honkanen, & Nissinen, 2002). This team can also identify relevant research findings and at-risk students; liaise between school and parents; and progress policy and procedures necessary to decrease bullying (Dwyer, Osher, & Hoffman, 2000).

Strategies for Good Practice: Committed and Engaged Leadership

1. The principal and the leadership team communicate to the whole-school community a clear vision for increasing social skills and reducing bullying as a priority commitment.
2. The principal and the leadership team are actively engaged in leading school action to reduce bullying.
3. The principal and the leadership team enable and encourage all members of the whole-school community (staff, students, families) to actively participate in planning and decision making about school action to reduce bullying through regular, planned monitoring and feedback.
4. The principal and the leadership team develop and promote an effective and clear whole-school policy, outlining strategies, structures, and systems to reduce bullying.
5. Key staff, led by a coordinator, take responsibility for helping other staff implement school strategies to reduce bullying.
6. The principal and the leadership team engage the support of wider systems to provide leadership, mentoring, and support to the school in its actions to reduce bullying.

1　**The principal and the leadership team communicate to the whole-school community a clear vision for increasing social skills and reducing bullying as a priority commitment.**

As with any priority integrated into a school system, its success is directly related to the clear commitment and support demonstrated by the principal and the leadership team. This includes creating a vision for a safe and supportive school environment that encourages social behavior that does not accept bullying behaviors. To achieve this outcome, the school vision needs to be developed collaboratively with students, staff, and parents in a way that provides a common understanding of what behavioral expectations are within the school community and what is not acceptable behavior. This vision must be clearly and consistently communicated by the principal and the leadership team through a number of mediums such as the school website, newsletters (see Supportive School Culture toolkit 3.1 for examples), assemblies (see Supportive School Culture toolkit 3.2 for examples), staff meetings, and school planning processes (see chapter 4 for more information) to ensure this vision and these values are recognized as priorities in the school.

2　**The principal and the leadership team are actively engaged in leading school action to reduce bullying.**

The principal's and the leadership team's involvement is pivotal to the success of the policy development and implementation process and, in particular, implementation of whole-school activities. School leaders who are proactive in the development and promotion of the whole-school policy outlining strategies, structures, and systems for the prevention of and response to bullying provide a whole-school perspective necessary to ensure effective implementation across the school community. Seeing leaders in the school "walk the talk" demonstrates to the school community that the principal and the leadership team are highly committed to making the school a safer and more supportive environment for students.

3 **The principal and the leadership team enable and encourage all members of the whole-school community (staff, students, families) to actively participate in planning and decision making about school action to reduce bullying through regular, planned monitoring and feedback.**

As well as being involved in the policy development process, staff, students, and families need to be given the opportunity to provide feedback about its implementation and ideas for improvement. Consultation with whole-school community members ensures fairness of participation and embraces the principles of equal opportunity and social justice. To encourage and facilitate this level of participation in school planning and decision making, clear mechanisms are required. Surveys with students and staff, for example, can inform how, where, and what types of bullying incidents may be occurring in the school. Building Capacity toolkit 2.1 provides information about whole-school surveys related to bullying behavior and the schools' strategies to prevent and reduce this behavior. Surveys can also provide feedback on the effectiveness of current strategies and suggestions for change. Additionally, a student suggestion box and allocated time at staff meetings can be used to obtain feedback and monitor actions being implemented in the school.

4 **The principal and the leadership team develop and promote an effective and clear whole-school policy, outlining strategies, structures, and systems to reduce bullying.**

A policy that addresses bullying is crucial to providing the school with a framework for action. It clearly identifies how the school feels about bullying behaviors and student well-being and outlines strategies, structures, and systems for reducing these behaviors and increasing student support. It is important that the principal and leadership team invest in a process that ensures the policy is implemented well. This may involve training key staff with the skills and knowledge required for policy development and implementation and allocating time for staff to collect information to determine school needs. Commitment by the principal and the leadership team at this stage can determine how well the staff receive and implement the policy.

5 **Key staff, led by a coordinator, take responsibility for helping other staff implement school strategies to reduce bullying.**

In addition to the school principal and leadership team demonstrating their support, a school team that involves other key staff and champions is crucial. These staff members act as knowledge brokers to establish common understandings within the school community of what bullying is and the agreed actions to address this issue in the school. See chapter 5 for more detailed information about key understandings relating to social skill development and bullying prevention. Success is more likely when this team has a coordinator to provide leadership and facilitate consistent action. The coordinator is most effective when given formal recognition of and specific time to work in this role. The team typically comprises teacher representatives from across grade levels, at least one administrator (principal or vice principal), parent representatives whose children represent different grade levels, and other key members from counseling and student services. Some schools involved in Friendly Schools, Friendly Families research reported they found it easier to have a smaller core team that met regularly, supplemented by advisers who were called on when required (for example, parent groups, student services team, school psychologist, school nurse) as well as a student reference committee.

Chapter 2

The school team is most successful when it is (Gingiss, Roberts-Gray, & Boerm, 2006):

- Provided with information to establish common and consistent understandings about bullying
- Provided with background information about the school and students' needs
- Provided with information about the content and process of developing and reviewing, implementing, and promoting the policy
- Committed to the safety and well-being of students, staff, and parents, and acts on behalf of the whole-school community

Actions for the school team:

- Identify the team coordinator.
- Define the structure and roles of the team.
- Hold informal discussions with key staff (administrators, teachers, support staff) to establish interest and support.
- Provide potential members with the key information they need to make an informed decision about their participation and role on the team.
- Establish the team and give it a title and focus, for example, Student Well-Being team or Safe and Supportive team.
- Identify the skills and knowledge required by the team to establish common and consistent understandings about social skill development and bullying behaviors.
- Introduce the team to the whole staff, and define its role, which may include:
  - Working with the school community to establish common understandings and consistent school responses to incidents of bullying
  - Facilitating the development and review of the policies that promote positive social relations and safe and supportive learning environments for all members of the school community
  - Reflecting on and reviewing school actions to reduce bullying

Figure 7: Actions for the school team.

6 **The principal and the leadership team engage the support of wider systems to provide leadership, mentoring, and support to the school in its actions to reduce bullying.**

Creating a safe and supportive school environment that does not accept bullying behaviors requires support from wider systems such as regional and state-based education supports, and health and community sectors. School leaders that seek supporting policies, professional learning opportunities, and mentors will empower their staff and students to initiate and take responsibility for safe school initiatives, ensuring staff feel supported and see the need for their efforts. Presenting the school's policy within current state or national policy gives it relevance and justification for its importance. Identifying external supports, for instance professional learning provided by local education authorities, can encourage staff to try new ideas and build confidence to overcome sustainability issues.

Planning for System Support and Resources

School processes, such as providing adequate time for the team coordinator to plan and provide leadership, adequate planning time for team staff, accessible intervention materials to all staff, intervention plans that are incorporated into school planning processes, adequate training support for schools, technical assistance and coaching, and quality monitoring, feedback, and communication channels between team members are highlighted as important in facilitating successful program implementation (Bosworth, Gingiss, Potthoff, & Roberts-Gray, 1999). Facilitation processes such as these within schools have been shown to predict the quantity of school implementation activity (Damschroder et al., 2009).

The provision of adequate resources, including materials, staffing, facilities, funding, daily planning time, training, and longer time frames to test the strategies in the school (Roberts-Gray et al., 2007; Salmivalli et al., 2005; Smith, Schneider, et al., 2004), was linked to successful program outcomes in which greater efforts were achieved when sufficient resources were available (Roberts-Gray et al., 2007; Thaker et al., 2008). A study conducted with school principals identified that having adequate resources was directly linked to successful program outcomes in which the program "dose" was completely determined by sufficiency of resources (Smith, Schneider, et al., 2004). One of the key resource barriers identified by staff in the Friendly Schools, Friendly Families research was the competing demands on teacher time. Insufficient time for the school team to plan, teaching staff to teach, and school leaders to facilitate a whole-school approach meant actions were being implemented in small doses.

The following are some strategies suggested by schools to help address this issue.

- A Friendly Schools notice board was placed in the staff room for team members to communicate with each other and the whole-school staff and for staff to provide feedback on policy issues.
- Activities were monitored through teacher logs and in-staff performance management plans to formally acknowledge staff and faculty work and the time allocated for working on the implementation process.
- Teaching staff were given a half day off from teaching to use for training and planning time to incorporate the recommended learning activities into their classes.
- The policy was integrated with other priority programs in the school with similar goals to make planning and implementation easier. The policy implementation was then less likely to be seen by staff as just another thing to do.

Chapter 2

Strategies for Good Practice:
Planning for System and Resource Support

1. School actions to reduce bullying, and resources identified to implement them, are integrated into school strategic planning.
2. Strategies to reduce bullying are integrated into existing structures, programs, partnerships, and accountability processes where possible.
3. Adequate time to plan, implement, and sustain school action to reduce bullying is allowed (three to five years to initiate, five to seven years to sustain).
4. Adequate numbers of staff are part of the student well-being team to ensure the workload is shared and the impact on staff is minimized.
5. The team and the coordinator have adequate time to meet regularly, plan, and facilitate school action.
6. The principal and leadership team ensure teaching staff have allocated time in the curriculum to develop students' key understandings and competencies to encourage positive social behavior.

1　**School actions to reduce bullying, and resources identified to implement them, are integrated into school strategic planning.**

Strategies to prevent and respond to bullying and build positive relationships must be included in school behavior management planning and priority processes. Identification of current state- and district-level education policies and guidelines that are consistent with the schools' proposed objectives can help justify and support this issue as a high priority. Planning for the provision of funding to support implementation of these school activities is also essential to enable them to proceed. Identification of the potential funds and additional resources required for each stage of policy development and implementation and subsequent strategies was important in turning the school vision into practice for those schools involved in CHPRC research. Staff time to facilitate change in promoting a positive school culture was listed by schools involved in CHPRC research as the most important resource support. If financial resources are required, then processes to evaluate the impact of this expenditure would also be necessary.

2　**Strategies to reduce bullying are integrated into existing structures, programs, partnerships, and accountability processes where possible.**

When a new strategy or initiative is proposed in a school, the benefit of integrating its activities within existing structures and priorities is clear. Pooling resources and staff time to achieve similar objectives can mean less time and energy by staff are needed and the likelihood of sustainability is increased. Many schools involved in CHPRC research had existing committees that were responsible for student health and well-being, or values education within the school. Using these teams to also include bullying prevention and management strategies as part of their role meant they were ready to implement change much faster with partnerships with key staff and outside agencies and with accountability processes already in place. School leaders can review their school development plan to assess current priorities and possible links between the bullying prevention and management and other relevant policies, for example, behavior management policy, social justice and equity policy, mobile phone and technology policy, or field trip policy to evaluate opportunities of best fit.

3 **Adequate time to plan, implement, and sustain school action to reduce bullying is allowed (three to five years to initiate, five to seven years to sustain).**

The benefits of the bullying prevention and management policy and its implementation depend largely on the stage at which the school started. Previous CHPRC research suggests that at least three years is a realistic timeline to see positive change. Feedback from these schools suggests that the first year is mostly spent in reviewing and developing the policy with some planning while the second and third years tend to focus on the implementation and promotion of the policy. The following years are focused on sustaining the strategies, monitoring and adjusting the policy according to the success or failure of the strategies, and response from the school community. In subsequent years, the policy should not need the intensive time required at the start of the process; however, a review of social skill building and bullying prevention and response strategies within the school needs to be carried out at the start of each year. After five years, it is thought that the new strategy is sufficiently diffused into the school organization and can take up to seven years to be sustained to a point where the impact on student outcomes is realized. Small objectives and steps that are set yearly will ensure that successes are celebrated along the way and that it is a manageable process for schools to build on over time.

4 **Adequate number of staff are part of the student well-being team to ensure the workload is shared and the impact on staff is minimized.**

As the effectiveness of a program is related to the length of time it is implemented in the school, strategies that address shared staff workload and turnover are important. Ensuring the team has representatives across the school community by positions or roles can help in selecting new staff to replace those who leave. For example, having a coordinator of grade level positions connected to the team means that all grade levels are represented and staff in these positions are automatically nominated. It also creates an opportunity for staff who may not initially be interested in the team's objectives, such as improving guidance practices, to be engaged by being part of the process. Once positions are designated to the team, responsibilities and activities should be discussed and shared among the members to prevent burden on a small number of staff. Where possible, these responsibilities need to be written into staff performance management plans so that this work is recognized and rewarded, expectations are clear, and potential support needs are identified. It is useful to have an induction and mentoring process for new staff who may be interested in taking up positions on the team in the future.

5 **The team and the coordinator have adequate time to meet regularly, plan, and facilitate school action.**

A key part of successful implementation is having a team that functions effectively and is adequately resourced. Adequate planning time allocated to the coordinator and team members to meet and facilitate the school action plan is one of the main barriers to successful implementation CHPRC research schools reported. This is particularly necessary at the initial planning and policy development stages in the exploring and engaging parts of the implementation process. The coordinator requires additional time to provide leadership and support to other team members, with a half day per week recommended by these schools as sufficient time. First tasks for the team would be to prepare a timeline of action for the policy development and its implementation so it is clear what invested time is required and when tasks would need to be completed. While set times for the team to meet regularly are essential, identifying numerous channels of communication between team members means that actions can move along without the need to meet face to face as often. For example, school IT communications such as emails are an obvious way to facilitate discussions, allowing face-to-face meetings to be reserved for decision making. In addition to team meetings, mechanisms for regular monitoring and feedback from all staff to the team are important. CHPRC research schools use staff room notice boards to post updates and keep other staff informed and have a feedback box for staff to add suggestions for how things are working. A brief time slot in staff meetings is allocated for staff to provide feedback.

6 **The principal and leadership team ensure teaching staff have allocated time in the curriculum to develop students' key understandings and competencies to encourage positive social behavior.**

Developing a school culture that is supportive and does not tolerate bullying requires common understandings about bullying behaviors to be clearly communicated to the whole-school community. Plans to increase student competencies to put these understandings into practice are then essential to support the school's vision and culture. Lessons that build student social skills, positive bystander actions, and skills such as how to stop and report bullying behaviors are key to reducing bullying prevalence. Curriculum time dedicated to these understandings and competencies is the primary way to achieve this; however, competing demands in the curriculum timetable are a challenge for most schools. Students need a minimum of five hours of formal classroom teaching per year (one hour per focus area). If a school is serious about making a difference, then dedicated teaching time allocated by school management remains critical.

Ensuring Compatibility With School Community Needs

A school initiative is more likely to succeed if it is perceived by staff to be simple and easy to implement, is better than what they were doing before, and is compatible with school priorities, student needs, and school ethos (Smith, Schneider, et al., 2004; Roberts-Gray et al., 2007). Schools should conduct an assessment of their capacity to implement strategies to reduce and manage bullying and develop additional strategies that build structures, processes, and skills across the whole-school community. The Bridge-It model suggests implementation success is more likely when school staff are prepared for their role, committed, skilled and experienced, willing, have compatible job expectations, and believe in the relative advantage of the innovation over current practice (Roberts-Gray et al., 2007). The presence of a policy that addresses health education and promotion leads to higher perceptions from school staff that health is important within their school environment, and this in turn leads to a higher commitment to student health (Adamson, McAleavy, Donegan, & Shevlin, 2006). However, support for staff is needed to practice and enforce the policy. Training for staff is an important factor in achieving long-term sustainability or institutionalization of school-based programs (Hoelscher et al., 2004).

Strategies for Good Practice: Ensuring Compatibility With School and Community

1. Assessment of the school's capacity for implementing actions to reduce bullying is conducted to identify strengths, barriers, and new opportunities.
2. Pre-existing capacities and successful practices within the school to reduce bullying are valued and promoted to encourage a sense of collective self-efficacy in the school community.
3. Surveys of staff and students are conducted regularly to evaluate and inform school action to reduce bullying.
4. Strategies chosen to reduce bullying are easy for the whole-school community to implement.
5. Any disruptions occurring inside and outside the school environment that will influence the success of school actions to reduce bullying are acknowledged, and ways to overcome these are discussed.

1 **Assessment of the school's capacity for implementing actions to reduce bullying is conducted to identify strengths, barriers, and new opportunities.**

Research in schooling and capacity building suggests that each school's context and capacities are unique and, therefore, no blueprint for action can be proposed for all schools. In addition, defining what capacities need to be strengthened requires having a specific program or strategy in mind. Once results from the student, staff, and parent surveys create a picture of what is happening in the school and strategies are chosen to target areas of need, a capacity assessment can help to identify areas requiring capacity development. Key implementation drivers such as leadership support and structures, competencies, and organizational supports are critical to review. Objectives for building staff capacity are necessary alongside program objectives to ensure staff are well supported to implement the strategies that target students and parents. Strategies to build capacity may include prioritizing the program in school planning documents, allocating resources such as staff time to plan strategies, and increasing knowledge and competencies through staff professional learning, student curriculum, and workshops for families as well as leadership structures to mentor and provide support to other staff. A description of the curriculum materials that form part of this program is provided in Key Understandings and Competencies toolkit 5.1. Capacity building is a long-term process that takes time to deliver change. It is vitally important for schools to realize that the school system will slip back into old patterns if the process of capacity building is not intentionally maintained and annual objectives set.

2 **Pre-existing capacities and successful practices within the school to reduce bullying are valued and promoted to encourage a sense of collective self-efficacy in the school community.**

Most schools are already implementing many activities to address school culture and student support services that aim to improve student learning and reduce time spent on behavior management. As well as surveys with the different groups in the school community, a review of past and current school practices is helpful to identify strategies that are working well and ones that have not worked well in the past. This may be a task for the school executive or selected key staff as part of discussions around the survey findings. Many CHPRC research schools were surprised by how many whole-school activities they were already implementing. Acknowledging this effort is important and provides a useful starting point to review these practices to determine their effectiveness relative to alternative and additional strategies. This review also allows opportunities for the new policy or program to be integrated into existing structures, partnerships, and accountability processes so that efforts are not duplicated and limited resources are maximized. Acknowledgment at staff meetings, in newsletters (see Supportive School Culture toolkit 3.1 for examples), at assemblies (see Supportive School Culture toolkit 3.3 for examples), via the school website, at parent nights, or as part of celebrations on a special day (such as International Friendship Day, described in School–Family–Community Partnerships toolkit 7.5), for example, can help build the collective self-efficacy of the school community to believe they can make a difference.

3 Surveys of staff and students are conducted regularly to evaluate and inform school action to reduce bullying.

Online or paper-based self-report surveys are a reliable way to determine the extent of an issue in the school and perceptions of staff and students to inform school planning and enable targeting of resources. Building Capacity toolkit 2.1 provides an overview of the information that can be collected in whole-school surveys. An understanding of students' bullying experiences in terms of prevalence, types of behaviors, location, duration, and help with seeking and reporting outcomes for those students being bullied and those engaging in bullying is important to identify specific areas of need. If the sample of students surveyed is large enough, differences between grade-level groups can also be detected and highlight which grade levels may need extra support. Staff surveys can determine their observations of bullying behaviors, perceptions of their knowledge and skills to deal with incidents, and what is currently working within the school. Staff professional learning can then be tailored to meet identified needs such as specifically preventing and responding to cyberbullying behaviors. Surveys can also be used to evaluate the effectiveness of counseling, peer support and bystanders' actions, school climate, and student connectedness to their school and teachers to determine protective or mediating factors against bullying behaviors and pointers for intervention. A review of the school bullying ethos; the perceptions of students, staff, and families of school policy; and the practices and vision regarding bullying behaviors also provide a mechanism to evaluate whether changes made within the school are making a difference. Ensuring the strategies implemented are compatible with school priorities, student needs, school ethos, and school structure, and evidence that school community efforts are a significant improvement on what the school was previously doing, will increase the likelihood of program sustainability.

4 Strategies chosen to reduce bullying are easy for the whole-school community to implement.

Once research can demonstrate the severity of the issue within the school community, staff, as primary implementers, need to be convinced that the proposed strategies are the most effective way to address the issues identified. Achieving staff buy-in is important and can be influenced by the perceived complexity and length of the intervention, staff perceptions of how it will fit with their current role, their perceptions that it will be better than what they were doing before, and their competency and understanding of the program's underlying principles to fulfill their part in implementation. Interventions for CHPRC research schools were always presented as a more effective and easier way to achieve necessary student outcomes while not adding to their already significant workloads. By streamlining ways the school prevents and responds to bullying incidents, staff time spent dealing with bullying issues should be reduced.

5 **Any disruptions occurring inside and outside the school environment that will influence the success of school actions to reduce bullying are acknowledged, and ways to overcome these are discussed.**

As schools are busy places, there will always be disruptions occurring in the school environment that will affect how well a new initiative is implemented. CHPRC research schools found the process of identifying those disruptions occurring inside and outside the school was useful to help explain why some strategies may not have worked as well as expected. It is important to acknowledge that the strategy itself may be effective when implemented at another time or in different circumstances and can assist with future planning. CHPRC research schools noted that in identifying these potential disruptions, solutions were often found to overcome these obstacles that reduced their impact on school operations.

Summary

The development of positive social skills and the prevention of bullying behaviors is a whole-school issue. However, little change will occur unless staff, students, and families have an understanding of what has happened previously in the school to reduce bullying and how successful this has been. Based on this knowledge, school leaders can engage the whole-school community to set actions and assemble resources to achieve change. Establishing timelines and implementing activities requires committed leadership support, adequate resource planning, and ensuring compatibility with school needs. Finally, evaluating school action is important not only to identify benefits relating to student behavioral outcomes but also staff, student, and family efficacy and perceptions of improvement over previous action.

Several toolkits included in this chapter and across this book will assist schools in building the capacity of their whole-school community to improve their ability to enhance student well-being and reduce bullying.

Chapter 2

Toolkits for Action

 ## Building Capacity Toolkit 2.1
Whole-School Surveys

Schools may wish to survey their whole-school community to develop an understanding of the social and emotional health and well-being of their students, the prevalence and nature of bullying behavior in their school, their staff and family capacity to respond to bullying situations, and their satisfaction with school prevention strategies and responses to bullying behavior.

It is important that information provided by survey respondents is treated as being strictly confidential and that strategies to ensure this confidentiality are communicated to respondents prior to their survey completion.

Staff Surveys

Objective: To provide schools with an understanding of their staff members' perspectives about their students' social and emotional learning (SEL) and bullying behaviors by measuring their:

- Perception of their key understandings
- Attitudes toward SEL and bullying behaviors
- Perception of their skills to teach SEL and prevent and manage bullying behaviors
- Self-efficacy to enhance students' social and emotional health and reduce bullying behaviors
- Perception of the effectiveness of their school's prevention, response, and support strategies
- Perception of their school's culture and their school and staff capacity to implement evidence-based strategies

Student Surveys

Objective: To provide schools with an understanding of students' social and emotional health and well-being experiences and behaviors by measuring students':

- Social and emotional competencies
- Perception of school climate, connectedness to school and teachers, safety at school, and peer support
- Perception of their school's actions to prevent, respond to, and support students experiencing bullying behaviors
- Experiences of different types of bullying behaviors
- Experiences of the duration and location of bullying behaviors
- Perception of how bullying behavior affected them
- Absences from school due to bullying experiences
- Actions after being bullied or bullying others and the type of support sought
- Perception of teachers' responses to bullying behavior
- Actions as a bystander

2.0 PLANNING TOOL: BUILDING CAPACITY FOR ACTION

Statement of Evidence for Building Capacity for Action

Schools that assess and improve capacity support to implement strategies to improve student outcomes such as well-being, counseling, social skills, and reduction in bullying help to ensure their actions are effective, sustainable, and systemwide. Sufficient leadership, organizational support, resources, and strategy compatibility with school needs are crucial to optimize impact.

Review Action 2.1—Committed and Engaged Leadership

	Not yet initiated	In planning	Preparing staff	Partially in place	Fully in place	Sustained practice
2.1.1 The principal and the leadership team communicate to the whole-school community a clear vision for increasing social skills and reducing bullying as a priority commitment.						
2.1.2 The principal and the leadership team are actively engaged in leading school action to reduce bullying.						
2.1.3 The principal and the leadership team enable and encourage all members of the whole-school community (staff, students, families) to actively participate in planning and decision making about school action to reduce bullying through regular, planned monitoring and feedback.						
2.1.4 The principal and the leadership team develop and promote an effective and clear whole-school policy to reduce bullying.						
2.1.5 Key staff interested in counseling, led by a coordinator, take responsibility for helping other staff implement school strategies to reduce bullying.						
2.1.6 The principal and the leadership team engage the support of wider systems to provide leadership, mentoring, and support to the school in their actions to reduce bullying.						

Plan Action 2.1—Committed and Engaged Leadership

What needs to be done?	Who is going to do it?	Status	Timeline		What do we need?	Comments and reflections
			Finish	Status		

continued →

Review Action 2.2—Planning for System and Resource Support

	Not yet initiated	In planning	Preparing staff	Partially in place	Fully in place	Sustained practice
2.2.1 School actions to reduce bullying and resources identified to implement them are <u>integrated into</u> <u>school strategic planning.</u>	Not yet initiated	In planning	Preparing staff	Partially in place	Fully in place	Sustained practice
2.2.2 Strategies to reduce bullying are <u>integrated into existing structures, programs, partnerships, and</u> <u>accountability processes</u> where possible.	Not yet initiated	In planning	Preparing staff	Partially in place	Fully in place	Sustained practice
2.2.3 <u>Adequate time</u> to plan, implement, and sustain school action to reduce bullying is allowed (three to five years to initiate, five to seven years to sustain).	Not yet initiated	In planning	Preparing staff	Partially in place	Fully in place	Sustained practice
2.2.4 <u>Adequate numbers of staff</u> are part of the student well-being team to ensure the workload is shared and the impact on staff is minimized.	Not yet initiated	In planning	Preparing staff	Partially in place	Fully in place	Sustained practice
2.2.5 The team and the coordinator have adequate time to meet regularly, plan, and facilitate school action.	Not yet initiated	In planning	Preparing staff	Partially in place	Fully in place	Sustained practice
2.2.6 The principal and leadership team ensure teaching staff have allocated time in the curriculum to develop students' key understandings and competencies to encourage positive social behavior.	Not yet initiated	In planning	Preparing staff	Partially in place	Fully in place	Sustained practice

Plan Action 2.2—Planning for System and Resource Support

What needs to be done?	Who is going to do it?	Timeline		What do we need?	Comments and reflections
		Status	Finish Status		

Review Action 2.3—Ensuring Compatibility With School Community Needs

	Not yet initiated	In planning	Preparing staff	Partially in place	Fully in place	Sustained practice
2.3.1 Assessment of the school's capacity for implementing actions to reduce bullying is conducted to identify strengths, barriers, and new opportunities.						
2.3.2 Pre-existing capacities and successful practices within the school to reduce bullying are valued and promoted to encourage a sense of collective self-efficacy in the school community.						
2.3.3 Surveys of staff and students are conducted regularly to evaluate and inform school action to reduce bullying.						
2.3.4 Strategies chosen to reduce bullying are easy for the whole-school community to implement.						
2.3.5 Any disruptions occurring inside and outside the school environment that will influence the success of school actions to reduce bullying are acknowledged and ways to overcome these are discussed.						

Plan Action 2.3—Ensuring Compatibility With School Community Needs

What needs to be done?	Who is going to do it?	Status	Timeline		What do we need?	Comments and reflections
			Finish	Status		

Chapter 3

Supportive School Culture

A supportive school culture provides safety, encourages open communication, supports a sense of connectedness to the school and connection between staff and students and among students, and also protects students from the risks of bullying. The quality of relationships between and among staff, students, and families is vital in fostering a safe, supportive, and engaging school environment. Positive student behavior should be encouraged and acknowledged at the whole-school level.

Evidence for Building a Supportive School Culture

Students who are bullied or cyberbullied, students who bully or cyberbully others, or students who are both victims and perpetrators are more likely than those not involved to report feeling unsafe at school (Burns, Cross, Alfonso, & Maycock, 2008). In contrast, schools that implement strategies that foster student safety have been found to reduce bullying behaviors (Andreou & Metallidou, 2004; Bradshaw, O'Brennan, & Sawyer, 2008). Williams and Guerra (2007), for example, found that if students perceive their friends as trustworthy, caring, and helpful, they are less likely to be involved in perpetrating bullying and cyberbullying. In this chapter, ways to foster a positive school culture, effective classroom practice and environment strategies, and the role of the peer group in building a supportive school culture are discussed.

Positive Whole-School Culture

Research has found students' perception of a positive school climate is associated with a reduced likelihood of bullying others (Lee, 2010). A key component of a supportive school culture is an ethos that bullying is not tolerated, with action taken to actively prevent or respond immediately and effectively to its occurrence. The increased use of technology by students means this ethos and associated actions need to be promoted in both online and offline environments. A positive whole-school culture is described in the following research.

- Schools express a culture of disapproval of bullying behavior by valuing "telling," responding consistently, and ensuring adequate follow-up. School staff can play a major role in the bullying dynamic by inadvertently fostering aggressive behavior by failing to speak out against it (Espelage & Swearer, 2003).
- From a bystander perspective, students need to know that supporting a person being bullied is promoted in the school and to have confidence that school staff will support their efforts to help the person being bullied, follow through on reports of bullying, and provide protection for those students who intervene to stop bullying (Craig et al., 2000; O'Connell et al., 1999). This is especially important given that the main reason students do not intervene to stop bullying is because they fear retaliation and becoming the next target of the bullying (Hazler, 1996; Slee, 1994).

Connectedness to School

Ensuring students feel connected to school is an important strategy to promote a positive school culture. Connectedness to school is the sense of belonging among students, families, school staff, and the wider school community (Rowe, Stewart, & Patterson, 2007). Lower levels of connectedness to school are associated with greater frequency of peer harassment (Eisenberg, Neumark-Sztainer, & Perry, 2003). Students who are bullied, who bully others, or who both bully and are bullied are more likely to report feeling a lack of connectedness to school compared to students with low or no involvement in bullying (Bradshaw et al., 2008). Similarly, students who report greater connectedness to school and a positive school climate have a reduced likelihood of bullying and cyberbullying others (Williams & Guerra, 2007). Furthermore, Bond et al. (2007) found that students who report higher levels of connectedness to school are more likely to have:

- Higher levels of academic competency, achievement, attitudes, and motives
- More positive attitudes toward themselves and others
- Increased participation and engagement
- Decreased rates of school dropout
- Decreased engagement in health risk behaviors

Also, Resnick et al. (1997) found that connectedness to school may be an important protective factor for adolescents experiencing emotional distress, suicidal thoughts and behaviors, violence, and substance use. Extracurricular activities, such as sports, recreation, music, arts, and service are important ways to increase connectedness to school (Hamilton, Cross, Hall, Resnicow, & Young, 2003; McBride, Midford, & James, 1995; McNeeley, Nonnemaker, & Blum, 2002). These activities provide opportunities for increased social networks and social support, which appears to help students who are cyberbullied, in particular, as they are more likely to report emotional and peer problems (Sourander et al., 2010).

Effective Classroom Practice and Environment

Research has found poor teacher management of the class (as viewed by students) is associated with a higher likelihood of students bullying others, whereas more effectively managed classrooms have lower rates of bullying (Roland & Galloway, 2002). Classroom management refers to the capacity of teachers to plan and organize classroom instruction, learning, and behaviors; actions to maintain order among students; promoting an environment where student-student and student-teacher cooperation is fostered; and maximizing student engagement in their learning (Emmer & Stough, 2001). Farrington and Ttofi (2009) found that an emphasis on classroom management techniques to respond to bullying and the use of classroom rules against bullying are key to reducing bullying behavior.

Teachers' personal characteristics, such as their level of supportiveness and warmth, were also found to be related to students' perceptions of the social climate of the school and had an important influence on the bullying behavior of students (Gini, 2006). Students who engage in the perpetration of bullying and cyberbullying as well as students who are the targets of cyberbullying, for example, were more likely to report negative perceptions of their relationships with their teachers and were more likely to feel uncared for by their teachers (Bacchini, Esposito, & Affuso, 2009).

Positive Peer-Group Influence

Schools that develop an ethos as well as policies and practices that encourage and support safe, positive bystander action help raise the level of bystander involvement. Providing students with opportunities to practice safe bystander skills can increase the efficacy and likelihood of students taking positive action when they see bullying occurring in their school. Younger students and girls are likely to show more positive attitudes toward students who are bullied (Gini et al., 2008) and are more likely to intervene to stop the bullying than are older students and boys (Rigby & Johnson, 2006; Trach et al., 2010).

Although many students do not agree with bullying, most do not intervene to stop the bullying but instead act in ways that enable and maintain bullying (Craig et al., 2000; O'Connell et al., 1999). Possible reasons for students' failure to help a person being bullied include:

- Their desire for peer acceptance (Burns, Maycock, et al., 2008)
- Uncertainty about what action to take (Hazler, Miller, Carney, & Green, 2001)
- Fear of becoming the next target of the bullying (Craig et al., 2000; Hazler et al., 2001)
- Lack of knowledge about appropriate strategies to use to intervene (Craig et al., 2000)
- Assuming another observer will take action to stop the situation (Darley & Latane, 1968)

Students who are bullied perceive positive actions from peers as more helpful than positive actions from adults or their own positive actions to address bullying (Davis & Nixon, 2010). When peers do decide to intervene to help a student being bullied:

- Bullying stops more quickly (Hawkins et al., 2001)
- They are less likely to experience interpersonal and intrapersonal problems, and there is less peer-reported victimization one year later (Sainio et al., 2009)
- Students are less likely to assign blame to the person being bullied (Gini et al., 2008)
- They report feeling good about themselves for attempting to intervene and are more likely to intervene again (Lodge & Frydenberg, 2005)

Chapter 3

Actions for Building a Supportive School Culture

Positive Whole-School Culture

"It is everything we say and everything we do" (Cross et al., 2009).

A school's culture is determined by the school community, including its leaders, educators, students, parents, and supporters. Encouraging positive values such as respect, trust, and equity is the foundation of the policies and programs that ultimately drive the vision of what the school community aims to achieve. Promoting connectedness to school for students, staff, and families in an environment where they feel emotionally and physically safe is a key part of developing and maintaining a positive school culture.

Strategies for Good Practice: Positive Whole-School Culture

1. The school culture supports a sense of connectedness and safety for all students, staff, and families through positive, trusting, and caring relationships.
2. The school treats bullying as a relationship issue and communicates a clear philosophy regarding how it feels about social relationships and bullying.
3. Positive social values such as respect, trust, fairness, and celebration of diversity are promoted across the school community.
4. The school recognizes that bullying can be reduced in the school environment and acknowledges everyone's responsibility to reduce bullying behavior.
5. Staff well-being is an important focus of the school's culture.
6. Appropriate social behaviors are formally and informally modeled by staff.
7. Students are actively involved in the promotion of a positive whole-school culture.
8. All staff are skilled to build positive relations among students and between themselves and their students.
9. Students are empowered to increase their safety and solve problems.
10. Prosocial, cooperative behavior is encouraged and acknowledged.

1 **The school culture supports a sense of connectedness and safety for all students, staff, and families through positive, trusting, and caring relationships.**

While families are an important source of support for students, teachers are important in facilitating students' connectedness to school as they offer guidance, information, interest, and attention, engaging students in the learning environment. In addition, peers play an important role in students' perceived connectedness to school, especially as students grow older. Because peers can positively and negatively influence students' behaviors, attitudes, achievement, and attention, opportunities need to be provided for positive peer interactions and the development of friendships.

While staff and students' relationships can be developed through formal and informal interactions, this is particularly important in secondary schools where opportunities to build relationships and connectedness are often fewer. For example, consider having "Mix It Up" days where students sit next to someone different for lunch to reduce lunchtime cliques. Participating in extracurricular activities also provides opportunities to enhance connectedness to school through the development of positive relationships with school staff and other students.

2 **The school treats bullying as a relationship issue and communicates a clear philosophy regarding how it feels about social relationships and bullying.**

Bullying is more than a relationship between students who perpetrate bullying and those who are bullied; it is a breakdown in a social relationship, involving group values and group standards of behavior, that requires collaborative and consistent action across the school community for positive change to occur. Some students who have not developed the ability to get along with others need to learn and practice skills to resolve conflict, empathize with others, play fairly, and treat others with kindness. Newsletter items included in the Supportive School Culture toolkit 3.1 provide an opportunity for schools to communicate the behaviors that constitute bullying and the school's response plan to bullying situations.

An awareness and shared understanding of bullying behavior needs to be developed by actively consulting with all members of the school community, including students. This awareness counters the view that bullying is an inevitable part of school life, challenges the attitudes of the community, and invites the community to examine its own social behavior and culture. This shared philosophy forms the basis for policies that address expected student, staff, family, and community behaviors. More information about policy review and development can be found in chapter 4. In particular, Proactive Policies and Practices toolkit 4.4 discusses the importance of and ways to identify the school's vision statement and guiding principles.

Chapter 3

3 **Positive social values such as respect, trust, fairness, and celebration of diversity are promoted across the school community.**

A welcoming and supportive environment can be achieved by school community members showing:

- Respect
- Trust
- Fairness
- Appreciation of diversity
- Thoughtfulness
- Engagement in school life

The social environment of a school is enhanced by strong leadership and the demonstration of clear expectations of what the school community hopes to achieve. A values clarification exercise can help identify core values important to each school community.

School Community Values Clarification Exercise

1. Provide staff, students, and families with clear information in accessible language about values, what they are, and why having school values is important.

2. Provide opportunities for consultation about the core values the school community sees as being important to its school.

3. Allocate time for consideration, feedback, and collation of nominated values.

4. Identify the core values the school will promote, and express them in language that is easily understood by staff, students, and families.

5. Promote the values often, clearly, and consistently, for example, at assemblies, in school handbooks, and on the school's website.

Figure 8: School community values clarification exercise.

In addition, schools may choose to promote their values through the school's newsletter. Supportive School Culture toolkits 3.1 and 3.2 include examples of assembly and newsletter items that discuss the school's values and expectations.

4 **The school recognizes bullying can be reduced in the school environment and acknowledges everyone's responsibility to reduce bullying behavior.**

A whole-school understanding about bullying and the development of concern for the safety and well-being of one another are key factors in the reduction of bullying behavior across school communities. Chapter 5 provides information about how to develop an awareness of bullying behavior and how it can be reduced.

Consistent actions will help increase feelings of safety and support among students and staff. Encourage students to identify key messages from the school's ethos or policy to help promote positive social skills and values. For example, a CHPRC research school uploaded winning key messages to its school's website and used them as school screensavers. In addition, the school laminated and displayed posters of the key messages in prominent places around the school to raise awareness of key issues.

Bullying involves more than the students who are bullied and those who bully others. Other students are observed to be present during most bullying and cyberbullying incidents at school. Bullying can continue because people who are involved do not talk about it or seek help. This includes bystanders to bullying situations. For more information about the role of, and ways to engage, bystanders, see Supportive School Culture toolkit 3.4.

5 **Staff well-being is an important focus of the school's culture.**

Happy, valued, and positive staff members are more likely to engage in policies, plans, and practices that ensure the long-term sustainability of programs such as those to reduce bullying behavior. This can be achieved by:

- Celebrating the different and unique knowledge and skills each staff member brings to the school
- Supporting school staff and rewarding their efforts to introduce and participate in programs that help reduce inappropriate, antisocial, and bullying behavior
- Equipping staff with information, resources, and training to build their capacity to implement these programs successfully
- Establishing a social committee that is responsible for fostering positive relationships between staff and enhancing staff connectedness to the school
- Considering unique ways of acknowledging staff for their contribution to the development of the whole-school culture

6 **Appropriate social behaviors are formally and informally modeled by staff.**

Students learn, feel, and act based on what they see others say and do. Staff can unknowingly behave in ways that actively support or condone bullying or in ways that promote the reduction and prevention of bullying. The messages students receive from school staff are important, as they provide constant, prosocial adult modeling (online and offline), particularly when students lack positive family role models.

By understanding what constitutes bullying behaviors (see chapter 5), staff can model appropriate social behavior, which in turn can be repeated by students.

Chapter 3

Students are actively involved in the promotion of a positive whole-school culture.

To promote student ownership and promotion of a supportive school climate, schools need to actively involve them in:

- Planning and decision making (see Proactive Policies and Practices toolkit 4.5)
- Developing positive messages of respect and support (see Supportive School Culture toolkit 3.2)
- Promoting and supporting positive and caring relationships (see Supportive School Culture toolkit 3.3)

Promoting social responsibility among students encourages peer groups to support students who are bullied and discourages bullying behavior through positive peer influence.

 All staff are skilled to build positive relations among students and between themselves and their students.

Teachers need to be provided with professional learning opportunities that:

- Increase their awareness and identification of bullying and its short- and long-term effects on students
- Enhance their knowledge and ability to integrate effective ways to prevent and respond to bullying in teaching and learning activities
- Encourage reflection on their own behavior and social interactions and the influence of these interactions on the values and behavior of their students
- Enhance their knowledge and ability to build positive social relations among students and between themselves and their students

The promotion of these understandings and skills is discussed in more detail in chapter 5.

9 Students are empowered to increase their safety and solve problems.

Fostering positive student relations, cooperative learning, and prosocial behavior will empower students to be aware of and take responsibility for their own safety and develop decision-making skills. This is likely to lead to increased levels of confidence in finding solutions to their problems. Empowered students know where and from whom to get help when they are experiencing difficulties. These social skills are addressed in the Friendly Schools Plus teaching and learning materials described in Key Understandings and Competencies toolkit 5.1.

Parents can also assist in the process by encouraging open and supportive communication with their children and discussing bullying behavior with them (see School–Family–Community Partnerships toolkits 7.2 and 7.3).

10 **Prosocial, cooperative behavior is encouraged and acknowledged.**

The more opportunities students have to develop their social skills, the more likely they are to make prosocial choices that will strengthen their interpersonal relationships and facilitate success in school. As an example, schools and parents can encourage the development of assertiveness among students to assist them in supporting students who are bullied by stepping in to stop the behavior and approaching an adult for help if they see bullying occurring. Supportive School Culture toolkit 3.5 describes assertive behavior and how schools and parents can support development of this social skill among students.

Effective Classroom Practice and Environment

An inclusive, trusting classroom environment will help students build care and empathy for others and provide cooperative and productive learning opportunities. Effective management of the classroom by teachers includes providing an environment in which students can be:

- Focused
- Attentive
- Conscientious
- Actively engaged
- Connected to teachers and fellow students (Emmer & Stough, 2001; McNeely et al., 2002)

Promoting a normative culture of disapproval of bullying within the classroom and using social skill building and bullying prevention and response strategies that are consistent with the school's positive approach maintain a safe and supportive school.

Strategies for Good Practice: Effective Classroom Practice and Environment

1. Students participate actively in the development of classroom rules about bullying behaviors, which are demonstrated consistently with the school policy.
2. Teachers have an understanding of their responsibility as behavioral role models.
3. Teachers use positive behavior expectation strategies in the classroom to promote effective learning.
4. Teachers use their classroom, curriculum, and knowledge of students to help those who are bullied and those who engage in bullying.
5. Behavior support strategies are implemented to help students develop self-control and responsibility.
6. A variety of group activities and structures are used to facilitate positive decision making about bullying situations.
7. Teachers engage students in cooperative learning methods and activities.

1   **Students participate actively in the development of classroom rules about bullying behaviors, which are demonstrated consistently with the school policy.**

Classroom rules—based on the school's behavioral policies and written as clear statements of expected behaviors—reflect the culture the school aims to promote. Student involvement in the development of these rules enhances their compliance, responsibility, and ownership. In secondary schools, this consultation with students may occur through the student leadership council and tutor group meetings. Learning activities can provide opportunities for identifying and practicing specific behaviors to support implementation of classroom rules.

Students may need help to encourage the reporting of bullying. The following statements may help students.

Asking for Help Versus Tattling

Asking for help is when someone feels the situation is out of his or her control and he or she is unable to deal with it alone and needs help.

"Tattling" is when a person tries to get attention or to get someone else into trouble.

Asking for help for yourself or others is always OK.

2 **Teachers have an understanding of their responsibility as behavioral role models.**

Teachers are responsible for ensuring the online and offline social behaviors they model encompass the core values promoted within the school community. When teachers model pro-social skills such as respect, compassion, and negotiation, students learn to use these skills in their own social situations. All staff need to have a strong understanding of expected staff and student behaviors, particularly with the growth in popularity of online social networking sites. Further, Proactive Policies and Practices toolkit 4.5 discusses opportunities for promotion of these understandings and competencies through the school's behavior expectations policy.

3 **Teachers use positive behavior expectation strategies in the classroom to promote effective learning.**

Staff who successfully develop positive behavioral expectations for students:

- Use positive recognition as a means of promoting the pro-social behavior of students
- Help students who engage in bullying behavior develop more appropriate modes of behaving
- Provide positive ways of using student leadership and peer support skills
- Encourage commitment to the values of trust and respect and a shared understanding of social rules and procedures

4 **Teachers use their classroom, curriculum, and knowledge of students to help those who are bullied and those who engage in bullying.**

Using strategic seating and grouping arrangements in the classroom can positively impact cohesion, academic satisfaction, and bullying behaviors. This may be particularly useful in secondary environments and at times of transition, when students choose their own groups and seating arrangements and may therefore be more vulnerable to exclusionary practices. Teachers can use their knowledge of the class's social relationships to group students in ways that will enhance constructive interaction, including:

- Set role grouping
- Vertical grouping
- Interest grouping
- Expertise grouping
- Experience grouping

Embedding bullying prevention and positive technology use content in the curriculum enables the development of a shared understanding of classroom and social expectations, which support those who are bullied and those who bully others. Key Understandings and Competencies toolkit 5.1 discusses the Friendly Schools Plus teaching and learning materials in more detail.

Chapter 3

Behavior support strategies are implemented to help students develop self-control and responsibility.

School staff can help to build students' capacity to manage their own emotions and behaviors, identify social goals and how to achieve them in a positive way, and view social experiences positively. These behavioral support strategies are best tailored to meet the strengths and needs of the school community.

Supportive School Culture toolkit 3.3 outlines peer support strategies that can be used to help students develop appropriate behavior when engaging with other students. In addition, the development of assertive social skills, as discussed in Supportive School Culture toolkit 3.5, enables students to communicate more clearly and effectively with others.

 A variety of group activities and structures are used to facilitate positive decision making about bullying situations.

To make informed decisions about bullying situations, students need to be provided with the opportunity to learn and practice decision-making skills. Providing students with a social decision-making framework allows a range of alternatives to be considered and explored before a decision is made. Students need to be encouraged to recognize their values and feelings toward the consequences of the decisions they make. Providing regular opportunities to practice decision making facilitates students' ability to use this process in bullying situations.

A group decision-making model including the following five components can be beneficial.

1. State the problem.
2. Gather information.
3. Examine the choices.
4. Consider the positive and negative consequences.
5. Decide, execute, and evaluate.

Decision making is a key theme promoted throughout the Friendly Schools Plus teaching and learning materials described in Key Understandings and Competencies toolkit 5.1.

7 Teachers engage students in cooperative learning methods and activities.

Schools that implement a cooperative curriculum encourage a shared understanding of social rules and procedures and enable positive outcomes relating to group interaction. These activities promote honest communication, understanding differing perspectives, and students' positive sense of self and concern for others.

Cooperative skills to promote in the classroom include:

- Respecting other people's opinions
- Sharing
- Including others
- Negotiating
- Solving and responding to fights and arguments
- Suggesting and persuading (versus bossing)
- Making group decisions

These skills can further be reinforced by parents and can be promoted through school newsletters (see Supportive School Culture toolkit 3.1), school assemblies (see Supportive School Culture toolkit 3.2), and family communication sheets (see School–Family–Community Partnerships toolkits 7.2 and 7.3).

Positive Peer Group Influence

Positive peer group influence includes the authentic participation of students in the planning, implementation, and evaluation of school actions, particularly those to reduce bullying. This can lead to increased student ownership and support and greater respect for systems and structures. Recognizing, valuing, and encouraging student participation fosters collaboration between students and staff, assists in ensuring school practices are relevant and helpful, and lets students know their voices are heard. Schools can foster positive peer group influence by:

- Offering education targeting specific strategies to provide support for students being bullied
- Encouraging peer intervention in bullying (such as the responsibilities of bystanders)
- Encouraging students to withhold the social rewards that may maintain bullying
- Promoting positive peer group influence and group norms that actively discourage bullying

Strategies for Good Practice: Positive Peer Group Influence

1. Students are valued as active participants in the development of school plans, policy, and practice to reduce bullying.
2. Opportunities for students to voice their opinions are valued, encouraged, and incorporated into school planning and activities.
3. Peer group actions to reduce bullying (such as positive bystander behaviors) are encouraged and commended at the whole-school level.
4. Support and empathy for students being bullied are encouraged.

 Students are valued as active participants in the development of school plans, policy, and practice to reduce bullying.

Students can be actively engaged in policy development by:

- Identifying how they would like to see staff respond to bullying situations
- Identifying where bullying occurs (potential hot spots)
- Identifying safer zones
- Reviewing the policy
- Identifying ways to distribute the policy
- Assisting with the design of the policy to make it engaging for students

The finished policy needs to be understood and accessible to all school community members. Chapter 4 discusses proactive policy development and implementation for the whole-school community. In particular, Proactive Policies and Practices toolkit 4.5 provides suggestions for reviewing the school's behavior expectation policies, including how to involve students in this process.

2   **Opportunities for students to voice their opinions are valued, encouraged, and incorporated into school planning and activities.**

Students have excellent ideas on how to promote positive behavior across the school community and solve problems. When the focus is on students taking action and accepting responsibility for the outcome, results can be more powerful and meaningful. While each school will have a unique way of engaging students, the following may provide some initial ideas:

- Student councils
- Student trainers for parents and younger students (especially in ICT)
- Students as researchers
- Students as interviewers
- Student events managers
- Student tour guides
- Students involved in policy writing
- Students leading learning (input into inspiring programs offered at the school)
- Student break time leaders (leading activities offered in break times)

It is not recommended that students are selected to play a formal role in resolving bullying situations (for example, peer mentoring). Students are well placed to encourage positive social behavior and contribute to strategies that provide a supportive environment for students, such as online and offline procedures that make it easy for students to report bullying (see Supportive School Culture toolkit 3.3 for a discussion of peer support strategies).

3 **Peer group actions to reduce bullying (such as positive bystander behaviors) are encouraged and commended at the whole-school level.**

Bullying behavior in the school usually takes place in the presence of other students (peers). Although many students do not agree with bullying, most do not intervene to stop the bullying, but instead act in ways that enable and maintain bullying (Craig et al., 2000; O'Connell et al., 1999). It is important that the onus for intervening in bullying incidents is not left to students alone, but rather, peer intervention efforts are viewed as complimentary to a whole-school approach to tackling bullying. Ensuring staff respond consistently increases students' ability and willingness to intervene as they know they will be supported.

Teachers and school administrators who model consistent responses to bullying behavior will see increased levels of peer intervention efforts. When students are mobilized to take action against bullying, they must feel secure that teachers understand their need to stay safe. For some students, in both primary and secondary schools, this means ensuring the information they share will not cause them to lose status in their peer group.

Leaders who provide opportunities for their staff to understand the reasons students may or may not be willing to intervene as bystanders increase their school's capacity to actively engage more students in positive bystander responses. Strategies for engaging bystanders are described in Supportive School Culture toolkit 3.4.

4 **Support and empathy for students being bullied are encouraged.**

To respect how another student is feeling and respond in a positive and supportive way are key to showing kindness, compassion, and friendship and are integral to a supportive school culture. It can be hard to understand another person's experience of a situation, especially if we have not experienced it ourselves. It is possible, however, to respect other people's feelings and opinions.

Commonly recognized means of exhibiting respect in a school include:

- Listening carefully
- Offering encouragement
- Being nonjudgmental
- Acknowledging experiences
- Allowing for privacy and personal space in times of distress
- Asking students to define what respect and support mean for them—what they look like, feel like, and sound like

Summary

This chapter has discussed ways to build a supportive school culture through the promotion of whole-school strategies to foster connectedness to school, effective classroom practice and environments, and positive peer group influence. To support the achievement of a supportive school culture, three school stories are provided as examples of how CHPRC research schools have taken action in this regard and the barriers and solutions they encountered in this process.

Chapter 3

Schools wishing to use the strategies outlined in this chapter to enhance the supportiveness of their school may find the toolkits that follow to be helpful in this endeavor:

- Supportive School Culture toolkit 3.1 includes eighteen newsletter items that aim to promote common understandings about bullying behavior and the school's approach to its prevention across the whole school.
- Supportive School Culture toolkit 3.2 provides examples of primary-school assembly items to promote a positive and supportive school culture. Secondary schools could support these assembly items through buddy programs with primary-school students.
- Supportive School Culture toolkit 3.3 discusses peer support strategies that contribute to students' and staff perceptions of a supportive school environment. All students have a responsibility to take action to reduce and prevent bullying behavior and support a positive school culture.
- Supportive School Culture toolkit 3.4 builds on this premise by highlighting the important role of bystanders in bullying situations and ways they can take positive action.
- Supportive School Culture toolkit 3.5 is included as an example of ways to encourage the development of positive social skills to build a supportive school culture.

Throughout this chapter, references have been made to toolkits featured in other chapters of this book. These toolkits may further help schools build a more supportive school culture for the reduction and prevention of bullying behaviors.

School Stories

School Story 3.1

Brief background to school initiative:

This school developed a consultative process to create a new policy on bullying and harassment.

School profile:

- Metropolitan private boys' school
- 1,210 students
- Grades: K–12
- Education support school—catering to learning difficulties

Action

This school stated in its bullying policy that an aim of the school was to "provide an environment in which each student is personally involved." To this end, it worked to establish a school community where everyone could feel valued and safe and where individual differences were understood and celebrated. Staff communicated to the school community that every student had the right to enjoy their time at school and that the school community expected respect for others and did not tolerate bullying or harassment.

The school promoted an ethos that valued individual differences. Assemblies were used to validate students' achievements. Modeling by staff and senior students was a valuable tool in promoting positive behavior. An example of an activity that promoted leadership and positive role modeling was the school's peer support program. The program integrated first-grade students with twelfth-grade students during physical education. Each twelfth-grade student was placed in charge of two first-grade boys to teach them swimming. The twelfth-grade students were evaluated on their teaching skills, with some attaining qualifications as swimming instructors for children at the primary and secondary level. The first-grade boys enhanced their swimming skills and made some "big friends."

The tutor system promoted the development of individual and social skills. The school was divided into houses, and within the houses were smaller vertically structured tutorial groups. Each tutorial group was made up of students from different grade levels. The house system ensured that each student had a home base in the school and that there was at least one staff member who knew what was going on in the student's day-to-day life. Students kept a diary that was signed each week by the tutor and the student's parents. This provided a line of communication between the students, their tutor, and their parents. The groups provided older students with the opportunity to show responsible stewardship and for younger students to learn from positive role models. Several other opportunities were provided to older students to further develop their leadership skills. For example, there was an annual camp for newly appointed student leaders, a training program for peer support program leaders, and volunteers that assist in eighth-grade camps. The peer support program consisted of small groups of eighth-grade students meeting with a trained eleventh-grade leader. The program built confidence and self-esteem, developed communication and relationship skills, and improved the students' ability to resist harmful peer pressures and make responsible decisions.

Reports of being bullied were responded to with listening and empathy. Staff reinforced to students that they had done nothing wrong by talking about the situation. Staff then made a judgment as to whether the student required additional help, for example, counseling. Students who engaged in bullying were directed to discussions with counselors. These discussions focused on what they could do to change their behavior. Parents were contacted to support the proposed changes.

The school viewed education as a partnership between a school and its students' parents. Effort was taken to clearly explain to parents the expectations of the school regarding its students.

What We Learned

Difficulties Encountered

A large number of the students' fathers were brought up under a different system—one that included "tit for tat" type retaliation. Many of the fathers felt that learning to "stand up for themselves" was a necessary part of growing up. Thus, much of the bullying behavior was perceived as a rite of passage, both for the person who bullied others and the person bullied. There was also a strong belief that "whatever you do, don't tattle on your friends."

Overcoming Difficulties

The school recognized these barriers and attempted to change them through the provision of knowledge. The school introduced the concept of *bystander power* to the students. The students were encouraged to participate and contribute to the antibullying policy.

Recommendations for Other Schools

Educate the staff, students, and parents about the importance of antibullying policies.

Sample Letter From School to Parents and Students

Dear parents and students,

It is not always easy to speak on behalf of the school, student leaders, and all my fellow seniors. On some topics, it is very hard to find consensus of opinion.

However, on the issue of bullying and harassment, there is unanimity of opinion. All seniors consider bullying in our school community to be totally unacceptable. They are glad that the issue is being aired. Furthermore, because it is sometimes difficult to be certain exactly what behavior is acceptable, they are pleased that there are now clearer published definitions as well as guidelines that will help everyone handle the problem.

The issue of bullying prevention has been given a high profile in the school to raise awareness and, in turn, to reduce its harm. We would like to make one point clear: the raising of awareness does not imply that there has been an increase in bullying. Rather, as one senior said during a long discussion of the issue late last year, "It is not that there is more bullying; there is instead more caring about how it can be stopped."

That is a positive sign. It is caring that will help us all build a more pleasant school community in the years ahead.

If anyone feels pressured, he or she must talk to a teacher, a student leader, or any senior student. Everybody is happy to help.

Yours sincerely,

Student Council President

Figure 9: Sample school letter.

More information about the strategies used by this school can be found in the following toolkits.

- Supportive School Culture toolkit 3.2
- Supportive School Culture toolkit 3.3
- Supportive School Culture toolkit 3.4
- Proactive Policies and Practices toolkit 4.4
- Proactive Policies and Practices toolkit 4.5

- School–Family–Community Partnerships toolkit 7.2
- School–Family–Community Partnerships toolkit 7.3

School Story 3.2

Brief background to school initiative:

This school helped students distinguish between telling and tattling and upheld the motto: "It's OK to tell."

School profile:
- Metropolitan co-ed public school
- 756 students
- Grades: 8–12
- Very multicultural

Action

In its "Stopping Bullying at School" pamphlet, this school defined tattling as telling on someone to deliberately get him or her into trouble, drawing attention to oneself, and acting helpless or making oneself look good. Telling, on the other hand, is asking for support to solve a problem you have been unable to resolve yourself.

Staff were trained in the Shared Concern method, which involved interviewing all individuals engaged in bullying incidents, including bystanders. The idea was to increase the empathy of those engaging in bullying behavior toward the students they bullied. Strategies were devised to change the behavior and attitudes of those involved in bullying incidents. Follow-up meetings were held with all participants to ensure the situation had changed positively for the bullied student. Some students needed individual counseling to help develop self-protection and risk-minimization strategies.

The "Strong Schools" lessons were taught in eighth-grade Studies of Society and Environment classes. This involved defining bullying behavior, examining how it is a problem for the school, and answering four questions.

1. Why is bullying serious?
2. Why do students bully?
3. What can be done if you are bullied?
4. What does the school do about bullying?

The modules were taught in the form of class discussion and worksheets with interesting activities. The examples included both direct bullying, such as name-calling and physical bullying, and indirect bullying, such as exclusion.

The school also ran a peer support program. Eighth-grade students were assigned an eleventh-grade buddy, who volunteered for the program in tenth grade. If the response was too great, staff selected the students who would become the peer support students. The eleventh graders were trained by staff. After the two-day training, the eleventh graders were matched up with an eighth-grade student. The eleventh-grade buddies supported groups of eighth graders during class time (half an hour per week for an entire semester). This time was used for discussion, games (trust), and personal development.

Chapter 3

What We Learned

If We Could Do It Over

The school would have liked to have adopted more of a whole-school approach.

Recommendations for Other Schools

Remain vigilant. Conduct regular ongoing awareness-raising activities with parents, students, and teachers. Emphasize correct bystander behavior.

More information about the strategies used by this school can be found in the following toolkits.

- Supportive School Culture toolkit 3.3
- Proactive Policies and Practices toolkit 4.3
- Key Understandings and Competencies toolkit 5.1
- School–Family–Community Partnerships toolkit 7.2
- School–Family–Community Partnerships toolkit 7.3

School Story 3.3

Brief background to school initiative:

Data collected by the school indicated that a social skills initiative was necessary. The teachers felt their students needed to understand that consequences for inappropriate behavior were directed at the behavior and not at the child. Also, the school experienced an influx of new teachers with skills in peer support. There was a realization that the number of fifteen- to twenty-five-year-olds in the area was rapidly increasing, and thus the number of students would likely increase too. All these factors were taken into consideration when planning and implementing the bullying prevention strategies.

School profile:

- Metropolitan public school
- 780 students
- Grades: K–7

Action

Input for the bullying prevention plan was received from both the staff and a student cohort. When revising the plan, the school organized parent coffee chats to discuss the proposed changes. If parents were unable to attend these chats, they were sent a flier outlining the changes.

The school organized a collaborative problem-solving team. The problem-solving team consisted of one administration representative and three teachers (one male, two female) from kindergarten, grade 4, and grade 7. Teachers who experienced difficulties in the classroom approached the problem-solving team to discuss the issue. The group discussed the problem and suggested potential strategies and methods for its resolution. The teachers and the problem-solving team also approached parents to discuss such situations and how they could assist in the reduction of the problem.

The school introduced a climate committee that involved the students and teachers. The committee ran regular features in the school newsletter, organized activities for Kindness Week, and organized a time capsule (that is to be opened in twenty-five years). The committee was set up with the help of the Lions Quest International. It aided in the production of some books and provided staff training. This involved a two-day professional development program, Skills for Working with Adolescents, which was paid for by the local Lions Club. In the first year, the training was only available to staff, and in the second year, parents were also able to attend. Additional staff training was provided by the Centre for Adolescent Mental Health and the school psychologist. The presentations discussed issues for adolescents (peer pressure, bullying) and their effects on students.

Classroom strategies included discussions, role play, and creative writing. For lower primary students, the period after lunch was used to sit in a circle and discuss what had happened on the playground, how it made others feel, and how things could be improved. Upper primary students also conducted discussion groups where they used examples from the media to discuss issues related to bullying and harassment. Teachers used drama, health, and language classes to act out and discuss issues of bullying without directly focusing on issues within the classroom.

The school established a student council and a peer-support program. Seventh-grade students chosen as peer supporters were given a whole day of training. It was held outside the school, and students learned skills such as negotiation, assertiveness, and team building through a variety of games and activities. At every lunch and recess break, two peer supporters patrolled the playground and resolved problems that were brought to them by other students.

The school has conducted several evaluation surveys. Both the peer supporters and parents were surveyed regarding all of the actions that the school had implemented throughout the school year. Staff meetings were held once a term to discuss issues relating to any of the programs and activities. If any changes were implemented, they were advertised in the school newsletter.

What We Learned

Difficulties Encountered

One of the main difficulties the school experienced was the mismatched expectations of parents compared to overall school expectations.

Overcoming Difficulties

Lots of talking and meetings were held with parents. One strategy used to help parents realize the true actions of their children in school was to talk to parents on the phone before students had a chance to get home and lie to parents to avoid punishment. Parents are reluctant to believe the school's side of events if it means believing their child has lied.

If We Could Do It Over

The school realized the need to focus on consequences for behavior, not punishment of the student. It is important to understand that you're not going to get rid of all bullying; support is the most important thing. Documentation is also helpful to remind parents of past discussions and actions taken.

Recommendations for Other Schools

Everyone must be involved and consistent if the program is to work. The school believes that bullying should be looked at under the umbrella of guidance counseling, as opposed to behavior management.

Next Steps

The school plans for its newly set up behavior management committee to review its hierarchy of consequences. The climate committee will also include students next year.

More information about the strategies used by this school can be found in the following toolkits.

- Supportive School Culture toolkit 3.1
- Supportive School Culture toolkit 3.3
- Supportive School Culture toolkit 3.5
- Proactive Policies and Practices toolkit 4.5
- Key Understandings and Competencies toolkit 5.1
- School–Family–Community Partnerships toolkit 7.5

Toolkits for Action

3.1 Supportive School Culture Toolkit 3.1
Newsletter Items

This toolkit contains a number of brief social and emotional messages in the form of newsletter items that can be used in the school's communication to families and other school community members. These are designed to give families information about actions that can be taken to enhance students' social skills and reduce student bullying. These messages can also be presented at assemblies to reiterate the school's commitment to encouraging positive social behaviors and discouraging bullying.

Aims of the newsletter items:

1. Introduce your school's goals and actions for creating a friendly school.
2. Encourage families to help create a supportive school culture.
3. Provide families with a definition of bullying.
4. Provide families with a definition of cyberbullying.
5. Provide families with strategies they can use to help their children if they are being bullied or cyberbullied.
6. Provide families with tips to communicate more effectively with their children about bullying.
7. Help families teach their children how to respond if they are being bullied at school.
8. Provide practical strategies families can use to discourage their children from bullying others.
9. Provide families with information about bystander roles and responsibilities.
10. Provide strategies for families to effectively support their children if they are being bullied at school.
11. Provide families with a rationale for the school's response to bullying incidents.
12. Provide families with an understanding of the Shared Concern method in managing bullying incidents.
13. Provide families with practical strategies to support the school to reduce bullying.
14. Discuss the importance of discipline in resolving bullying behaviors, and provide strategies for families to adopt at home.
15. Provide families with strategies to help their children develop and maintain friendships to reduce the likelihood they will be bullied at school.
16. Provide families with strategies to help them support their children if they are cyberbullied.
17. Provide families with strategies they can take to save and report evidence of cyberbullying.
18. Provide families with strategies to help their children be safer when online.

Visit **go.solution-tree.com/behavior** for reproducible copies of the newsletter items in this toolkit.

3.2 Supportive School Culture Toolkit 3.2
Assembly Items

Assemblies are a time when the whole-school community (including families) comes together to celebrate and discuss issues that concern the whole school. They provide the ideal platform to convey consistent messages about the school's behavior expectations policy and responses to bullying behaviors.

The assembly item examples provided in this toolkit offer examples of the types of activities that can be used during primary-school assemblies to promote messages that encourage supportive social behavior and discourage bullying and to promote the rights and responsibilities of all members of the school community.

To create a positive, empathetic culture at your school aimed at reducing bullying behaviors on- and offline, focus discussion topics at assemblies on:

- Sharing
- Respect
- Cooperation
- Friendship
- Positive recognition of achievements (academic and nonacademic)
- Rights and responsibilities of all school members
- Social skills

Some ways to incorporate these messages into whole-school assembly discussions include:

- Assigning a theme for each assembly (based on weekly values)
- School leaders acknowledging positive behavior and encouraging the rights and responsibilities of all students
- Focusing on the rights and responsibilities of all students, both online and offline
- Asking student representatives to describe times they have witnessed students displaying positive behaviors on the playground

3.3 Supportive School Culture Toolkit 3.3
Peer Support

Peer support initiatives help upperclass students and staff address issues affecting all students in a positive and productive manner. A training and supervision program enables upperclass students to develop their capacity to act as peer supporters.

What Is Peer Support?

Peer support strategies are based on the premise that young people, especially adolescents, seek out other young people for support and advice when they are experiencing some concern or worry, especially when they are cyberbullied.

Peer supporters are *not* professional counselors or therapists; they are young people who offer supervised support to other young people. They need to be trained to provide a nonjudgmental, active approach to listening that encourages others to express and explore their feelings or concerns.

How Can Peer Supporters Help?

Peer supporters may be involved in:

- Helping younger students with learning
- Helping younger or new students make the transition to a new school
- Assisting with bringing concerns of students to a teacher's attention
- Assisting students by listening in a nonjudgmental way

Peer supporters have the potential to be successful, as many students feel more comfortable talking to an older peer about being bullied (especially cyberbullying) than a teacher. They also promote prosocial behaviors that positively influence the social environment of the school and reduce bullying.

Peer supporters do, however, need to have:

- Suitable training
- Strong links to the school's student support programs
- Whole-staff support and action

Identifying Peer Supporters

The selection of peer supporters is the most important step in the establishment of such a program. Research suggests that students should select peers (vetted by teachers) from varying grades so students have a range of supporters they may feel comfortable talking with.

Some schools have used existing school leaders to be peer supporters. These students may not be the most appropriate choice, as they are typically high achievers and may be perceived by students as "good students" who may not represent the cross-section of students at the school.

Chapter 3

Training of Peer Supporters

Students should be trained—ideally by a counselor or other qualified person—and have the opportunity to practice:

- Active listening skills
- Problem-solving approaches
- Empathy building
- Acceptance of others
- Showing respect for those who talk to them
- Processes at the school for accessing help or progressing complaints or problems (such as what to do if a student is extremely upset or in need of help)
- Listening in a nonjudgmental way and providing students with the correct processes or staff to assist them
- The need for confidentiality
- Record keeping

How Does the Program Work?

Students who have been selected and trained as peer supporters should be identified to the whole-school community. These students must be known by their peers if they are to be accessed for support.

There are many ways in which the role of peer supporters can be used.

- Being informally present every day in the schoolyard in an unofficial capacity, unless approached by another student; while other peer supporters can be available at a "drop-in" room where students can speak with them in private. This drop-in room may be seen by students as a possible way to discuss challenges without being noticed by their school peers.
- Being responsible for showing new students around the campus during break times and generally looking out for them by making sure they have other students to play or sit with. This process provides new students with familiar and safe students they can go to if they feel alone or isolated during break times and can reduce the likelihood of being bullied.
- Having a regular spot at assemblies to discuss peer supporters' roles and the rights and responsibilities of each member of the school community.

Assign a duty teacher the task of providing assistance to the peer supporters.

Keeping It Successful

While peer support programs have been used successfully in schools, there are common issues that can threaten the integrity or existence of the program, including:

- Peer supporters clearly understand the boundaries of their role. Staff are responsible for ensuring these boundaries are observed, particularly if peer supporters begin providing advice beyond the scope of their training.
- Training of peer supporters should be thorough and ongoing. Training needs to be provided by staff with advanced skills in the fields of communication, behavior management, and counseling, with regular follow-up or booster trainings linked to specific needs.
- Whole-staff support for the peer supporters must be consistent, highly visible, and ongoing.

3.4 Supportive School Culture Toolkit 3.4
Bystanders—An Important Group

What Is a Bystander?

A bystander is someone who sees the bullying situation but is not the person being bullied or bullying others. Bystanders may act in many different ways, including:

- Watching what is going on and not getting involved
- Pretending not to see and ignoring the situation
- Choosing to get involved in the bullying
- Choosing to get involved and stop the bullying
- Choosing to get help

As bystanders, students can either support bullying in the way they behave or help to stop bullying. Many students don't know how to help or how to get help.

Talking With Students About Bystanders

Bullying can sometimes be made worse if students don't know what to do or who to turn to for help. School staff and parents can help by offering to talk and providing support. Everyone needs to take responsibility and respond to bullying behavior by not remaining silent but instead talking about the issue.

When some students were asked what stops them from helping other students who are bullied, the most common answers were: "It's none of my business" and "I didn't want to get involved."

Yet when asked if they wanted to stop the bullying, most students said, "Yes, I don't like to see people being bullied." These students don't like the bullying but are not sure if they should help and are unsure what to do to help the person being bullied.

What Can Bystanders Do?

If students see someone being bullied, they could:

- Let the person doing the bullying know that what he or she is doing is bullying
- Refuse to join in with the bullying and walk away
- Support the student who is being bullied
- Ask a teacher or support person for help
- Support their friends and protect them from bullying by being there for them. Students who are alone are more likely to be the target of bullying, so encourage students to be aware of other students who are left out or who are on their own in the schoolyard.

School staff and parents can support students by:

1. Discussing bullying (stories in books or on television can trigger discussion about bullying situations)

2. Listening to students' points of view on the topic of bullying

3. Helping students to discuss solutions and consequences to problems they see or are involved in (decision making)

4. Problem solving as a whole class or family—this can help students feel valued and supported as well as make other class and family members aware of problems and solutions

5. Providing advice on what might happen as a result of bullying and why it is important to tell someone

6. Developing a clear class and family policy that put-downs are not OK

7. Helping students understand the problem of bullying and showing empathy and understanding of how people might feel if they are bullied

Figure 10: How staff and parents can support students.

Sometimes students find themselves in a position of being bystanders to their friends bullying others. They will be torn between what they believe is the right thing to do and supporting their friends.

Peer Influence

Being part of a group offers security and a feeling of belonging. Students learn about social skills and relationships by being part of a group. Sometimes students can feel influenced by the group to do things or behave in ways that they do not agree with or feel comfortable with.

How Can School Staff and Parents Help Students Understand Peer Influence?

Explain to students:

- It is good to have friends and be part of a group
- Peers can sometimes try to persuade others to follow a decision that they may not agree with
- You can say "No" to your friends and still be friends with them (see possible responses)

Training in assertive responses can also help students resist pressure and respond in ways that do not promote bullying (see Supportive School Culture toolkit 3.5).

If a student wants another student to do something that he or she doesn't want to do, that student may use some powerful persuaders:

- Threatening to not be friends anymore
- Calling names (for example, *chicken, wimp*)
- Physical threats
- Rejection from the group

Activity—Possible Responses to Powerful Persuaders in Bullying Situations

You can role-play some pressure situations with students to practice possible responses, for example, a staff member or a parent role-plays another student trying to get someone to do something he or she doesn't want to do.

Parent: *Let's tease [student's name] about his new haircut.*

Ask students to think of a possible response to let the person know he or she doesn't want to do this. If they can't think of something to say, help them find a possible response from the following list.

Have students try practicing some of these responses to a bullying situation. After a bit of practice, students will find it easier to think of their own responses and will look and sound more confident when they speak.

General

- I don't want to do it.
- I don't believe in bullying.
- I don't see the point in hurting other people.
- Bullying is wrong.
- The more friends we have, the better.
- I am not going to help you bully someone.
- How would you feel if someone did that to you?

Leaving Someone Out

- Why not just let him or her join in?
- I don't see the need to make someone feel bad.
- I don't want to be mean to someone; that's not fair.
- Why can't we all be friends?

Teasing

- I don't think it is fair to tease someone about that.
- I don't like to call people mean names.
- I would feel terrible if someone did that to me, so I am not going to do it.
- Teasing people is not fun.

Threatening

- I don't want to be involved in this.
- Threatening people is wrong.

Gossip or Rumors

- How do you know this story is true?
- That is probably gossip.
- I don't want to be involved in spreading gossip.

Chapter 3

Physical

- I don't want to be involved in fighting.
- I've got something else going on at that time.
- I don't see the point in hurting someone.

During this activity, students quickly realize that a person who pressures them to do something they don't want to do is not behaving as a friend should. Friends accept their friends' decisions and don't try to pressure them to do something they feel uncomfortable about.

3.5 Supportive School Culture Toolkit 3.5 Assertiveness

Assertiveness training has been shown to increase self-esteem and confidence in a person being bullied. A person who has good self-esteem and confidence is less likely to be bullied.

What Is Assertiveness?

Being assertive is about saying what you think, feel, and want in a confident way and protecting your own rights while not infringing on the rights of others. It means saying what you want without shouting, glaring, being angry, or putting others down. It also means saying what you want without putting yourself down or letting others make you feel bad.

Assertive students:

- Can express their feelings calmly and are able to work out when it is the right time to do this
- Can accept feedback from others
- Are able to protect themselves without being hurtful to other students
- Are able to ask for help when they have difficulty dealing with a situation themselves
- Act with self-respect and confidence

The assertive response is just right (not too hard and not too soft).

- Speak in a firm but friendly way.
- Stand tall; make eye contact.
- Stand up for yourself politely.
- Smile or look calm.
- Feel positive, confident, and in control.
- Feel OK about yourself.

How Can School Staff and Parents Talk to Students About Dealing With Arguments?

Explain that everyone has arguments sometimes. Arguing with somebody doesn't necessarily mean that you don't like the person or that it is the end of the friendship. Point out that, during arguments, both people think they are right.

What Tips Can I Give Students to Help Them Deal With Arguments?

- Try to stay calm and talk through the problem using a normal voice.
- If either person is getting too angry or upset, say, "We are getting too angry and upset. Let's talk about this later." Then, walk away.
- Make sure you do talk about it later when you have both calmed down.
- Point out your view, and talk about your feelings (for example, "I felt bad when you told the rest of the team I was useless at football").
- Let the other person explain his or her point of view. Listen without interrupting.
- Apologize if necessary, and try to find a way to be friends.

Chapter 3

3.0 PLANNING TOOL: SUPPORTIVE SCHOOL CULTURE

Statement of Evidence for Building a Supportive School Culture

A supportive school culture provides safety, encourages open communication, and supports a sense of connectedness to the school that protects students from the risks of bullying. The quality of relationships between and among staff, students, and families is vital in fostering a safe, supportive, and engaging school environment. Positive student behavior should be encouraged and rewarded at the whole-school level.

Review Action 3.1—Positive Whole-School Culture

	Not yet initiated	In planning	Preparing staff	Partially in place	Fully in place	Sustained practice
3.1.1 The school culture supports a sense of connectedness and safety for all students, staff, and families through positive, trusting, and caring relationships.						
3.1.2 The school treats bullying as a relationship issue and communicates a clear philosophy regarding how it feels about social relationships and bullying.						
3.1.3 Positive social values such as respect, trust, fairness, and celebration of diversity are promoted across the school community.						
3.1.4 The school recognizes that bullying can be reduced in the school environment and acknowledges everyone's responsibility to reduce bullying behavior.						
3.1.5 Staff well-being is an important focus of the school's culture.						
3.1.6 Appropriate social behaviors are formally and informally modeled by staff.						
3.1.7 Students are actively involved in the promotion of a positive whole-school culture.						
3.1.8 All staff have the skills to build positive relations among students and between themselves and their students.						
3.1.9 Students are empowered to increase their safety and solve problems.						
3.1.10 Pro-social, cooperative behavior is encouraged and acknowledged.						

Plan Action 3.1—Positive Whole-School Culture

What needs to be done?	Who is going to do it?	Timeline			What do we need?	Comments and reflections
		Status	Finish	Status		

continued →

Review Action 3.2—Effective Classroom Practice and Environment

	Not yet initiated	In planning	Preparing staff	Partially in place	Fully in place	Sustained practice
3.2.1 Students participate actively in the development of classroom rules about bullying behaviors, and the rules are consistent with the school policy.	Not yet initiated	In planning	Preparing staff	Partially in place	Fully in place	Sustained practice
3.2.2 Teachers have an understanding of their responsibility as behavioral role models.	Not yet initiated	In planning	Preparing staff	Partially in place	Fully in place	Sustained practice
3.2.3 Teachers use positive behavior expectation strategies in the classroom to promote effective learning.	Not yet initiated	In planning	Preparing staff	Partially in place	Fully in place	Sustained practice
3.2.4 Teachers use their classroom, curriculum, and knowledge of students to help those who are bullied and those who engage in bullying.	Not yet initiated	In planning	Preparing staff	Partially in place	Fully in place	Sustained practice
3.2.5 Behavior support strategies are implemented to help students develop self-control and responsibility.	Not yet initiated	In planning	Preparing staff	Partially in place	Fully in place	Sustained practice
3.2.6 A variety of group activities and structures are used to facilitate positive decision making about bullying situations.	Not yet initiated	In planning	Preparing staff	Partially in place	Fully in place	Sustained practice
3.2.7 Teachers engage students in cooperative learning methods and activities.	Not yet initiated	In planning	Preparing staff	Partially in place	Fully in place	Sustained practice

Plan Action 3.2—Effective Classroom Practice and Environment

What needs to be done?	Who is going to do it?	Timeline		What do we need?	Comments and reflections
		Status	Finish Status		

Review Action 3.3—Positive Peer Group Influence

	Not yet initiated	In planning	Preparing staff	Partially in place	Fully in place	Sustained practice
3.3.1 Students are valued as active participants in the development of school plans, policy, and practice to reduce bullying.						
3.3.2 Opportunities for students to voice their opinions are valued, encouraged, and incorporated into school planning and activities.						
3.3.3 Peer group actions to reduce bullying (such as positive bystander behaviors) are encouraged and commended at the whole-school level.						
3.3.4 Support and empathy for students being bullied is encouraged.						

Plan Action 3.3—Positive Peer Group Influence

What needs to be done?	Who is going to do it?	Timeline			What do we need?	Comments and reflections
		Status	Finish	Status		

Chapter 4

Proactive Policies and Practices

Schools with clear and consistent policies and procedures send a strong message to the whole-school community about the school's mission, values, and actions to build a safe and supportive school environment. School policies should be promoted to the whole-school community, particularly at times of higher risk, such as orientation and transition. Positive student behavior needs to be encouraged and rewarded at the whole-school level.

Evidence for Proactive School Policies and Practices

International research has found school policies and procedures are important in reducing bullying (McBride et al., 1995; Sourander et al., 2010). The development of a clear and consistent policy provides a basis for action and behavior change throughout the school community. Active consultation should be sought with all members of the school community including teaching staff, nonteaching staff, students, parents, and the wider community. Establishing clear policy and practice is the first step in managing bullying within a school. This chapter provides information, guidelines, and strategies to help schools engage in discussion and planning toward a whole-school response to bullying.

While an international review of fifty school-based bullying prevention studies (Farrington & Ttofi, 2009) found one of the program elements associated with a reduction in being bullied was the presence of a formal school antibullying policy, the presence of a bullying policy alone will not lead to reduced bullying. Policies need to be developed with the involvement of students, staff, and families (Smith & Sharp, 1994), promoted to the whole-school community, implemented consistently, and monitored to be effective.

Promotion of the Policy to Students, Staff, and Families

The promotion of the school policy and procedures to reduce bullying appears to be especially important during times of orientation and transition to school. There are many different structures in schools, and each school may have differing periods of transition. In addition to students' first entry to school, which is an obvious point for transition, consider other transition points, such as when students move from elementary to middle school or to high school.

Several studies have observed a peak in bullying following student transition from primary to secondary school (Cross et al., 2009; Rigby, 1997). From 2005 to 2007, the CHPRC developed and evaluated the Supportive Schools Project to enhance the capacity of secondary schools to develop and implement a whole-school bullying reduction intervention, including strategies to enhance student transition to secondary school. Results from the project indicated the intervention reduced regular bullying behavior among students, reduced their sense of loneliness at school, improved their perceptions of school safety, and, if they were bullied, improved their perception of staff and peer support (Cross, Hall, Waters, et al., 2008). A key component of the Supportive Schools Project was the development of whole-school policies involving the school community, active promotion of the policy to students, their parents, and staff, and consistent implementation by staff, especially with the seventh-grade students and their parents, prior to, and following, their transition to secondary school.

Responding to Bullying

Clear and consistent procedures for reporting and managing bullying need to be outlined in school policies. Of particular importance are the actions staff members are required to take when a student reports being bullied and the outcomes of these staff actions for students. The procedures a school uses to respond to bullying need to be described and communicated clearly to the school community to ensure consistent implementation. Communication of the behavioral expectations and the consequences of poor behavior is essential so all members of the school community are aware of the actions that will be taken.

Smith and Shu (2000) found that of those students who told a teacher they were bullied, approximately 80 percent reported the teacher had attempted to stop the bullying, while the remainder indicated the teachers had taken no action. Students reported teachers successfully stopped the bullying in 27 percent of cases and were able to reduce the level of bullying a student was experiencing in approximately 29 percent of cases. Students reported that in just over a quarter of the bullying cases, the bullying behavior did not change, and in 16 percent of cases, the bullying increased. This study found there was no significant reduction in bullying experienced by students when they told their teachers about the bullying, compared to when students told their families about the bullying.

Similarly, an Australian study found that when students reported being bullied, school personnel, including teachers and counselors, were the group least likely to be told (Rigby & Barnes, 2002). Recent evidence suggests that students who are cyberbullied are less likely to tell adults compared to when they are bullied by noncyber methods (Dooley, Gradinger, Strohmeier, Cross, & Spiel, 2010). Further, Rigby found that older students are less likely to have positive outcomes, with approximately 50 percent of secondary school students aged sixteen to seventeen reporting no change in their bullying situation after reporting the bullying to teachers (Rigby & Barnes, 2002). To encourage more students to seek support or help, they need to feel confident their disclosure of bullying will be addressed appropriately and discreetly by school staff, will not exacerbate the bullying situation, and that staff will listen to how students would like the situation to be resolved.

School staff may be unsure of what action to take when bullying, especially cyberbullying, is reported to them. Teachers report even more uncertainty about how to address this behavior (Cross, Hall, Waters, et al., 2008) and are also less likely to intervene in situations of covert bullying (Bauman & Del Rio, 2006; Casey-Cannon, Hayward, & Gowen, 2001; Hazler et al., 2001; MacNeil & Newell, 2004; Yoon & Kerber, 2003). School staff report they have less confidence responding to covert bullying, including cyberbullying, than verbal and physical bullying; they are unsure if it is their duty to intervene and what is the best action to take (Bauman & Del Rio, 2006).

In the Australian Covert Bullying Prevalence Study, over half of the teachers surveyed (57 percent) reported their school had whole-school bullying prevention strategies in place that were moderately or very effective in reducing covert bullying (Cross, Hall, Waters, et al., 2008). The study found that while 39 percent of teachers had knowledge of their school's bullying policy that addressed covert bullying, 28 percent reported their school had a bullying policy that did not include explicit reference to covert bullying, including cyberbullying.

Easy-to-access reporting procedures such as online reporting and appropriate follow-up by school staff are also more likely to encourage students to report bullying.

Punitive Versus Nonpunitive Approaches

Whereas a large proportion of school staff (71 percent) feel they can justify the use of punitive approaches to address bullying, there exists considerable disagreement over which of these strategies should be used with the student who is engaging in the bullying (Rigby & Bauman, 2009). Importantly, however, the effectiveness of punishment as a means to address bullying in schools has many potential limitations that have a basis in psychological theory (Rigby & Bauman, 2009):

- Punishment may only suppress behavior temporarily, rather than in the longer term.
- The effectiveness of punitive approaches is dependent on how the student responds to the consequence (in some cases, suspensions may be desired by students). Often, suspensions have little or no link to the behavior that invoked this form of consequence, making the learning from the suspension of less value.

Chapter 4

- Punishment applied toward a student who is engaging in bullying others and who feels undeserving of the punishment may inspire the student to feel resentful and act spitefully, such as in cases where there are provocative victims involved.
- Punishment for bullying behavior may lead students to resort to more covert forms of bullying, which are less detectable by adults.
- If students receive approval by peers for their inappropriate bullying behavior, this is likely to outweigh the disapproval (and punishment) by the school, which then influences their subsequent behavior.

According to the United Nations *Convention on the Rights of the Child* (1991), discipline in schools should respect children's dignity. While the Farrington and Ttofi (2009) meta-analysis found some support for the use of firm sanctions, the long-term effectiveness of this is unknown. However, the use of punitive approaches is almost certain to be harmful to the school climate and students' perception of safety at school, and is contrary to valuing students as active participants of the school community and encouraging student voice in all aspects of the school's functioning. Moreover, rewarding positive behavior rather than punishing poor behavior is related to decreased student discipline problems, including bullying (Luiselli, Putnam, Handler, & Feinberg, 2005). Punitive responses to bullying seem even less useful in cases of cyberbullying. Students often fail to report instances of cyberbullying to adults for fear the technology will be taken away from them (Campbell, 2005; Dooley et al., 2010), causing social isolation that could further complicate their experiences. Banning the use of such technologies in or out of school is unlikely to eradicate the problem as the effects of cyberbullying infiltrate the school environment (Smith et al., 2008). Furthermore, students' high rates of mobile phone usage mean students can access websites outside the school network and privacy filters.

Kajs's (2006) research suggests that firm and inflexible disciplinary sanctions against bullying, such as zero-tolerance policies, don't take into account relevant explanations for student infractions. This research suggests the disciplinary sanctions applied should be appropriate to the offense and age of students and should not create additional barriers to resolving the original issue. Constructive responses to inappropriate student behaviors such as bullying should be applied fairly and consistently, and with administrator discretion, to promote a policy of fairness and respect (Skiba & Peterson, 2000). School disciplinary responses should also seek to teach students how to constructively resolve social problems to prevent similar incidents in the future (Hazler et al., 2001).

CHPRC research and research conducted by Rigby and Bauman (2009) has found the Support Group method and the Shared Concern method to be promising in resolving some cases of bullying. Other methods, such as motivational interviewing traditionally used to treat drug-use problems and eating disorders, may also be effective in changing the behavior of students who regularly engage in bullying behaviors. The CHPRC is conducting research to determine the effectiveness of this approach. Proactive Policies and Practices toolkits 4.1, 4.2, and 4.3 describe the types of conversations that comprise these techniques. It should be noted the Shared Concern method and the Support Group method are best used with perpetrators who have some capacity for empathy, whereas motivational interviewing is useful for students who have other motivations for their bullying behavior.

Actions for Developing Proactive Policies and Practices

Strategies for Good Practice: Proactive Policies and Practices

1. Policy development
2. Policy framework and implementation—prevention, early response, and case management
3. Integrated focus on orientation and transition

 Policy Development

Schools with clear and consistent policies and procedures for practice send a strong message to the whole-school community about the school's beliefs and actions to encourage a safe and supportive school environment.

Strategies for good practice:

1.1 Policies to reduce bullying are collaboratively developed with staff, students, and families.

1.2 Policy development includes an ongoing collaborative planning and review process.

1.3 Policies are distributed and promoted to all staff, students, families, and relevant community members through a range of channels, such as seminars, workshops, newsletters, assembly items, home activities, emails, school website or intranet, curriculum, student diaries, parent handbooks, and information meetings.

1.4 Policies are always accessible to staff, students, and families.

1.5 Professional learning is provided for all staff to implement and enforce the policies.

1.6 An agreement for responsible use of the information and communications technology is implemented between school and students.

1.7 Plans for student behavior management during out-of-school and after-hours activities, including management of bullying (including cyberbullying) incidents, are developed.

1.8 School policies determine and are consistent with staff roles in supervision.

1.9 School policies support national, state, and district policies and mandates.

School policies that are developed and implemented to reduce bullying behavior can sometimes be complex because effectively addressing student bullying behavior is a complex problem. However, if the school community is to understand and consistently act in accordance with the school's behavioral expectations related to preventing and discouraging bullying, then these policies need to be simple and accessible to all. This doesn't just mean the policies are available on the school website or in student handbooks. It also means they are easy to understand and implement. Most importantly, everyone, especially students, clearly knows and understands the standard of behaviors the school expects. This clarity also encourages consistency on the part of the staff members who are required to implement these policies. Clear policies that encourage positive behavior also build on the responsibilities and rights of students to meet the normative expectations of the school community.

Proactive Policies and Practices toolkit 4.4 discusses the importance of establishing a clear vision statement while Proactive Policies and Practices toolkit 4.5 outlines a policy review process to assist schools in developing and reviewing their behavior expectations policy to include clear and consistent policies and procedures for a safe and supportive school environment.

2 Policy Framework and Implementation—Prevention, Early Response, and Case Management

Proactive policies provide a framework to guide school action for the prevention, early response, and case management of bullying.

Strategies for good practice:

2.1 Policies explicitly include prevention, early response, and case management actions that students, staff, and families can follow to prevent, identify, respond to, and report bullying behaviors consistently across the school community.

2.2 Policies specifically include—

  - Links to whole-school vision statement and guiding principles for achieving that vision
  - Whole-school agreement that states the school's clear intention to take bullying seriously
  - Policy rationale and objectives and purpose
  - Common understandings about prosocial behaviors and bullying and cyberbullying behaviors (definitions)
  - Rights and responsibilities of school community members
  - Clear actions for preventing and responding (including reporting and case management procedures) to bullying behaviors

2.3 Positive theory and evidence-informed approaches to responding to bullying incidents are adopted, such as restorative approaches.

2.4 A clear understanding of the positive response strategies adopted by the school is achieved by staff to ensure consistent implementation.

2.5 Behavior expectations used in the classroom are consistent with the school's selected approaches.

2.6 Behavior expectation strategies recognize that the determinants of cyberbullying behavior are part of the whole-school response to bullying and not the technology in which it is being manifested, for example, focus on relationships and social skill building rather than removing access to technology.

2.7 A behavior expectations team is established that is made up of staff who regularly deal with the behavior of school students.

2.8 The behavior expectations team is trained to identify signs of bullying and to use specific counseling approaches, problem-solving methods, and restorative practices.

2.9 The behavior expectations team has methods of recording and collating data per school policies.

2.10 The behavior expectations team provides support for students involved in bullying situations to develop positive behaviors (including students who are bullied, students who bully others, and bystanders to bullying).

2.11 Support to students and families identified as being in need is ongoing, and follow-up support is sought from outside support services if required.

Preparing the school community to actively work together to resolve incidents of bullying behavior when they occur can be done in three phases: pre-event, event, and postevent.

Pre-Event

The following points may be considered when preparing an early response.

- There is a common understanding of what bullying and cyberbullying are and an understanding about the range of behaviors so staff, students, families, and school community members can identify these behaviors.
- There are clear procedures and a variety of methods for staff, students, families, and school community members to report bullying and cyberbullying behavior, incorporating both online and offline reporting mechanisms.
- There is a common understanding among all school community members, including students, staff, family members, and the broader community, that any reports of bullying or cyberbullying will be taken seriously and actions per the school policy will result.
- Proactive Policies and Practices toolkit 4.5 discusses how these points can be incorporated in behavior expectations policies.

Event

Each situation is unique; there will be individual circumstances surrounding the event as well as those involved in the bullying event. Each incident will need to be assessed, and the severity and impact of the situation used to determine the level of intervention required for both the victimized student and the student engaging in the bullying behavior. Proactive Policies and Practices toolkit 4.6 is an example of one way in which you could think about how you assess harm in your school.

A response to the event that supports all involved can include:

- Inviting all those involved with the incident (the student who was bullying others, the student being bullied, bystanders, and so on) to discuss the incident (strategies such as those used for the Co-LATE model may be used for these discussions as demonstrated in Proactive Policies and Practices toolkit 4.7).
- Helping all the students involved express their feelings about the incident by being approachable and nonjudgmental
- Talking about which behavior expectations have been broken and what harm has been done
- Discussing strategies for making amends and stopping the bullying from occurring again

Chapter 4

- Formalized reporting that is critical when addressing bullying incidences
- Ensuring all staff members are aware of the reporting mechanisms outlined within the policy and that these are followed. Reporting may include—
  - Writing a report on the student's record
  - Informing families involved of the situation
  - Informing other teaching staff who need to be made aware
  - Informing the school administration team
- Consequences for breaking school rules that can be applied according to the severity of the situation
- Consequences that are most appropriate when closely linked to the action that invoked the consequence, for example, if the incident occurred when using technology. These may include:
  - A formal apology
  - Loss of social privileges such as spending time with friends during break times
  - School community service
  - In-school suspension
  - Separate meetings with staff, families, and students involved in the bullying situation
  - Accurate summaries and descriptions of all discussions being recorded and placed in student files

Postevent

Monitoring the effectiveness of a response strategy after each incident and ensuring this monitoring is recorded and tracked as a part of the school record management system are essential given that more than half of students who were bullied reported that the situation got worse or did not improve after reporting it to teachers (Cross, Hall, Waters, et al., 2008). Follow-up sessions need to gather information from:

- Students directly involved
- Bystanders
- Any staff involved
- Families

Case Management for Students Persistently Involved in Bullying

Case management is provided to students who have a history of being involved in bullying or who need support to maintain their role in a safe and supportive school environment. A clear case management plan may include:

- A problem-solving approach for those involved in the incident
- Follow-up to ensure the longer-term safety of the student who is bullied and the occurrence of change
- Procedures to inform and involve families when appropriate
- Clear recording of incidents through formalized procedures
- Clear ongoing monitoring mechanisms
- Referring students to other support services, such as psychologists external to the school, when necessary

3   Integrated Focus on Orientation and Transition

School policies are promoted to the whole-school community, particularly at times of higher student risk, such as during orientation and transition.

Strategies for good practice:

3.1 Orientation days include information about the relevant policies to students and their families.

3.2 Students are provided with quality support to improve their social interactions at times of orientation and transition (when there is a higher risk for bullying).

3.3 Principal and leadership team present and discuss relevant policies, procedures, and information about bullying with new staff and relief staff.

3.4 Structures are used to support student connectedness and well-being such as cross-year group homerooms.

Orientation of new staff, students, and parents is an ideal time to disseminate the policy. This ensures that everyone arriving in the school has a copy and a good understanding of the policy and the school's vision of a safe and supportive school environment. Effective strategies suggested by schools involved in CHPRC research to raise awareness about their bullying policy are outlined in Proactive Policies and Practices toolkit 4.5 and could include the following.

Staff:

- Discussions and raising awareness of policy at staff meetings
- Offering training to staff in the implementation of the policy and strategies to address bullying
- Using professional learning time to provide a thorough overview of current research and successful practices to ensure everyone has the same capacity and there are consistent understandings
- Providing opportunities to show teachers who have not been involved in implementing the classroom curriculum what has and is being done
- Inducting new teachers by ensuring they receive a copy of the bullying policy

Students:

- Discussions and raising awareness of policy during assemblies (see Supportive School Culture toolkit 3.2)
- Discussions and learning activities addressing bullying in classes (see Key Understandings and Competencies toolkit 5.1)
- Having teachers draw attention to the bullying policy during their discussions of classroom policies with their students

Parents and the wider community:

- Issuing the bullying policy to all families at the start of the year
- Discussing the bullying policy at parent nights
- Using newsletter items for promotion of the policy to parents and the wider community (see Supportive School Culture toolkit 3.1)
- Displaying posters developed as part of the curriculum in every teaching area
- Introducing the policy at parent-teacher association meetings for parents and the wider community

Summary

This chapter has outlined the importance of consistent policy and practice for the reduction and prevention of bullying behaviors. Having a clear and consistent policy and set of practices and procedures sends a strong message to the whole-school community about the school's beliefs and actions to encourage a safe and supportive school environment. In addition, proactive policies provide a framework for the prevention, early response, and case management of bullying behavior. School policies need to be promoted throughout the whole-school community to ensure a shared understanding and consistent response to bullying behaviors.

Two school stories are included with this chapter to demonstrate how CHPRC research schools have sought to implement proactive policies and practices. In addition, eight toolkits are included to help schools take proactive action in developing and reviewing policies and practices for the reduction of bullying behavior, as follows.

- Proactive Policies and Practices toolkits 4.1, 4.2, and 4.3 describe the Shared Concern method, the Support Group method, motivational interviewing, and the Critical Thinking Line, respectively, as restorative strategies schools may use to resolve bullying situations.
- Proactive Policies and Practices toolkit 4.4 is included to assist with the identification of a school's vision statement and associated guiding principles while Proactive Policies and Practices toolkit 4.5 provides advice regarding the policy review process. In particular, information about which policies may need to be developed or reviewed, what needs to be included in these policies, and reviewing and implementing these policies is included.
- Proactive Policies and Practices toolkit 4.6 provides a framework for assisting schools in preparing the whole-school community to resolve bullying incidents.
- Proactive Policies and Practices toolkit 4.7 describes the Co-LATE model, a strategy that can be used by all members of the school community when responding to the reporting of bullying behaviors.

Throughout this chapter, reference is made to toolkits located in other chapters of this book. These toolkits may further assist schools to develop or review policies and practices relating to behavior expectations and the prevention of bullying behavior.

School Stories

> ### School Story 4.1
>
> **Brief background to school initiative:**
>
> The school had a philosophy of openness about bullying and introduced clear processes for student complaints and peer support. The school developed learning programs to address myths surrounding bullying. The principal prompted action when he reinvigorated a no put-down program.
>
> **School profile**
>
> - Metropolitan private boys' school
> - Grades: K–12
> - 895 students
> - This school has a significant boarding school population and a large number of students of Asian descent.

Action

The school believed that bullying should not be a hidden issue. It wanted to dispel the conspiracy of silence by increasing awareness and understanding of the behavior. The school created an advice pamphlet for families and students that outlined what bullying was, how parents could spot the signs, information for siblings and friends, how the school could be contacted, and the school's response to bullying. During a semester-long antibullying program, students asked adults about their experiences of bullying, particularly when they were in school. The responses were recorded, used for discussion, and compiled in a learning resource.

The school believed that only punishing students who engaged in bullying could make matters worse. Students who bullied also needed help coming to terms with different ways to behave or through building an understanding of the effects of their actions. The school decided that in the first instance, students who bullied would not be punished. The initial action was conciliatory and nonpunitive, encouraging an "OK to tell" atmosphere, partnership between parents and the school, and the development of social responsibility. The school's primary concern was to protect the person being bullied. Initially, the school worked separately with both the student being bullied and the student bullying to find a solution to the conflict. Incidents of bullying were recorded, including the date, time, place, and nature of the incident; the students involved; the follow-up action; and the name of the person who made the report. The records were reviewed on a weekly basis, and recurring names were noted. Students who were named frequently were interviewed and counseled, and their parents were informed. The school's priority was to stop bullying at an early stage rather than waiting until it became serious enough for students engaging in bullying to be punished.

Peer support was used as an educative tool to promote positive values and relationships. Eleventh-grade students volunteered to act as group leaders to small groups of eighth-grade students. The program gave the older students opportunities for self-development. They developed communication and leadership skills and a greater awareness of their own abilities. Younger students were provided with a supportive environment, security, and friendship.

Chapter 4

All implemented strategies were evaluated using pre- and postevent surveys. The school collected informal comments from teachers, parents, and the school council revealing that a significant change in behavior and attitude had been achieved as well as a significant reduction in the amount and type of bullying behavior.

What We Learned

Difficulties Encountered

It was difficult to sustain the initial impetus of the program. Changes in staff were particularly detrimental to maintaining the program's momentum.

Overcoming Difficulties

Bullying was an ongoing issue. The school needed to remain vigilant in its response to the issue and maintain communication between parents, students, and staff.

If We Could Do It Over

A change in administration unfortunately resulted in a loss of momentum. The school would have liked greater parental involvement earlier in the process.

Recommendations for Other Schools

Ensure that the administration and parents are fully committed to the program. To facilitate this, there needs to be an emphasis on educating staff and parents on the impact that bullying and harassment have on a child's life. The school must commit to a short-, mid-, and long-term plan, as it takes years to achieve a cultural change. Funding is essential, as a whole-school approach requires additional resources and staffing, including bringing in external expertise.

More information about the strategies used by this school can be found in the following materials.

- Supportive School Culture toolkit 3.3
- Proactive Policies and Practices toolkit 4.1
- Proactive Policies and Practices toolkit 4.2
- Proactive Policies and Practices toolkit 4.3
- Chapter 5: Key Understandings and Competencies

School Story 4.2

Background to school initiative:

When the principal arrived at this school, there was a hostile atmosphere. There was an oppositional culture and a general feeling of teachers versus students on the playground. There was also an expectation from parents of severe punishment for their children in any instance in which they were contacted by the school.

School profile:

- Metropolitan primary school
- 680 students
- Grades: K–7
- This was generally a low-socioeconomic area with a high proportion of racial and ethnic minorities. This was not necessarily a factor in the strategies used, but racial taunts were something that teachers and staff wanted to address.

Action

The school adopted a proactive stance toward behavior management, aiming to minimize reactive strategies. The school exposed its students to practices that develop a sense of self-respect and a clear understanding of the school motto: "Care, Respect, Trust." To facilitate ownership, the students were involved in the creation and the design of the new motto.

To promote team spirit within the school, a challenge was created. Tokens in each of the four team colors were used by teachers, assistants, and administration personnel to reward positive behavior. Every two weeks, the winning team was announced at an assembly and received ten minutes of extra recess time. A raffle was also conducted during the assembly, with five names being drawn at random and the winners receiving an ice cream. At the end of each term, the most successful team had its name placed on a memorial shield. To culminate the challenge, if all teams met a predetermined quota of tokens each term together, everyone received a small prize. The challenge, therefore, rewarded students at the whole-school, team, and individual levels.

To further recognize and reward positive behavior, students were rewarded with a special event at the end of each school term, known as reward days. All students were invited to attend provided that they had not received more than two detentions during the current term. However, negotiations occurred if detentions were received early in the term or it was apparent the student had demonstrated considerable improvement in behavior and attitude.

Games carts were used to reward individual classes for positive classroom behavior. The school purchased numerous high-quality children's board games and puzzles. Each class was challenged to earn five reward cards from its teacher and from each teaching specialist for positive classroom behavior. If the class achieved this goal, it was allowed to use the games cart for half a day.

A buddy program operated at the school. This program consisted of twice-weekly class visits by grade 1, 4, and 5 students. Half of one class would go to the other class and share activities, such as making and building things and playing games. This was organized between class teachers.

Chapter 4

The school encouraged and promoted an ethos of working with parents. This school emphasized the importance of being aware of the family and cultural attitudes of the district. It found that parents sometimes encouraged retaliation and physical fighting and that weekend conflicts were spilling into the school environment. The school encouraged parents to resolve problems through the school rather than approach other students' parents or the student themselves. The school encouraged parents to trust that bullying and behavioral management issues would be dealt with and that it was not up to individual parents to settle the score with students who were bullying others, or their parents.

The school encouraged teachers and administrators to act as role models and avoid engaging in bullying behavior themselves. The school considered it important for the school community to know that the principal and teachers did not bully others. The school's ethos statement reinforced that all students and parents have the right to talk and share their points of view.

A midyear survey revealed the school and teachers scored a high rate of approval among parents, who were confident that the school, principal, and teachers were "firm but fair." The survey showed that parents trusted the school and teachers much more than they previously did and understood that the school would deal with any negative behavior. Staff attitudes also changed positively with regard to discipline. In the past, teachers had the attitude that, because it was a big school, student behavior was going to be hard to manage. Now the problem is not seen as being the large school size, but the relationships. There is an emphasis on promoting friendly, respectful behavior toward people from all parts of the school community including administration, teachers, general staff, and students.

What We Learned

Difficulties Encountered

Teachers, staff, and parents accepted bullying as part of the school environment. Sixth- and seventh-grade students had experienced hostility from older students when they were in lower grades and had developed an attitude that it was their turn to dominate the younger students in the school.

Overcoming Difficulties

The school believed in the selection of local staff as well as ensuring that new staff members were right for the school. The school ethos was an important first step in establishing this supportive school culture.

By concentrating on the attitude of the lower primary students, the school was able to ensure that the hostile attitude of the older students did not influence the younger grades, thus interrupting the cycle of negative behavior. Many problems were overcome through the promotion of positive behavior from both staff and students. When teachers set an example of a comfortable, happy working environment, this filtered through to teacher-student relationships and to student-student relationships.

More information about the strategies used by this school can be found in the following toolkits.

- Supportive School Culture toolkit 3.3
- Proactive Policies and Practices toolkit 4.4
- Proactive Policies and Practices toolkit 4.5
- School–Family–Community Partnerships toolkit 7.2
- School–Family–Community Partnerships toolkit 7.3
- School–Family–Community Partnerships toolkit 7.5

Toolkits for Action

4.1   ## Proactive Policies and Practices Toolkit 4.1

This information has been modified from the Shared Concern method originally developed by Professor Anatol Pikas.

The Shared Concern Method

Description

The Shared Concern method aims to change the causes of the behavior of students involved in bullying within their social groups and to improve the situation for the student or students being bullied. The method employs a nonpunitive problem-solving approach to addressing reported incidents of bullying involving groups who are bullying others. Due to the nondisciplinary nature of the method, the process of responding to a report of bullying is not slowed down by needing to determine if the bullying actually occurred, who may be guilty of what part in the bullying, or even that the student reportedly bullied is free of having contributed to the circumstances affecting him or her.

The method targets the dynamics within groups carrying out bullying. Often groups who bully others use power and subtle reinforcing pressures or even open threats to maintain the cooperation of their own group members. The threat of expulsion from the group is a significant reinforcer for the participation of each member in bullying others. The Shared Concern method equalizes power imbalances inherent in group bullying and then allows the resolution of any underlying social problems with all of the parties involved.

The goals of the Shared Concern method are:

- To elicit empathy and a sense of cooperation toward the bullied student or students from the students involved in the bullying
- To work with the students involved in the bullying to shift the group dynamics that allowed and sustained the bullying behaviors in the first place
- To empower the bullied student or students by ensuring they are party to solving the social problems affecting them

The Shared Concern method is designed to get the students involved in the bullying to have *empathy* for the bullied student's situation and to really want to do something about it. Empathy reduces the attitudes that support bullying behaviors. Thinking of something they could do to improve the situation encourages students to take on a more positive attitude.

Each student involved in the bullying participates in a series of individual discussions with a staff member. Clearly defined steps are used to reach the point where each student involved in the bullying of others agrees that there is a problem for the bullied student or students and that the situation warrants concern. The student or students who are bullying are then encouraged to suggest ways to help improve the situation for the student or students being bullied. The student being bullied is also provided with an opportunity to discuss what is happening to him or her and encouraged to consider ways the situation could be improved, including any actions they could take to help themselves (Bauman & Del Rio, 2006; Hazler et al., 2001).

Key Points

The method is used with students who have the capacity to develop empathic responses toward the individual or individuals being bullied.

- Those involved in the bullying are first interviewed individually.
- The facilitator or teacher elicits, from each student involved in the bullying, concern for what is happening for the bullied student or students.
- The facilitator or teacher invites and supports the students who are bullying to then generate ideas they could undertake to improve the situation.
- The bullied student or students are then given an opportunity to discuss the situation.
- The students who previously bullied others then meet with the facilitator or teacher to follow up on the outcomes of their individual actions.
- If the target of the bullying is comfortable doing so the students who bullied and the student or students who were bullied are then invited to meet to report against the outcomes of their actions, resolve any ongoing concerns, and develop some common understandings around how they will talk to each other in the future.

While the Shared Concern method appears useful as an action to support students who are bullied, to be successful in the longer term, it is important that it be embedded within a whole-school approach to bullying prevention and management. Consultation with the whole-school community and formalization of this and other methods in a whole-school bullying approach enable a consistent and effective response to bullying issues.

A brief outline and suggested scripts follow that may be used to guide Shared Concern method sessions with both those who are targets of bullying and those who perpetrate bullying. If a school intends to implement the method, it is highly recommended that the staff using the method get training and undertake more detailed reading. Incorrect implementation will make the method ineffective.

Meeting With Each Student Who Is Suspected of Bullying Others

Step 1

"Thank you for coming to see me; I am meeting with a number of students because I have heard that some unpleasant things have been happening for *X*."

- Give space for the student to respond.
- If the student doesn't respond, ask, "Do you know *X*? What can you tell me about him or her that might help us?"
- Do not try to force the student to own up or admit to his or her involvement; simply try to encourage him or her to acknowledge that there is a situation that is making *X* unhappy.
- If the student complains about *X*, don't question; just let the student explain the situation.

Step 2

"So it sounds like *X* is having a bit of a tough time."

- Give space for the student to respond.
- As soon as the student agrees or acknowledges that *X* is having a hard time, move to step 3.
- If the student says that *X* is to blame, accept the point but suggest that "it still sounds like the situation is not good, is that correct?"

Step 3

"Well, I was wondering what you could do to help improve the situation for *X*?"

- Accept any reasonable suggestions with positive feedback.
- If the suggestions are negative, ask the student whether he or she thinks this would help *X* feel better about what is happening.
- If the student can't think of anything to do or is resistant to the idea, ask him or her to take some time to think about something he or she could do to help make *X* feel better, and then move to step 4.

Step 4

"OK, I'll see you in a few days to find out how you are getting on."

- If the student had an idea, then say you will see him or her to "discuss how your idea went when you tried it."
- If he or she didn't have an idea, then say you will see him or her to "discuss the idea you have come up with."

Meeting With the Student Who Has Reportedly Been the Target of Bullying

Step 1

"Thank you for coming to speak with me. I have heard that some things have been happening that are making you feel unhappy at school."

- Give space for the student to respond.
- Let the student explain his or her situation, and acknowledge how it is affecting him or her.

Step 2

"I have spoken to a few students about the situation, and they have made some good suggestions to improve things."

- If the student is concerned about this, reassure him or her that you will be keeping a close eye on what is happening.
- Let the student know that there may be a few changes in some students' behavior toward him or her.
- If you feel the student could help the situation by changing some of his or her behaviors, move to step 3.

Step 3

"I was wondering if there is anything you can think of doing that may improve the situation."

- Accept any reasonable suggestions with positive feedback.
- If the suggestions are negative, ask the student, "How do you think that will work?"
- If the student does not offer any ideas, ask, "What have you tried already?" and "How did that work for you?"
- If the student can't think of anything to do or is resistant to the idea, ask him or her to take some time to think about something he or she could do, and then move to step 4.

Step 4

"OK, I'll catch up with you again in a few days to find out how you are getting on."

- If the student had an idea, then say you will see him or her to "discuss how your idea went when you tried it."
- If the student didn't have an idea, then say you will see him or her to "discuss the idea you have come up with."
- Say, "Remember to keep an eye out for any positive changes that may be happening, and let me know what you have noticed when we meet again."

Plan follow-up meetings with the individuals to check on progress following this process. A final step may be a group meeting of the students doing the bullying followed by a summit meeting that includes the bullied student to report on positive outcomes, develop a plan, and create ideas about how it can be maintained. This meeting should only occur if and when the target of the bullying feels comfortable being involved; it should not be forced on the target. A plan is also put into place to look for early warning signs and deal with any future relationship issues.

It is preferable to have thorough knowledge and training in the Shared Concern method before implementing it, as it is easy to fall back into persuasive coercion approaches rather than a more neutral attitude that is required for it to be effective.

4.2 Proactive Policies and Practices Toolkit 4.2

Support Group Method

This technique aims to encourage students who are bullied and students who bully others to work together to try to decide on a mutually agreeable way to deal with the bullying.

Key Points

- This method is best used when the facilitator or teacher feels that the students bullying, as well as the students who are bullied, want the bullying to stop.
- The facilitator or teacher who intervenes avoids blaming anyone for the problem.

This approach works best in less serious cases of bullying when the students who are bullied and the students who bully may have previously been friends but this friendship has ended. It is unlikely to work if the students who bully are picking on students they don't know or care about, and if the patterns of bullying are so well established that the bullying itself has become a reward for the students who bully. CHPRC research has found this method to be most effective when bullying occurs within a social group, particularly girls, who are having friendship difficulties (for example, exclusion and teasing). By developing empathy for the feelings of the person being bullied, the groups are able to resolve this behavior and determine ways to prevent it from reoccurring.

When bullying has been observed or reported, the following steps can be taken.

Step 1

Interview the person being bullied.

When the facilitator or teacher finds out that bullying has occurred, he or she begins the process by talking to the student being bullied about his or her feelings. The teacher does not question him or her about the incident but does need to know who was involved.

Step 2

Convene a meeting with the people involved.

The facilitator or teacher arranges to meet with the student or students involved. This will include some bystanders who joined in but did not initiate any bullying.

Step 3

Explain the problem.

The facilitator or teacher talks about the way the person being bullied is feeling and might use a piece of writing or a drawing to emphasize his or her distress. At no time does the teacher discuss the details of the incidents or assign blame to the group.

Step 4

Share responsibility.

The facilitator or teacher does not attribute blame but states that he or she knows the group is responsible and can do something about it.

Step 5

Ask the group for its ideas.

Each member of the group is encouraged to suggest a way in which the person being bullied could be helped to feel happier. The facilitator or teacher gives some positive responses but does not go on to extract a promise of improved behavior.

Step 6

Leave it up to them.

The facilitator or teacher ends the meeting by passing over the responsibility to the group members to solve the problem and arranges to meet with them again to see how things are going.

Step 7

Meet with them again.

About a week later, the facilitator or teacher discusses with each student, including the person being bullied, how things have been going. This allows the teacher to monitor the bullying and keeps everyone involved in the process.

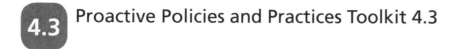

4.3   Proactive Policies and Practices Toolkit 4.3

Motivational Interviewing and the Critical-Thinking Line

Motivational interviewing and the critical-thinking line can be used in conjunction with the Shared Concern method or when a student has limited capacity to empathize with the person who has been bullied. These strategies help students who bully others talk about why they engage in this behavior.

Motivational Interviewing

Key Points

- This strategy is best used with students who bully who are not responding well to the Shared Concern method or who have limited empathy for the person they bullied.
- Motivational interviewing will not work with all students and may be less effective with individuals who are not willing to talk about their bullying behavior.

Interviewing Students Who Bully

Always begin by asking the student who bullies others if it is OK to talk about bullying. You need his or her permission to proceed. Explain that all discussion is confidential and if he or she prefers not to talk about bullying, he or she can read the school's behavior expectations policy.

Step 1

Getting Permission

Involve students in the conversation, and get their permission before getting started.

- "I'd like to spend a few minutes talking about your behavior. Is that OK with you?"

Step 2

Open-Ended Questions

To get the ball rolling, students may need to be drawn into conversation. Open-ended questions require more than single-word responses and may provide opportunities to explore students' issues. The following question stems may help.

Ask open-ended questions, such as:

- "To what extent . . ."
- "How often . . ."
- "Why . . ."
- "Tell me about . . ."
- "Help me understand . . ."

Avoid asking closed questions, such as:

- "Did you . . ."
- "Will you . . ."

Step 3

Reflective Listening

Asking more than three questions in a row may stop the conversation; reflections demonstrate that you have been listening to the student. They usually involve a statement restating, rephrasing, paraphrasing, or deducing from the information given to you (a reflection that slightly understates may work best). Reflections result in affirming or validating the student and keeping the student talking and thinking.

The following are safe reflections:

- "It sounds like this has been tough for you . . ."
- "It sounds like you're not happy with . . ."
- "It sounds like you're a bit uncomfortable about . . ."
- "It sounds like you're not ready to . . ."
- "It sounds like you're having a problem with . . ."

Step 4

Summarizing

At natural breaks, summarize the conversation. These summaries allow all facts to be considered and gives the student the opportunity to correct or add to the story so far. For example:

- "Let me see if I understand what you've told me so far . . ."
- "OK, this is what I've heard so far . . ."

Follow up with:

- "OK, how did I do?"
- "What have I missed?"
- "Is there anything you want to correct or add?"

Step 5

Self-Motivational Statements

The aim is to allow the student to discover discrepancies in his or her behavior. The interviewer encourages students to voice their own motivation for behavior change and helps students find solutions to the barriers they have created. For example:

- "Could you tell me some of the things you like about . . ."
- "Could you tell me some of the things you don't like about . . ."
- "Could you tell me some of the reasons why you might want to change your . . ."
- "Could you tell me some of the reasons why you may not want to change . . . (fears, barriers)"
- "How might your life be different if you . . ."

Remember that bullying is seen by the person doing the bullying as having both benefits and disadvantages. Help students clarify for themselves their own barriers to, and benefits of, stopping the bullying behavior.

What do you like about, or get out of, bullying someone? (barriers to stopping)

_____

What makes it hard for you to stop?

_____

What are some things that you think aren't so good about bullying? (advantages of stopping)

_____

If the student cannot think of any advantages of stopping, ask the student to role-play someone convincing you not to bully. For example, "If I were bullying someone, how would you convince me to stop?"

When the advantages and disadvantages of bullying have been identified, summarize both sides of the issue. For example, "On one hand you want to bully because . . . but you also say that it is the best way to deal with the situation because . . . . What do you think about this?"

Step 6

Offering Advice

Allow students time to explore their barriers. Ask students to identify who could help them stop using bullying behavior and where and when they might need help. (Again, you may have to ask students to imagine that they want to stop.)

Summarize what they have said. "So, what you are telling me is that . . . is that right?"

If students are interested, ask for permission to offer tips. "Would you like to hear some things other students have found useful for changing their behavior so they don't bully others?"

It is important not to offer unsolicited information or advice. There may be times when students require information or suggestions. Information or advice should only be provided when:

- The student asks for it
- The student gives you permission to provide it

When possible, offer only the facts, and ask the student to interpret them.

Students may need help to identify the best strategies. If the student asks for suggestions or provides permission, you may provide a range of strategies others have used (for example, decision-making techniques). However, when possible, ask the student to identify strategies that have worked previously for him or her or that he or she has observed others using.

Remind the student that there are people in the school and the community who can help them with information and support for their behavior change.

Chapter 4

Sample Questions for Motivational Interviewing

1. Positives and benefits (good things):

   - What are some of the good things about your bullying behavior?
   - What do you enjoy about bullying?
   - How important are these things to you?

2. Less positive and costs (not-so-good things):

   - What is there about your bullying behavior that you or other people might see as reasons for concern?
   - What worries you about your bullying behavior? What can you imagine happening to you?
   - What do you think might happen if you don't make a change?

3. Life goals:

   - How do you see yourself?
   - Can you describe to me what sort of person you are?
   - How do your friends, teachers, and parents see you?
   - What would be the advantages of making a change?

4. Compare with current unchanged behavior:

   - How would you like things to be different in the future?
   - You'd like to be . . ., so what do you think is stopping you?
   - You've told me something about yourself and your bullying behavior, but how would you like to see yourself in three months' time?

5. Ask for a decision:

   - Where does that leave you now?
   - What do you think you might want to do now?

6. Plan a short-term goal.

Figure 11: Sample questions for motivational interviewing.

Visit **go.solution-tree.com/behavior** for a reproducible version of this figure.

Reminder Cards

Schools involved in CHPRC research found it useful to print the following cards to keep with them while on duty as prompts for discussing bullying situations with students. They also enlarged them and displayed them on their office walls to assist student discussions without appearing to look up information or question ideas.

Sentence Starters

- "Tell me about . . ."
- "OK, this is what I've heard so far . . ."
- "It sounds like this has been tough for you . . ."
- "Because . . ."
- "Give me a recent example . . ."
- "What's your next step?"

Key Skills and Strategies

- Asking permission (supports student autonomy)
- Open-ended questions
- Reflective listening (keep it rolling)
- Summarizing (stop, assess, move on)
- Elicit change talk (student decision to change)
- Build empathy
- Avoid arguments (roll with resistance)
- Provide information (but let student interpret it)

Motivational Interviewing

+ (good things about . . .)

– (not-so-good things about . . .)

S Summarize

A Assess balance of + and –

G Goal set

S Support

Figure 12: Reminder cards.

Visit **go.solution-tree.com/behavior** for a reproducible version of this figure.

Critical-Thinking Line

The critical-thinking line is based on a number line and can be used for many purposes. For younger students, the line can be used to help students consider the intensity of their feelings. For example, *"You are feeling angry. Look at the critical-thinking line, and tell me how angry you feel."* In class, students can think of the things that make them feel most angry and mark these on the line. This allows students to see how others feel and their levels of response to those feelings.

The critical-thinking line can also be used when talking to students about bullying. It is best used in conjunction with the Shared Concern method or motivational interviewing as a means to establish, for example, some feelings of empathy for the student being bullied.

The interviewer asks the student to consider how he or she feels about the person he or she has been bullying. Then ask the student, on a scale of 1–10, how strong that feeling is. On this scale, 1 is low, and 10 is high.

For example:

"On a scale of 1–10, how do you feel about _____?"

Very few students have been found to answer 0. But if this happens, ask the student why, and continue with the process you are using—either the Shared Concern method or motivational interviewing.

A student might say, *"He's about a 4."*

The interviewer then replies, *"OK, about a 4. What was it about that person that made you decide on a 4 rather than a lower score like a 3?"* (At this point, you are trying to get the student bullying to identify some positive characteristics about the student being bullied.) For example, the student might reply, *"Well he's not the worst kid I ever met."* From this point, the interviewer can attempt to establish some positive attributes of the bullied student.

The interviewer then asks why the student bullying didn't give the other student a higher score, for instance a 5. At this point, the student will usually point out the reasons why this particular student was targeted for bullying. This is an important starting point for discussion relating to the characteristics and feelings of the other person and how the bullying may be affecting that student.

This method of getting the student to think critically about the person he or she is bullying helps to develop an awareness of how the bullying situation developed and may provide ideas as to how this problem could be addressed.

4.4   Proactive Policies and Practices Toolkit 4.4

Vision Statement and Guiding Principles

Prior to reviewing school behavior expectations policies that encourage students' positive social behavior and aim to reduce student bullying, it is important to consider how this policy links to the school's vision statement and guiding principles. The following checklist of ideas and examples was found by schools involved in CHPRC research to be useful when developing a vision statement and guiding principles.

Developing Your Whole-School Community Vision Statement

Developing a vision statement for the safety and well-being of school community members accounts for their values, priorities, and common understandings.

To develop a vision statement, the following questions may be helpful.

In five years' time:

- What would it be like to be part of this school?
- How would you feel as you walk into the school?
- What would the school look like as you move around?
- What would people be saying about your school and its staff, parents, and students?

Vision statements are most effective when they are worded positively. Outline what is to be achieved in simple terms that are easy to recall, and convey messages everyone can understand and relate to.

Caring and respect are the foundations of a school community that is free from bullying and harassment.

Identifying the Guiding Principles to Achieve Your Vision

Guiding principles provide the foundations for the development of a comprehensive, schoolwide effort to promote a safe, inclusive, and supportive learning environment. The guiding principles define how the school plans to implement the whole-school community vision. For example, the National Safe Schools Framework (Ministerial Council on Education, Employment, Training and Youth Affairs, 2011) guiding principles provide a useful starting point.

Also consider how the school will achieve the whole-school community vision, for example:

- Everyone has the right to feel safe and to be safe
- Every member of our school community is treated with respect
- Everyone feels part of the whole-school community and is included in its vision
- Common goals are clearly articulated and prioritized
- Everyone knows his or her role in the school and has the skills and knowledge to fulfill that role
- Written documentation provides the school community with a consistent approach to addressing bullying strategies and is in place to prevent and respond effectively to situations that may impact the well-being of school community members

These ideas could be used in the formulation of principles to determine how the school could achieve its vision.

The following is an example of guiding principles developed and tested by schools involved in CHPRC research.

Chapter 4

The school:

- Affirms the right of all school community members to feel safe and supported in a school environment where diversity is valued and everyone is treated with respect, fairness, and dignity

- Ensures all community members understand their responsibility to ensure everyone feels physically and psychologically safe

- Promotes a clear, well-defined, agreed understanding that bullying and cyberbullying are not acceptable behavior

- Promotes well-defined and agreed understanding of acceptable behavior for all members of the school community, both online and offline

- Establishes and endorses a shared responsibility between the whole-school community to prevent and report incidences of bullying and cyberbullying

- Develops and consistently implements student behavior policies that articulate programs and processes for promoting a safe and supportive environment

- Encourages active participation of staff, students, families, and the whole-school community to plan, implement, and evaluate school policies, procedures, and practices

- Ensures that the roles and responsibilities of all members of the school community outlined in the policy are explicit and clearly understood and the actions associated with these roles are consistently implemented

- Recognizes that leadership that is committed to a shared vision through policy and practice is essential for establishing a safe and supportive school environment

- Focuses on evidence-based intervention and management strategies and incorporates procedures and programs that are restorative and solution focused

- Implements universal, whole-school prevention and intervention programs including formal and informal activities in the curriculum, school ethos and environment, student support, and family links to ensure all members of the school community have common levels of awareness and consistent responses to bullying and cyberbullying

- Provides professional learning and support for staff to implement the student behavior policies

- Regularly monitors and evaluates policies and programs so evidence-based practice supports decisions and guides improvement

Figure 13: Example of school guiding principles.

Visit **go.solution-tree.com/behavior** for a reproducible version of this figure.

Proactive Policies and Practices Toolkit 4.5

Policy Review Process

Permeate School Vision Through Policy Documents

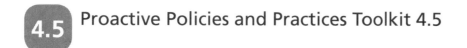

Figure 14: Policy review process.

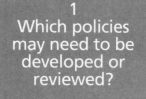 **Which policies may need to be developed or reviewed?**

When considering the writing or review of policy that addresses the expected behaviors of members of the school community, it is important to consider the context for this policy relative to other related school policies. Policy documents are easier to understand and implement if the messages are consistent in all policy documents.

These policies may include:

- Enrollment policy
- Bullying and cyberbullying policy
- Student expectations agreement
- Expected behavior policy
- Excursion policy
- Communication policies
- Mobile phone policy
- Technology use agreement
- Staff guidelines
- Parent expectations

Chapter 4

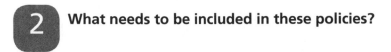

2 What needs to be included in these policies?

Policies addressing the expected behaviors of school community members are closely linked to the school's overarching vision. Once the whole-school vision and guiding principles are established, the next stage is to develop policies to guide practice in the school.

The name given to the school policy outlining expected behaviors varies in each school. While these policy documents may specifically address bullying, it is critical for this document to be framed positively. School community members are more likely to respond to a policy that expects they will behave well at all times rather than the reverse. The following section will assist in writing a school's expected behavior policy. The policy may include:

2.1 Whole-school community agreement

2.2 Policy rationale

2.3 Policy objectives

2.4 Whole-school common understandings about prosocial behavior, bullying, and cyberbullying

2.5 Rights and responsibilities of the school community

2.6 Preventing and responding to bullying and cyberbullying behavior

2.1 Whole-School Community Agreement

Effective policies state a clear intention to take bullying involving any member of the school community very seriously and respond to it effectively. Students, teachers, parents, caregivers, and members of the wider school community have a shared responsibility to create a safe and happy environment, free from all forms of bullying. A shared responsibility between all school community members to prevent bullying and actively work together to resolve incidents of bullying behavior when they occur is most effective when clearly articulated and described in a way that is understood by all members of the school community.

2.2 Policy Rationale

A clear statement of purpose regarding bullying prevention and management is articulated in the policy. It should clearly but succinctly state what this policy is for and emphasize the school's positive goals.

2.3 Policy Objectives

The objectives of an expected behavior policy outline the outcomes the school wishes to achieve by implementing this policy. When writing these, consider how the outcomes will be measured and whether they can be used in the ongoing monitoring and evaluation of the effectiveness of policy implementation.

2.4 Whole-School Common Understandings About Prosocial Behavior, Bullying, and Cyberbullying

It is important for all members of the school community to share common understandings about what is bullying and what is not bullying. Clear definitions developed by the school community will help to clearly identify the types of social behaviors that are expected within the school and the types of behaviors that are not. These understandings will also enhance the quality and consistency of response to bullying by the school community. Common understandings typically found in a school policy include:

- Definition of bullying and cyberbullying
- Types and examples of bullying and cyberbullying
- Information about actions that should be taken by the person being victimized and bystanders to the bullying and cyberbullying behavior

The following provides an example of what could be included in the school's behavior expectations policy.

Definition of Bullying and Cyberbullying

Bullying is a repeated behavior that may be physical, verbal, written, or psychological; where there is intent to cause fear, distress, or harm to another; conducted by a more powerful individual or group against a less powerful individual or group of individuals who are unable to stop this from happening.

Power: A person who engages in bullying may display power through various means—physical size and strength, status within a peer group, and recruitment within the peer group so as to exclude others.

Frequency: Bullying is not a random act—it is characterized by being repetitive. Students who are bullied not only have to endure the humiliation of the bullying, but many live in fear of its re-occurrence.

Intent to harm: People who engage in bullying and cyberbullying behavior usually deny any intent to harm others and may not always be fully conscious of the harm they cause. Causing physical and emotional harm, however, is usually a deliberate act. It puts the person who is bullied in a position of oppression by the person who is engaging in the bullying.

Cyberbullying is when, over a period of time, an individual or a group uses information and communication technologies to intentionally harm a person who finds it hard to stop this bullying from continuing.

Figure 15: Example definition of bullying and cyberbullying.

Chapter 4

Types and Examples of Bullying and Cyberbullying

Physical Bullying

Repeatedly and deliberately:

- Bumping, pulling, shoving, or tripping someone
- Throwing things at someone to hurt, annoy, or upset him or her
- Hitting, punching, slapping, pinching, biting, or scratching someone
- Touching someone who doesn't want to be touched

Verbal Bullying

Repeatedly and deliberately:

- Calling people names or offensive nicknames
- Making racist comments about someone and his or her family
- Making rude comments or jokes about someone's religion
- Teasing someone or being sarcastic in a way that is hurtful and upsetting
- Making comments that are hurtful about the way someone may look or behave
- Making nasty comments about someone's sexual orientation, perceived or otherwise

Threatening

Repeatedly and deliberately:

- Making someone feel afraid that he or she is going to be hurt
- Pressuring someone to do things he or she doesn't want to do
- Making aggressive gestures or looks that make someone afraid
- Forcing students to do hurtful or embarrassing things
- Forcing someone to give you money, food, or belongings

Property Abuse

Repeatedly and deliberately:

- Damaging someone's belongings
- Stealing someone's money
- Taking things away from someone
- Taking or hiding someone's belongings

Emotional Bullying

Repeatedly and deliberately:

- Ignoring someone or keeping him or her out of group conversations (known as exclusion)
- Leaving someone out by encouraging others not to have anything to do with him or her
- Spreading lies or stories about someone to try to get others to dislike someone
- Making things up to get someone into trouble
- Stalking someone by continually following him or her or giving unwanted attention, for example, staring

Cyberbullying

Repeatedly and deliberately:

- Ignoring someone or sending nasty messages through social media such as Facebook
- Sharing electronic images of people without their permission
- Sending harassing, abusive, or offensive messages online, for example, through social media or by phone
- Making silent or abusive phone calls
- Spreading rumors online, for example, through social media or by phone

Figure 16: Types and examples of bullying and cyberbullying.

Bystanders to Bullying and Cyberbullying

A bystander is someone who sees the bullying or knows that it is happening. Bystanders can be identified in the following categories:

- **Supporters** support the person bullying either by helping him or her bully the other person or by encouraging the person bullying
- **Spectators** gather or deliberately stay to watch the incident (sometimes from concern and sometimes for enjoyment)
- **Witnesses** are aware that the incident is occurring (know about the bullying or see it from a distance)
- **Defenders** support the person being bullied either directly or indirectly

It is expected that all students in the school would take some positive action to support the person being bullied directly (for example, by inviting the person being bullied to join their group or letting him or her know what happened was wrong) or indirectly (for example, by asking an adult for help).

Figure 17: Definition of a bystander.

Visit **go.solution-tree.com/behavior** for a reproducible version of this figure.

2.5 Rights and Responsibilities of the School Community

Individual and shared responsibilities of students, families, and school staff when addressing bullying behavior are best understood when outlined in the school policy. For example, an acknowledgment can be made that it is the responsibility of the whole-school community to encourage positive social behavior and discourage bullying.

Rights

A statement of the rights of students, staff, and families with respect to bullying at school, including:

- A declaration of the rights of individuals in the whole-school community to be free of bullying
- A statement of rights of students, staff, families, and the wider school community with respect to prosocial behavior and types of bullying

Responsibilities

A statement of the shared responsibilities of staff, students, and families to model positive social behaviors and to prevent and respond to reports and observations of bullying

Examples

Schools have a responsibility to inform staff, students, families, and the wider school community about the expected behavior policy, including:

- Providing families and students with clear information about strategies that promote appropriate behavior and the consequences of inappropriate behavior
- Providing students with strategies to respond assertively (not aggressively) to incidents of bullying behavior, including responsibilities as bystanders to bullying situations
- Communicating to families the important role they play in encouraging prosocial behaviors and resolving incidents of bullying behavior involving their children
- Outlining how the school leadership team will support, promote, enact, maintain, and review the policy and procedures

Students, staff, and families have a shared responsibility to:

- Promote positive relationships that respect individual differences in the school community
- Acknowledge their responsibility as role models of positive, caring, and respectful behavior
- Be familiar with the school's expected behavior policy and procedures
- Be observant of signs and symptoms of bullying
- Report incidents of bullying
- Actively work together to resolve incidents of bullying behavior when they occur
- Support families to be open in their discussions about bullying in the school, being observant of signs of bullying, treating reports of bullying seriously, supporting their children in developing positive responses to incidents of bullying consistent with the school's expectations, and supporting the school to effectively address bullying through the strategies outlined in the school's policy documents
- Respond in an appropriate, timely, and consistent manner to incidents of bullying by recording and following up on incidents of bullying in accordance with the school's policy documents

2.6 Preventing and Responding to Bullying and Cyberbullying Behavior

Preventing Bullying and Cyberbullying Behavior

The following checklist of bullying and cyberbullying prevention strategies can be consistently implemented through the school's behavior expectations policies.

Whole-school ethos:

✓ The school has an ethos that enables safety, care, support, and respect for all school community members.

Student behavior policy:

✓ A whole-school behavior expectations policy is developed and implemented to encourage the promotion of positive social behavior and the prevention and establishment of effective responses to bullying and cyberbullying.

Staff professional learning:

✓ All school staff members have a consistent understanding about bullying and cyberbullying and how to respond to situations.

Orientation:

✓ The behavior expectations policy is promoted during the orientation and provided to all new students, parents, staff, relief staff, and other school community members, including externally contracted staff such as bus drivers and providers of extracurricular activities.

Classroom:

✓ The classroom environment and curriculum are used to establish common understandings about bullying and cyberbullying and how to respond effectively while building positive social skills—online and offline—with students.

Peer support:

✓ The peer group is encouraged to provide support for students being bullied and fosters positive peer group influence to discourage bullying and cyberbullying.

School physical environment:

✓ The school provides a safe, well-supervised school environment with opportunities for positive social interaction, both online and offline, that promote support and respect.

Family links:

✓ Families are actively involved in the school and its response to bullying.

Responding to Bullying and Cyberbullying Behavior

The following seven-step response plan provides an outline of actions that need to be considered by schools once they identify students who have been involved in bullying.

		Responding to a Bullying Incident
R E S P E C T	**1. Co-LATE model** (See Proactive Policies and Practices toolkit 4.7.)	Listen to students involved to understand the situation and any history that may be relevant to the incident. Ensure notes are taken during this process (this must be the case for every stage). Discuss the situation with: • Students directly involved • Bystanders • Staff involved • Families (as necessary) • Administration staff (depending on harm or risk involved)
	2. Assess risk	Assess the level of risk or harm (consider the frequency, intensity, type, and duration of the bullying behavior) associated with the incident, and triage as high, moderate, or low.
R E S P O N D	**3. Report** (See Proactive Policies and Practices toolkits 4.6 and 4.7.)	Use the contact recommendations to determine who needs to be contacted, including: • Governance structures—system level or school board • Principal—administration team • Guidance counselors • Families • External support agencies • Teachers and tutors of young people involved • School support services—psychologist, nurse
	4. Record	Collect, record, and store all information related to each case. Ensure each stage has been recorded.
R E C O N C I L E	**5. Selection of restorative technique** (See Proactive Policies and Practices toolkits 4.1, 4.2, 4.3, and 4.4.)	Discuss restorative technique options with relevant staff, families, and students. Determine which technique to use based on the school policy and the triage guide (see pages 132–133) to determine technique, such as the Shared Concern method, Co-LATE model, motivational interviewing, Support Group method, or individual behavior plans. Agree on the plan to be implemented.
	6. Implement plan	Implement the agreed plan of action. Reinforce positive behavior. Ensure all vested parties (as determined in the report phase) have a copy of the agreed plan and are working together to reinforce positive behaviors.
	7. Additional support	Bullying incidences appear to resurface. Check in with all parties involved in the incident at regular predetermined intervals. Offer additional support to those students who are experiencing difficulties adhering to the terms of the agreed plan.

Figure 18: Responding to a bullying incident.

Visit **go.solution-tree.com/behavior** for a reproducible version of this figure.

Triage for Restorative Responses to Bullying Behavior

The Friendly Schools Plus triage response plan is a guide to help school staff determine under what circumstances one response to bullying behavior may be chosen instead of another. In many circumstances, the decision will be based on the school's values and policies related to student behavior and the school's capacity, and in particular, its resources and staff skills. If the school's culture and policies are more discipline based, then it is more likely it will select a disciplinary model of response, whereas a school with a culture and policies related to caring for students may be more likely to choose a restorative response. The triage proposed here has assumed the use of a more caring approach—one that is more restorative. However, in severe or extreme bullying cases, legal or firm disciplinary action may be necessary, no matter what the school's approach.

Try This First

The simplest of these techniques is called the Co-LATE model (see Proactive Policies and Practices toolkit 4.7). This technique can easily be used by all school staff to help students to feel safe and listened to by adults. The Co-LATE model was tested as part of the KIT+ Project conducted by the CHPRC and was found, qualitatively, to be very useful for encouraging students to talk with teachers and other adults about any issue, but particularly bullying. Co-LATE has value as an immediate response to students who report bullying, prior to them engaging in more formal counseling.

What Next?

While every student and situation is different in many ways, the following general triage guide may help school staff decide which restorative method to begin with. The diagram has attempted to profile the students (both targets and perpetrators who may benefit the most from these techniques). Students may also require a behavior expectations plan to support positive behavior change. A small proportion of students, however, will require psychological treatment beyond the scope of school services, especially in schools with limited access to qualified counseling staff. These students need to be linked via their families to these services as soon as possible.

Possible Restorative Approaches for Students Who Bully Others

Restorative Approach	Triage Checklist—Perpetrator
Shared Concern Method (Proactive Policies and Practices toolkit 4.1) **Age:** upper primary and lower secondary students For cases that are low to moderate severity	• Willingness to change behavior • Groups of students identified as bullying others • Feels remorse, capacity for empathy • Also bullied by others (bully/victim) • Multiple targets • Agreeable to participating in a series of meetings
Support Group Method (Proactive Policies and Practices toolkit 4.2) **Age:** middle to upper primary students For cases that are low to low-moderate severity	• Currently or previously a friend of target • Girls bullying girls • Target has other supportive friends • Feels remorse, has capacity for empathy • Influenced by group norms and normative expectations • Agreeable to participating in a series of meetings
Motivational Interviewing (Proactive Policies and Practices toolkit 4.3) **Age:** all secondary students For cases that are low to moderate severity	• Does not feel remorse, limited capacity for empathy • Also bullied by others (bully/victim) • Popular or high self-esteem • Willing to talk about behavior • Multiple targets • Agreeable to participating in a series of meetings

Figure 19: Restorative approaches to students who bully.

Possible Restorative Approaches for Students Who Are Targets of Bullying

Counseling Approach	Triage Checklist—Target
Shared Concern Method (Proactive Policies and Practices toolkit 4.1) **Age:** upper primary and lower secondary students For cases that are low to moderate severity	• Provocative target • Multiple perpetrators or bullied for extended length of time • Also a perpetrator (bully/victim) • Lower self-esteem • Agreeable to participating in a series of meetings
Support Group Method (Proactive Policies and Practices toolkit 4.2) **Age:** middle to upper primary students For cases that are low to low-moderate severity	• Currently or previously a friend of perpetrator • Girls bullying girls • Target has other supportive friends • Agreeable to participating in a series of meetings
Motivational Interviewing (Proactive Policies and Practices toolkit 4.3) **Age:** all secondary students For cases that are low to moderate severity	• High motivation to take action to stop bullying • Willingness to help themselves • Multiple perpetrators or bullied for extended length of time • Provocative target • Also a perpetrator (bully/victim) • Agreeable to participating in a series of meetings

Figure 20: Restorative approaches to students who are bullying targets.

 Reviewing and Implementing Policy

The policy review process will help school communities reflect on current practices and determine the need to review, refine, or improve specific aspects of the policy. The process involves using data from a number of sources to objectively review the whole-school processes and environment. Some schools will already have effective policies and procedures in place to respond to bullying situations while other schools will still be planning and developing these areas.

It is important for schools to conduct a review involving their school community to effectively:

- Understand the problems associated with bullying and cyberbullying
- Develop common commitment to the reduction of bullying and cyberbullying
- Motivate the community to support and promote positive behaviors
- Develop a plan of action specific to the school's needs

Whole-School Community Review of Policy

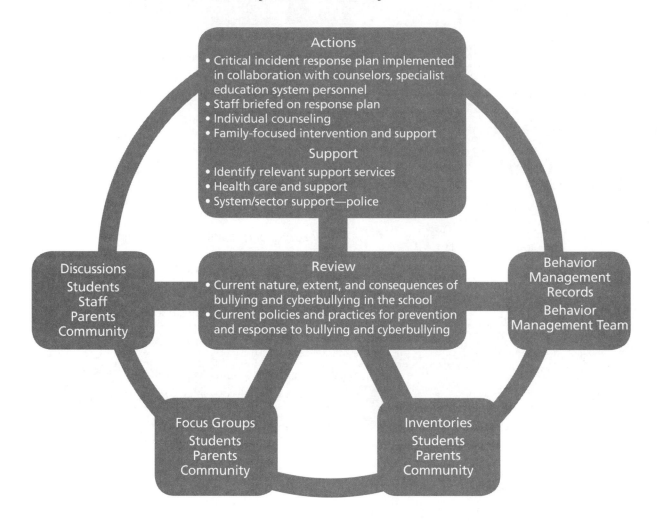

Figure 21: Whole-school community policy review.

3.1 Gathering Information

The development of the whole-school plan for addressing bullying and cyberbullying can be part of an ongoing, collaborative planning and review process, including specific methods of:

- Monitoring the whole-school policy that includes input from students, families, staff, education officers, and community agencies, and a timeline for review and modification, for example, an annual review
- Maintaining awareness-raising activities to regularly reaffirm the school's philosophy on prosocial behavior and bullying
- Keeping action on bullying a high priority
- Identifying resources (including staff and time) committed to support the recommendations from this process

Collecting and Analyzing Appropriate Data on the Nature and Extent of Bullying and Cyberbullying

A variety of methods of data collection will provide the most thorough understanding of the current school climate. It is useful to collect the following information from students, staff, families, and the broader school community.

- The nature and extent of bullying
- The impact of bullying on students
- Which students are most affected
- What is being done by the school to encourage positive social behavior and reduce bullying
- The outcomes of the school's response to bullying
- Satisfaction with the school's response to bullying

These data can be used to inform the review of the school policy to ensure it is understood and is relevant to students' current behaviors and experiences.

Information can be gathered from general observations of the relationships and social interactions within the school community. However, the use of an anonymous questionnaire (especially online) can be a useful way to collect information about the bullying and cyberbullying experiences of students. The examples described are ways schools have collected data from students, parents, and staff to help inform the development and review of the school's policies. For more information about questionnaire development, please see Building Capacity toolkit 2.1.

Questionnaires

Questionnaires can be excellent sources of data to inform planning decisions. If possible, it is a good idea to use a pre-existing survey that has been tested for validity (how accurately each question measures what it was trying to measure) and reliability (how consistently each question is perceived by the group of respondents). It is useful to repeat the survey each year to track social behaviors, both online and offline, within the school community. Longitudinal data (data collected in consecutive years) will provide valuable trend information compared to cross-sectional data (one-time data collection).

Chapter 4

Student Behavior Records

Analysis of student behavior records that describe the name of the students, the time, the location, the consequences, and follow-up for each reported incident of bullying will identify the kinds of behaviors and behavioral trends that may be occurring in the school. This information can be used to propose prevention and response strategies for the future as well as provide insight into possible behaviors that may have been overlooked without data.

The types of student behavior record information that can be analyzed include:

- Who are the students who repeatedly get into trouble?
- What is the nature of their bullying and cyberbullying behavior?
- How serious were these behaviors?
- Is there a trend in the type of behaviors and grade levels or gender involvement?
- When (time of day) do students most often bully?
- What months or days of the week are office referrals most common?
- Where does the bullying and cyberbullying behavior most often take place?
- Did these behaviors result in referral to the case management team or administration team?
- Are there behaviors that are handled differently by some teachers (for example, handled in their classrooms), while other teachers use referrals to case management teams?
- Who refers students most often?
- Is there consistency in response across the school?
- Are there consequences that seem to reduce referrals? If so, what?
- Do these consequences work differently for different groups of students (for example, boys and girls, younger or older)?
- Is there a sequence of responses that work best?
- How have bystanders been involved?

Focus Groups

A focus group is a group interview involving approximately eight to twelve participants that is used to collect qualitative information through group discussion of the issues. The one- to two-hour discussion is facilitated by a moderator who asks carefully constructed nonleading questions that encourage group discussion and interaction. Open-ended questions work best, for example, *What sort of consequences should be given to students who break the rules with regard to their use of technology?* Simple scenarios to accompany the questions are sometimes helpful. Parents are more likely to attend school focus groups when they are specifically invited (principal sends a letter of invitation), if the focus group is hosted as a breakfast or dinner meeting, and if students encourage parents to attend.

Intercept Interviews

Parents waiting for their children after school or at sports events may be willing to provide a random selection of responses. Students can also be trained to conduct interviews with peers or adults, which may result in more candid and honest responses. It may be useful for interviewees to have a digital recorder so they don't have to worry about taking notes while listening.

3.2 Review of Current School Policy and Practice

At a school level, decide how often the policy will be reviewed to determine the success of elements of the policy documents. Some areas to consider when reviewing a policy are:

- Who will be involved in the policy review?
- What specific areas of the policy will be examined based on the information gathered (for example, types or rates of prosocial behavior or bullying and cyberbullying among specific year groups, gender groups, and so on)?
- Which areas in the policy may become priorities for the following year?
- How will the review recommendations be implemented?
- How will the review recommendations be communicated?
- Is the date for the next policy review written into the policy?

Strategies for Consultation and Collaboration

As school policies related to prosocial behavior and bullying need to be owned by the school community and represent the beliefs and values of the school community, it is ideal for all members of the whole-school community to have an opportunity to contribute to their development or review. Students need to also be included in the feedback process. Each participant needs to feel respected and valued for his or her contribution to the policy development process. Indicate a realistic deadline for feedback and, when possible, hold meetings to discuss the content. Schools that consult widely in the development of their behavioral policies achieve better policy compliance.

Feedback on the draft policy can be obtained by:

- Making copies available in the office and advertising in the school newsletter and at assemblies that the policy is available to be reviewed
- Distributing copies to all staff (teaching and nonteaching)
- Presenting the draft policy at various meetings of different groups (staff meetings, student council, school board, PTA)
- Approaching community reference groups or individuals and requesting their feedback
- Attaching and distributing by mail or email a short questionnaire with the draft policy

Consider involving those groups that may have difficulty giving feedback by personally contacting those families who may lack confidence approaching the school. For example, when possible, have the policy translated for those families who speak English as a second language. Seek out those that may be opposed to what is being proposed, and involve them directly in the process of review. When possible, identify issues early in the review process that may be controversial, and engage appropriate community members who can help resolve these issues.

Incorporating the Feedback

Collate the feedback from school community members, and identify the main points and general themes of the responses. It may be necessary to investigate some of the responses further and gather more information or advice to address any concerns raised in the feedback.

Feedback collected from the school community could be incorporated into a second draft. Inform the school community that the policy is being rewritten to incorporate their feedback. Issues for further discussion may need to be raised at staff and parent meetings and assemblies. Circulate the second draft among the leadership team, counselors, students, staff, and interested members or groups from the school community. There may be a number of iterations following this procedure, as new feedback is collated and incorporated into a workable document. This process works well for schools developing new mobile phone or social media use policies, in which there can be many vested and opposing interests.

Have the Policy Endorsed

Endorsement of the policy allows the school community to confirm that it is aware of, and understands, the policy. This process is more likely to lead to whole-school ownership and therefore implementation of and compliance with the policy. Once the final draft policy is produced, the school's project team can determine who is most appropriate to endorse the policy. It is best to have a range of people from the school community to endorse the policy. Consider endorsement from the school board, school management team, student council, staff, and parent-teacher groups.

3.3 Implementing the Policy

Publishing the Policy

After developing or reviewing the behavior policies, it is important they are published and distributed to all staff, students, parents, and community members in a way that is easily accessed and understood. Most schools develop a detailed, formal policy as the official master document that is available to all school community members. It is worthwhile working with students to develop simplified versions in online or offline brochure or pamphlet format that present key information in an easy-to-read layout for other students and families. Students can help present the policy in language they understand.

Disseminating the Policy

Policy Launch

Schools may consider officially launching the policy during a bullying or positive social behavior awareness campaign, such as a bullying awareness week or by contacting the local community newspaper to publish an article. Provide a date the policy will come into effect, and make copies available in the library and school office. Consider putting abridged versions (perhaps developed by students) of the policy in the school handbook, on the website, and other places accessed by the school community.

Orientation

The orientation of new staff, students, and families is an ideal time to disseminate policies. This ensures everyone arriving in the school has a copy and an understanding of the school's position and action on key issues.

In summary, school dissemination strategies might include:

- Sending key policies home with all students at the start of the school year
- Including key policies in orientation packets or information provided to all new students and their families
- Including key policies on the school website and in student newsletters and handbooks
- Increasing the awareness of all staff (including library, cafeteria, and all other support staff) by explaining key policies at the start of a new school year
- Discussing students' rights and responsibilities at the first assembly of the year with students, staff, and families present if possible
- Providing key policies to all relief staff and new staff who start during the year

Policy Promotion

While structured activities raise general awareness of the school's key policies, it is important that brief, regular reminders of the policy are incorporated into whole-school activity. Strategies to raise awareness about policies related to encouraging prosocial behavior and reducing bullying may include:

- Discussing at assemblies school expectations regarding prosocial behaviors
- Discussions and learning activities addressing bullying in classes
- Developing a process for school administration staff to track incidents
- Offering training to staff in strategies to encourage prosocial behaviors and reduce bullying
- Enhancing the peer support or buddy system in the school
- Reviewing how students are recognized and rewarded for supportive behavior
- Training teachers in positive uses of technology and other cyberbullying prevention strategies
- Discussing with staff how the positive messages in the behavioral policies can be addressed in every learning area
- Discussing the behavioral expectations for the whole-school community at parent nights

Policy Into Practice

Adopting any policy where changes to school operations are necessary is best accomplished in stages. Plans to implement the policy can be made public so the community has ample time to prepare for the upcoming changes.

Chapter 4

4.6 Proactive Policies and Practices Toolkit 4.6

Preparing the School Community to Resolve Incidents of Bullying

HIGH-LEVEL HARM

Co-LATE model

- Triage—student ability to show empathy assessed
- External support services sourced (in discussion with family)
- Consequences as per policy recommendations
- Motivational interviewing
- Shared Concern method (if capacity for empathy)/Support Group method
- Individual behavior plan

Should consequence be school suspension, then a strategy for the student's return to school should be developed and discussed with student and family.

MANAGED BY BEHAVIOR EXPECTATIONS TEAM AND ADMINISTRATION

Contact recommendations— severe incidents

- System level or governance contacts, such as school board, especially if suspended
- Principal—administration team
- Guidance counselors
- Families

MODERATE HARM

Co-LATE model

- Triage—student ability to show empathy assessed
- Motivational interviewing
- Consequences as per policy recommendations
- Individual behavior plan (ratified by student, family, and staff)
- Shared Concern method (if capacity for empathy)/Support Group method

MANAGED BY BEHAVIOR EXPECTATIONS TEAM AND ADMINISTRATION

Contact recommendations— serious incidents

- Principal—administration team
- Guidance counselors
- Families
- Teachers and tutors of young people involved

MODERATE HARM

Co-LATE model

- Shared Concern method (if capacity for empathy)/Support Group method
- Low-level consequence as per policy recommendation

MANAGED BY TEACHER

Contact recommendations— low-level incidents

- Families
- Teachers and tutors of young people involved

Figure 22: Preparing the school community to resolve bullying incidents.

Visit **go.solution-tree.com/behavior** for a reproducible version of this figure.

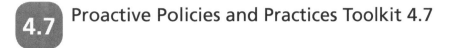

4.7 Proactive Policies and Practices Toolkit 4.7

Co-LATE Model

CHPRC research schools report finding the Co-LATE model helpful when talking to students about personal issues, including relationship difficulties and bullying behavior. The model is simple and can be used by all school staff, regardless of their role in the school. The Co-LATE model is based on the work of Michael Tunnecliffe (2008) and comprises five steps:

Confidentiality

Listen

Acknowledge concerns

Talk about the options

End with encouragement

Confidentiality

Students involved in CHPRC research express concern that school staff will discuss their interactions with other staff members. To address this, school staff can be clear with students about when they may need to talk to other adults about the content of their conversation (for example, duty of disclosure). If staff need to consult other staff about student interactions, it is important to do so in a confidential location (not by the photocopier), and with the permission of the student concerned. In addition, the location of student health and well-being services at the school can affect the likelihood of student access. Locating these services in areas used by students for a variety of purposes means that students can access them without other students knowing which service they are attending.

Listen

Students involved in CHPRC research acknowledge the importance of good listening skills. Active listening enables school staff to confirm they have understood the details of the conversation accurately, as well as demonstrate to students they have been paying attention to them. Avoiding behaviors that demonstrate to students that staff do not have time to talk to them can enhance students' confidence in approaching staff. These may include watching the clock, shuffling papers, and interrupting students.

Acknowledge Concerns

School staff can acknowledge students' concerns, even if they do not agree with them. Acknowledging takes the form of paraphrasing students' concerns and their reaction to the situation. For example, *"So you are concerned that if you don't forward the email you have received about Sam, your friends might not want to have you around. I can see how that would upset you a lot."* Comments about opportunities to make new friends and dismissing students' concerns are usually ineffective and demonstrate to students you don't understand the situation they are in. Hence, students may discontinue the conversation at this point.

Chapter 4

Talk About the Options

This step is likely to be most effective when school staff encourage students to identify solutions to their own concerns. This does not mean that staff cannot offer their own suggestions, but solutions suggested by, and endorsed by, students will likely be put into action faster than those suggested by staff. When identifying responses with students, it is important to also discuss the positive and negative consequences of each to enable students to make an informed decision about how to proceed with the situation.

End With Encouragement

Ending the conversation with a summary of what was discussed can help students make a decision about how to proceed with their situation. In addition, it provides an opportunity for school staff to give encouragement to the student for deciding to implement his or her chosen response strategy. While school staff cannot guarantee the outcome of students' actions or that they will resolve the situation, encouragement enables students to feel confident in trying to respond. At this point, it may also be helpful to establish a time to have a follow-up meeting with the student to discuss the effectiveness of implementing his or her strategy. If no follow-up is required, school staff can reassure students that they can reconnect if the situation is not resolved or if they need more support to take further action.

4.0 PLANNING TOOL: PROACTIVE POLICIES AND PRACTICES

Statement of Evidence for Proactive Policies and Practices

Schools with clear and consistent policies and procedures send a strong message to the whole-school community about the school's beliefs and actions to create a safe and supportive school environment. This provides the school with a framework to guide school action for the prevention, early response, and case management of bullying. School policies should be promoted to the whole-school community, particularly at times of higher risk such as orientation and transition. Positive student behavior should be encouraged and rewarded at the whole-school level.

Review Action 4.1—Policy Development	Not yet initiated	In planning	Preparing staff	Partially in place	Fully in place	Sustained practice
4.1.1 Policies to reduce bullying are collaboratively developed with staff, students, and families.	Not yet initiated	In planning	Preparing staff	Partially in place	Fully in place	Sustained practice
4.1.2 Policy development includes an ongoing collaborative planning and review process.	Not yet initiated	In planning	Preparing staff	Partially in place	Fully in place	Sustained practice
4.1.3 Policies are distributed and promoted to all staff, students, families, and relevant community members through a range of channels, such as seminars or workshops, newsletters, assembly items, home activities, emails, school website or intranet, curriculum, student diaries, parent handbooks, and information meetings.	Not yet initiated	In planning	Preparing staff	Partially in place	Fully in place	Sustained practice
4.1.4 Policies are always accessible to staff, students, and families.	Not yet initiated	In planning	Preparing staff	Partially in place	Fully in place	Sustained practice
4.1.5 Professional learning is provided for all staff to implement and enforce the policies.	Not yet initiated	In planning	Preparing staff	Partially in place	Fully in place	Sustained practice
4.1.6 An agreement for responsible use of the information and communications technology is implemented between school and students.	Not yet initiated	In planning	Preparing staff	Partially in place	Fully in place	Sustained practice
4.1.7 Plans for student behavior management during out-of-school and after-hours activities, including management of bullying (including cyberbullying) incidents are developed.	Not yet initiated	In planning	Preparing staff	Partially in place	Fully in place	Sustained practice
4.1.8 School policies determine and are consistent with staff roles in supervision.	Not yet initiated	In planning	Preparing staff	Partially in place	Fully in place	Sustained practice
4.1.9 School policies support national, state, and district policies and mandates.	Not yet initiated	In planning	Preparing staff	Partially in place	Fully in place	Sustained practice

continued →

Plan Action 4.1—Policy Development

What needs to be done?	Who is going to do it?	Timeline			What do we need?	Comments and reflections
		Status	Finish	Status		

Review Action 4.2—Policy Framework and Implementation: Prevention, Early Response, and Case Management

	Not yet initiated	In planning	Preparing staff	Partially in place	Fully in place	Sustained practice
4.2.1 Policies explicitly include prevention, early response, and case management actions that students, staff, and families can follow to prevent, identify, respond to, and report bullying behaviors consistently across the school community.						
4.2.2 Policies specifically include:	Not yet initiated	In planning	Preparing staff	Partially in place	Fully in place	Sustained practice
Links to whole-school vision statement and guiding principles for achieving that vision	Not yet initiated	In planning	Preparing staff	Partially in place	Fully in place	Sustained practice
Whole-school agreement that states the schools' clear intention to take bullying seriously	Not yet initiated	In planning	Preparing staff	Partially in place	Fully in place	Sustained practice
Policy rationale and objectives and purpose	Not yet initiated	In planning	Preparing staff	Partially in place	Fully in place	Sustained practice
Common understandings about prosocial behaviors and bullying and cyberbullying behaviors (definitions)	Not yet initiated	In planning	Preparing staff	Partially in place	Fully in place	Sustained practice
Rights and responsibilities of school community members	Not yet initiated	In planning	Preparing staff	Partially in place	Fully in place	Sustained practice
Clear actions for preventing and responding (including reporting and case management procedures) to bullying behaviors	Not yet initiated	In planning	Preparing staff	Partially in place	Fully in place	Sustained practice
4.2.3 Positive theory and evidence-informed approaches to responding to bullying incidents are adopted, such as restorative approaches.	Not yet initiated	In planning	Preparing staff	Partially in place	Fully in place	Sustained practice
4.2.4 A clear understanding of the positive response strategies adopted by the school is achieved by staff to ensure consistent implementation.	Not yet initiated	In planning	Preparing staff	Partially in place	Fully in place	Sustained practice
4.2.5 Behavior expectations used in the classroom are consistent with the school's selected approaches.	Not yet initiated	In planning	Preparing staff	Partially in place	Fully in place	Sustained practice
4.2.6 Behavior expectation strategies recognize that the determinants of cyberbullying behavior are part of the whole-school response to bullying and not the technology in which it is being manifested, for example, focus on relationships and social skill building rather than removing access to technology.	Not yet initiated	In planning	Preparing staff	Partially in place	Fully in place	Sustained practice
4.2.7 A behavior expectations team is established that is made up of staff who regularly deal with the behavior of school students.	Not yet initiated	In planning	Preparing staff	Partially in place	Fully in place	Sustained practice
4.2.8 The behavior expectations team is trained to identify signs of bullying, specific counseling approaches, problem-solving methods, and restorative practices.	Not yet initiated	In planning	Preparing staff	Partially in place	Fully in place	Sustained practice

continued →

	Not yet initiated	In planning	Preparing staff	Partially in place	Fully in place	Sustained practice
4.2.9 The behavior expectations team has methods of recording and collating data per school policies.						
4.2.10 The behavior expectations team provides support for students involved in bullying situations to develop positive behaviors (including students who are bullied, students who bully others, and bystanders to bullying).						
4.2.11 Support to students and families identified as being in need is ongoing, and follow-up support is sought from outside support services if required.						

Plan Action 4.2—Policy Framework and Implementation: Prevention, Early Response, and Case Management

What needs to be done?	Who is going to do it?	Timeline		What do we need?	Comments and reflections
		Status	Finish		
			Status		

Review Action 4.3—Integrated Focus on Orientation and Transition

	Not yet initiated	In planning	Preparing staff	Partially in place	Fully in place	Sustained practice
4.3.1 Orientation days include information about the relevant policies to students and their families.	Not yet initiated	In planning	Preparing staff	Partially in place	Fully in place	Sustained practice
4.3.2 Students are provided with quality support to improve their social interactions at times of orientation and transition (when there is a higher risk for bullying).	Not yet initiated	In planning	Preparing staff	Partially in place	Fully in place	Sustained practice
4.3.3 Principal and leadership team present and discuss relevant policies, procedures, and information about bullying with new staff and relief staff.	Not yet initiated	In planning	Preparing staff	Partially in place	Fully in place	Sustained practice
4.3.4 Structures are used to support student connectedness and well-being such as cross-year group homerooms.	Not yet initiated	In planning	Preparing staff	Partially in place	Fully in place	Sustained practice

Plan Action 4.3—Integrated Focus on Orientation and Transition

What needs to be done?	Who is going to do it?	Timeline		What do we need?	Comments and reflections
		Status	Finish	Status	

Key Understandings and Competencies

Schools that promote staff, students,' and families' understandings and skills to ensure students' social development are more likely to enhance students' social development and effectively reduce bullying behaviors. Key common understandings about bullying include the nature, prevalence, and types of bullying as well as information about how bystanders can reduce the prevalence of bullying. Key understandings are supported with skills or competencies needed to prevent, identify, and respond to bullying incidents effectively and consistently.

Evidence for Building Key Understandings and Competencies

Raising awareness and teaching common understandings about bullying is an important factor in equipping the whole-school community with the knowledge required to take positive action to prevent bullying and respond effectively when bullying does occur. All members of the school, including teaching and nonteaching staff, students, and their families, need to be the target of education efforts to build the knowledge and skills to prevent, identify, and respond effectively to bullying behavior. This chapter discusses how staff professional learning, curriculum content, and family communication can be used to ensure common, consistent understandings across the whole-school community.

Staff Professional Learning

When bullying behaviors within a school are tolerated actively or passively by teachers, it is likely these behaviors will persist over time (Espelage & Swearer, 2003). This demonstrates the need for comprehensive professional learning for all staff to help them feel confident in assisting students with bullying-related matters. This training needs to be part of a whole-school response to bullying and should be linked to the school's bullying-related policy and response plan. In a meta-analysis by Farrington and Ttofi (2009) of the effective components of school-based bullying interventions, teacher training was identified as one of the program elements significantly associated with reducing the prevalence of students bullying others. The vast majority of staff disapproves of bullying and perceives themselves as having a responsibility to reduce and prevent school bullying. However, many staff report they feel other teachers at their school need more training to improve their skills related to covert bullying, including cyberbullying (Cross et al., 2009). Developing school staff's knowledge about the forms and functions of technology may be particularly important in reducing cyberbullying (Hanewald, 2008). The digital generation gap between young people and their teachers (Palfrey & Gasser, 2008; Tapscott, 1998) may be a potential barrier in attempts to help students who are cyberbullied (Bhat, 2008). Findings from an Australian study demonstrate school staff are less able to recognize and more uncertain about how to address bullying involving technology, compared with other forms of bullying (Cross et al., 2009). In a study of preservice teachers' perceptions about cyberbullying, the vast majority of those surveyed reported they generally lacked the confidence to identify or manage cyberbullying, possibly because this form of bullying is easily concealed and does not result in physical effects that can be recognized as indicators of bullying (Li, 2008). Further, some research has reported that students do not perceive adults at school as being able to help if they were to report cyberbullying to them (Agatston, Kowalski, & Limber, 2007).

Explicit Student Learning Through the Curriculum

Improving students' key understandings, skills, and competencies to prevent and respond to bullying, especially as a bystander, also needs to be an essential element of school action to support students who do not seek help from school staff. Students' responses to bullying situations are associated with their self-esteem (Salmivalli, Kaukiainen, Kaistaniemi, & Lagerspetz, 1999), attitudes toward bullying (Salmivalli & Voeten, 2004), empathy (Gini, Albiero, Benelli, & Altoé, 2007), moral perceptions of bullying (Agatston et al., 2007), and social skills (Fox & Boulton, 2005) as well as their expectations about the outcomes arising from bullying others (Hall, Hezberger, & Skowronski, 1998). Accordingly, it is recommended that the curriculum raise students' awareness about bullying and its harmful effects and the rights and responsibilities of all students regarding bullying situations. Curricula should also provide students with opportunities to develop their social skills and strategies enhancing self-esteem. It is important that strategies teaching students about safer online behaviors are embedded into the curriculum, rather than as stand-alone messages, to enable students to refine their skills over time and to foster lasting behavior change.

In Farrington and Ttofi's meta-analysis, the use of antibullying videos to raise students' awareness about bullying was associated with a reduction in students being bullied (Espelage & Swearer, 2003). However, the same meta-analysis found that student curriculum was not significantly related to reductions in bullying. This may suggest that education efforts directed toward students should be more engaging and interactive and should be integrated throughout the school curriculum to be most effective in reducing bullying.

Educating students about technical and cyber safety strategies to prevent, respond to, and report cyberbullying is essential, as much cyberbullying behavior occurs out of sight of adults. Although students demonstrate knowledge of technical strategies to deal with cyberbullying, such as blocking the sender or ignoring the bullying, they may be less educated about other strategies such as how to remove harmful websites (Li, 2008). Knowing and using these strategies, however, are two different matters, as another study found only a minority of students responded to cyberbullying behaviors by using technical strategies such as blocking the sender, changing their screen name, or sending warnings (Juvonen & Gross, 2008).

Teaching students strategies specific to overcoming and preventing cyberbullying is an important focus of school action to reduce all types of bullying behavior. A recent meta-analysis of interventions to prevent cyber abuse found psycho-educational Internet safety programs were effective in increasing students' Internet safety knowledge (Mishna, Cook, Saini, Wu, & MacFadden, 2010). Students should be educated about their rights and responsibilities in cyberspace and encouraged to adopt positive attitudes toward technology and develop good digital citizenship skills.

Effective Family Communication

Opportunities for parents, caregivers, and other family members to further their knowledge about preventing and responding to all forms of bullying will support the schools' efforts in this regard. This recommendation is made on the basis of research demonstrating the links between family functioning and bullying behavior. For instance, poor supervision and lack of attention in the home (Ary et al., 1999; Oliver & Oaks, 1994), parental acceptance of aggressive behavior (Olweus, 1993), harsh discipline (Ary et al., 1999), and parent modeling of aggressive behavior (Baldry, 2003; Espelage, Bosworth, & Simon, 2000) are all associated with bullying behavior (Rigby, 1994). Conversely, students with higher parental support (Wang, Iannotti, & Nansel, 2009) and a good relationship with parents (Aman-Back & Björkqvist, 2007) are less likely to be involved in bullying. Moreover, high parental support may protect against symptoms of depression among students who are victimized or who bully others (Conners-Burrow, Johnson, Whiteside-Mansell, McKelvey, & Gargus, 2009).

Farrington and Ttofi (2009) also found information for parents (for example, information about the bullying prevention initiatives at their school or general tips about bullying) was an important program element related to reducing the proportion of students bullying others. Parent training (information nights, parent-teacher meetings) was also significantly associated with both a decrease in students bullying and being bullied.

As a result of the digital divide between young people and adults (Palfrey & Gasser, 2008; Tapscott, 1998), parents may feel limited in ways they can support their child to prevent and respond to cyberbullying appropriately and effectively. An Australian study by Campbell and Gardner (2005) showed many students believe adults are unaware of the existence of students' online lives. Moreover, students are unlikely to report instances of cyberbullying to adults (Juvonen & Gross, 2008; Li, 2007; Patchin & Hinduja, 2006; Smith et al., 2008), probably because adults appear to be less informed about the issues surrounding cyberbullying (Li, 2007), and because students fear having their computers or mobile phones taken away, causing further isolation (National Children's Home, 2002; Patchin & Hinduja, 2006). Given that cyberbullying has generally been found to occur more outside school hours rather than during school (Li, 2007; Slonje & Smith, 2008), developing parents' awareness about cyberbullying is crucial.

Actions for Building Key Understandings and Competencies

Staff Professional Learning

Ongoing professional learning opportunities about bullying enable staff members to feel prepared and motivated to implement the school bullying prevention and management policy. This is especially true for professional learning that focuses on specific strategies for cyberbullying prevention and management, including opportunities to learn about new technologies and their positive and negative uses.

School leaders who extend professional learning opportunities to nonteaching staff such as administration, cafeteria workers, custodians, and bus drivers encourage consistent responses to bullying behavior across the whole school and recognize that bullying, including cyberbullying, can occur at break times or on the way to and from school, where teaching staff may not be present (Cross et al., 2009).

Strategies for Good Practice: Staff Professional Learning

1. All school staff are enabled and encouraged through ongoing, regular, evidence-based professional learning to actively support school action to reduce bullying.
2. Specialized professional learning opportunities are provided for key counseling staff to effectively enable student behavior change.
3. All school staff are informed of their legal responsibilities to protect students from bullying-related harm.
4. Staff professional learning comprises a range of key understandings and skills.
5. School staff are provided with opportunities to promote their professional learning related to bullying prevention by networking with other schools and staff.

1 **All school staff are enabled and encouraged through ongoing, regular, evidence-based professional learning to actively support school action to reduce bullying.**

All school staff (including grounds staff, custodians, bus drivers, and cafeteria employees) need to be aware of their responsibility and be provided with professional learning to support school actions to reduce bullying behavior. As bullying behavior often occurs on students' journeys to and from school and during break times when supervision ratios (teacher to student) are lower, nonteaching staff can provide support for the schools' bullying-prevention-related policies and guidelines. Ensuring students are aware of the role non-teaching staff play in preventing and responding to bullying situations increases their credibility among students and supports their commitment to intervene when appropriate.

Some school staff members have particular responsibilities in the school for providing student support services. Students, however, often approach the staff with whom they are more familiar to seek support and advice. School leaders can support staff by ensuring they:

- Are familiar with the policies relating to student support services
- Are aware of and are comfortable with their role
- Understand role boundaries
- Know how to effectively refer students to appropriate internal and external services if needed

Schools can increase their understanding of the issues students face by conducting regular surveys of the whole-school community.

 Specialized professional learning opportunities are provided for key counseling staff to effectively enable student behavior change.

Quality, up-to-date professional learning for counseling staff increases their capacity to respond effectively to student needs. Because some students may not seek help, support, or advice from staff in traditional counseling roles, it may be beneficial to expand these professional learning opportunities to additional staff such as tutors. An expanded guidance staff with current training increases student access to support and also increases the likelihood that students will receive quality outcomes.

Some professional learning areas requested during CHPRC research include how the counseling staff can:

- Collaborate with school community members to identify and promote a shared vision of a safe and supportive school environment
- Encourage and enable whole-school community members to participate in school planning and decision making
- Make decisions fairly and ethically and embrace the principles of equal opportunity and social justice
- Be proactive in the development and promotion of an effective and well-executed whole-school policy outlining strategies, structures, and systems for the prevention and management of bullying
- Consult and negotiate with whole-school community members, ensuring fairness of participation and equity in input in the development of whole-school policies and planning
- Empower staff to initiate and take responsibility for safer and friendly school strategies

3 **All school staff are informed of their legal responsibilities to protect students from bullying-related harm.**

Staff will benefit from having an understanding of not only their legal requirements but also some relevant topics that apply to this area, for example, staff negligence regarding their responsibility to students such as students sexting in school.

Seek assistance from the superintendent's office or the state board of education if you need more information regarding legal responsibilities.

Chapter 5

Staff professional learning comprises a range of key understandings and skills.

The following areas are considered key understandings that the whole-school community needs to know and act on consistently.

- What constitutes bullying (definition of bullying, including cyberbullying)
- How to identify bullying (including overt, covert, cyber)
- The effects of bullying on students
- How to effectively respond to all forms of bullying behavior
- Opportunities to learn about information and communication technologies and their positive and negative uses
- How to appropriately monitor and supervise students' online behavior
- Referral to credible sources for further information and support about bullying and related issues, such as cyber safety resources and mental health support
- Ways to access current research on bullying and evidence-based approaches to reducing school bullying

Chapter 1 contains information about these points, and examples of how this information can be incorporated in behavior expectations policies are provided in Proactive Policies and Practices toolkit 4.5.

 School staff are provided with opportunities to promote their professional learning related to bullying prevention by networking with other schools and staff.

School leaders can facilitate the sharing of knowledge and practices by providing and supporting opportunities for staff to network with each other and surrounding schools on a regular basis. Networking opportunities provide:

- An exchange of ideas
- Motivation for improvement and change
- Affirmation of staff's efforts in responding to bullying-related issues
- Insight into how others have responded to issues
- Learning about the effectiveness of programs, practices, and policies implemented in other settings
- Engagement with other professionals in an informal setting that helps facilitate open discussion and cross-institutional collaboration
- The possibility of sharing resources

Explicit Student Learning Through the Curriculum

An effective curriculum is part of a whole-class approach to facilitate changes in the attitudes and dynamics of the group, creating common understandings of bullying and how to respond, while simultaneously building the social skills of students. An interactive and engaging curriculum for students includes activities that target the risk and protective factors associated with bullying behavior, comprising self-esteem building, promoting respect and care for self and others, moral perceptions, and behavior expectations. Cyber-specific strategies include technical strategies to respond to and report cyberbullying, principles of cyber safety, and digital citizenship skills.

Strategies for Good Practice: Explicit Student Learning Through the Curriculum

1. A developmentally appropriate, comprehensive, and engaging social and emotional learning curriculum is taught across all grade levels.
2. Student curriculum comprises a range of key understandings and skills.

1 **A developmentally appropriate, comprehensive, and engaging social and emotional learning curriculum is taught across all grade levels.**

Addressing bullying behavior through the curriculum enables primary and secondary schools to openly discuss the issue with students in consistent, developmentally appropriate ways. Use of activities that engage students regularly over time and involve cooperative teaching and learning strategies within a whole-school approach can lead to positive and lasting change. Students' bullying behaviors need to be targeted through formal teaching and learning prior to them becoming most prevalent. CHPRC research suggests that students need to receive targeted social skills development and bullying prevention content in every grade level but particularly prior to fourth grade and immediately prior to, and following transition to, high school.

Schools can develop students' prosocial desires for bullying to stop and their inclinations to help people being bullied by advocating for positive peer influence. This encourages greater student support and confidence in application of bystander strategies. Implementing teaching and learning activities based on a social and emotional learning model:

- Enhances students' social skills
- Maximizes learning opportunities
- Promotes cooperative behaviors
- Develops a supportive school culture where students, staff, and families feel valued

Key Understandings and Competencies toolkit 5.1 discusses the contents of the Friendly Schools and Supportive Schools teaching and learning materials.

2   **Student curriculum comprises a range of key understandings and skills.**

Schools that provide a developmentally appropriate curriculum that includes targeted, practical strategies explicitly for students enable a shared understanding about social and emotional learning and bullying behaviors that is consistently modeled and conveyed. This also provides students with the opportunity to practice making thoughtful, effective choices about their social and personal behavior in whole-school environments. In a secondary setting, being given the opportunity to learn how to set privacy settings and disable geotagging, for example, can be an effective tool for students knowing how to prevent and manage cyberbullying incidents. Key understandings for students include:

- What constitutes bullying
- How to identify bullying (including overt, covert, cyber)
- The effects of bullying on all students
- Building skills to enhance positive, healthy relationships online and offline
- Building skills to effectively respond to bullying behavior online and offline (bystander behavior)
- Building skills to develop social responsibility online and offline
- Providing opportunities for self-reflection
- Providing "real-life" experiential activities to reinforce learning, such as role play, and opportunities for positive online social interaction

Key Understandings and Competencies toolkit 5.1 describes the Friendly Schools and Supportive Schools teaching and learning materials and how these can be included in the curriculum to promote positive social skill development and bullying prevention.

Effective Family Communication

Schools that provide learning opportunities to students' families empower them to help their child respond to bullying and implement strategies for the prevention of bullying. This may be in the form of information for caregivers or families, parent-teacher conferences, and information nights for families. Families can play an important role in monitoring their child's behavior and communicating with their child about bullying. Given the disparities in technological knowledge among students and their parents or caregivers, providing families with opportunities to learn about the latest information and communication technologies and their positive and negative uses is a crucial component of effective family communication.

Strategies for Good Practice: Effective Family Communication

1. Multiple channels are used to communicate information and provide educational learning opportunities to families.
2. Parent information mirrors teacher knowledge and student learning to ensure common understandings and skills across a range of topics.

1 **Multiple channels are used to communicate information and provide educational learning opportunities to families.**

Leaders who seek to actively involve families in school efforts to prevent and reduce bullying behavior encourage ownership and support among the parent body, ensuring students receive a consistent message. Schools can be innovative in the ways in which they engage families in school activities, including:

- Getting to know the families in the school in both formal and informal settings
- Ensuring that the school policy on bullying is presented in ways that are accessible to all families
- Encouraging all staff to maintain regular, positive contact with families to establish supportive relationships
- Advertising and hosting school functions using multiple channels to raise awareness of events, with enough notice to facilitate attendance
- Hosting school functions at times that maximize family attendance
- Considering the provision of childcare support during school events to enable meaningful adult participation
- Surveying families about desired content for family information sessions
- Providing the school newsletter in an accessible format
- Finding ways to celebrate successes with the families in the school community

Several toolkits in this book provide examples of how to engage and communicate with families. These include Supportive School Culture toolkits 3.1 and 3.2 and School–Family–Community Partnerships toolkits 7.1, 7.2, 7.3, and 7.5.

2 **Parent information mirrors teacher knowledge and student learning to ensure common understandings and skills across a range of topics.**

Consistent messages are important in reinforcing student learning and behavior engagement. Schools can provide opportunities for families to develop their understandings about the following.

- What constitutes bullying
- How to identify bullying (including overt, covert, cyber)
- The effects of bullying
- How to effectively communicate with their child about bullying
- How to appropriately monitor and supervise their child's online behavior
- Developmental stages of child and adolescent social and emotional learning
- The role of bystanders in discouraging bullying behavior
- Skills for parents to respond effectively to bullying (including specific strategies for overt, covert, and cyberbullying)
- Opportunities to learn about information and communication technologies such as social media, social networking, instant messaging, chat rooms, blogs, online gaming, mobile phones, and websites and their positive and negative uses
- Skills for their child to build positive, healthy relationships
- Skills for their child to effectively respond to bullying behavior online and offline
- Skills for their child to develop social responsibility online and offline
- Referral to credible sources for further information and support about bullying and related issues, such as cyber safety resources and mental health support

For examples of how to enhance families' understanding and skills, see Supportive School Culture toolkits 3.1 and 3.2.

Summary

It is important to improve student, staff, and family understandings and competencies to positively impact the reduction of bullying behavior. In particular, common understandings about the types, prevalence, and nature of bullying, as well as students' role in bullying situations, are important to realize behavior change. To support the establishment of common understandings and competencies related to bullying situations, schools can implement developmentally appropriate curriculum, offer targeted professional learning opportunities, distribute newsletter items, and present social skills and values-related assembly items.

Two school stories are provided to illustrate how CHPRC research schools sought to enhance common understandings and competencies related to bullying situations. Schools that wish to implement strategies to improve the bullying-related understandings and competencies of their whole-school community may find further information in Key Understandings and Competencies toolkit 5.1 and Building Capacity toolkit 2.1.

- Key Understandings and Competencies toolkit 5.1 outlines the developmentally appropriate curriculum materials comprising the Friendly Schools and Supportive Schools Program.
- Building Capacity toolkit 2.1 describes how schools can survey their whole-school community to understand bullying-related knowledge, attitudes, and skills.

In addition, toolkits from other chapters of this book will help support the development of common understandings and competencies across the whole school, and chapter 1 contains definitions and background information to support this.

School Stories

School Story 5.1

Background to school initiative:

The issue of bullying was regarded as important to the school and general community. It was beginning to create problems within the school by affecting students' learning. The school began by surveying students about bullying and ensured open and consistent communication with parents, staff, and students about the level of bullying that was occurring at the school.

School profile:

- Nonmetropolitan public school
- 500 students
- Grades: K–7

Action

This school believed that raising the awareness of its students, staff, and parents was the first step in addressing bullying behavior. To begin, the school conducted a bullying behavior awareness week. The school took a collaborative and cross-curricular approach for the week. Collaborative teams of teachers were provided with a half day to plan activities around the theme of bullying.

Activities included:

- Songs and poems about bullying, poster making, puppet making for use in plays, and role-playing based on the theme
- Examining body language across different cultures and storytelling
- Science activities such as drawing scientific comparisons between nurturing human relationships and nurturing relationships in society and nature
- Math activities conducting graphing exercises based on the bullying survey and creating tallies of positive and negative incidents in the classroom
- Creating books that exemplify positive approaches to bullying (which were used in buddy reading), drawing cartoons depicting responses to bullying, diary entries guided by the theme, and letter writing
- Comparisons of schoolyard bullying to bullying in the workplace, lessons on conflict resolution skills, and role playing
- Behavior modification games
- Planting a friendship garden with friendship rocks

A staff survey was conducted following this week. The results of the survey suggested that teachers enjoyed the week and the opportunity to plan activities with colleagues. Teachers believed the week had raised the awareness of both students and teachers but also of parents. The school reported that students enjoyed the collaborative approach, particularly the opportunities it provided and the common theme between classes. Staff also received positive feedback from parents who appreciated the open and honest manner in which the school was dealing with the issue.

Following this week, the school developed a policy on bullying in collaboration with students, parents, and teachers to ensure the whole-school community would have greater ownership of the policy. All teachers were asked to discuss with their class what bullying is, how they felt about bullying, what they could do if bullied, what students, teachers, and parents could do to prevent bullying at the school, and what could be done to make sure the policy was working. The policy was developed from these responses and worded in the vernacular of the students.

The school adopted a whole-school positive incentive plan. This included the distribution of tokens for positive behavior, honor certificates, "Student of the Month" awards, positive visits to the principal, work displayed at the community center and the front office, and positive behavior banners awarded to the class with the most cards. Throughout the process, communication between parents, staff, students, and the community was a high priority. This was achieved through newsletters, articles, school assemblies, community displays, and representation in the press.

What We Learned

Difficulties Encountered

Getting all staff to accept the program and the additional effort required was initially a problem at the school.

Overcoming Difficulties

These initial problems were overcome by giving staff time to collaborate and discuss policy, plans, and activities, and setting realistic and achievable goals. Having parents involved and showing an interest also highlighted the importance of the program to staff. This was achieved through the involvement of the PTA as well as during parent-teacher conferences.

More information about the strategies used by this school can be found in the following toolkits.

- Supportive School Culture toolkit 3.1
- Supportive School Culture toolkit 3.2
- Supportive School Culture toolkit 3.3
- Proactive Policies and Practices toolkit 4.5
- Key Understandings and Competencies toolkit 5.1

School Story 5.2

Brief background to school initiative:

It became evident that bullying was a problem at this school. There was a significant amount of media attention on the issue at that time and, subsequently, the school psychologist and vice principal decided to take some positive action. The school adopted a whole-school approach to combat bullying behavior. They placed an emphasis on cooperation with colleagues, communication, and consistency in consequences and a commitment to creating a positive classroom atmosphere.

School profile:

- Public school
- 720 students
- Grades: 8–12

Action

The school introduced the Treat Everyone Decently (TED) program as the cornerstone of its antibullying policy. The TED school committee trained people, including teachers, and managed student behavior, rewards, issues of tolerance, and an overall review. It also addressed the school assemblies. The program was designed to enhance self-esteem and positive behavior. Prizes in the form of letters of commendation and other rewards were included.

The TED program was taught as a core subject to emphasize the importance that the school placed on the matter. The same teachers taught it each year and were, therefore, able to build on the students' knowledge. Bullying was addressed in the eighth-grade component of the program and revised in ninth and tenth grade. The four sessions defined what bullying was and the school's policy on bullying, and examined ways bullying could be reported and what students could do about bullying. Sessions were interactive and encouraged students to ask questions and brainstorm solutions. Each school department was asked to integrate the TED messages into its curriculum. The school provided staff professional learning to facilitate this process.

The school also ran a TED Plus program in which teachers acted as mentors and were matched with students who had behavioral problems or learning difficulties or were unhappy at school. The students met daily with their mentors, and both completed behavior cards. The behavioral expectations were explained in simple terms, for example, the student will not interrupt in class, will not constantly talk to the person next to him, and will listen to instructions. By concentrating on a small part of a student's behavior, this process provided attainable goals for the student. The program ran for four weeks, and at the end of that time, the student's behavior was reviewed. The students knew that their mentor was not going to judge them, but rather work with them through every situation that arose. This system was extremely successful. The school made an attempt to use friends to monitor students' behavior, as students usually respond well to their own peers. For example, in a particular group of friends, one girl was exerting her power over the others and on one girl in particular. The student doing the bullying was taken aside, and it was pointed out that through her behavior she stood the risk of losing all of her friends. She was then asked to choose two friends to monitor her behavior and report to the teachers. This had a significant impact on the level of bullying that was occurring.

What We Learned

Difficulties Encountered

The school struggled to recruit enough people to run the program. There were unsuccessful attempts to get teachers to take on the responsibility of the program. Furthermore, initially not all bullying incidents were dealt with consistently; teachers did not always follow the procedures.

Recommendations for Other Schools

This school emphasized the need to get parents involved as early as possible, as their support was essential to the success of the antibullying program. It also suggested that there be a program launch with high levels of publicity and information, suggesting something like a whole-school barbeque. This serves two purposes; it makes the program look important (if it looks important, people tend to think it is important), and it provides a great opportunity for the whole school to come together with teachers, students, and parents and receive information. The school also suggested setting realistic targets for teachers instead of overloading them.

More information about the strategies used by this school can be found in the following toolkit.

- Key Understandings and Competencies toolkit 5.1

Chapter 5

Toolkits for Action

5.1 **Key Understandings and Competencies Toolkit 5.1**
Friendly Schools Plus Teaching and Learning Materials

EARLY RESEARCH INTO SCHOOL BULLYING
WAS MARRED BY EXTREME PERFORMANCE ANXIETY

The social, emotional, cognitive, and physical aspects of a person's development are interrelated. Each influences and is influenced by the others. Consequently, it is not uncommon for students who have difficulty managing their emotions and behavior to face great challenges meeting the demands of schooling. This relationship between student behavior and academic problems is not always clear in terms of which comes first, but what is clear is that the presence of one greatly increases the risk of the other. Supporting children's emotional, social, and behavioral development thus enables students to more effectively engage in their learning.

The Friendly Schools Plus program is designed to address three key aspects of students' school experiences shown to be related to improved social and emotional development: (1) promoting positive peer relationships, (2) promoting positive teacher-child relationships, and (3) explicit teaching related to emotions, social knowledge, and social skills. The program aims to develop students' social and emotional competencies to enable them to recognize and control their emotions, build positive relationships, show consideration for others, make thoughtful and sensible choices, and cope successfully with difficult situations. These outcomes are developed through the following five focus areas in this resource:

1. Self-awareness
2. Self-management
3. Social awareness
4. Relationship skills
5. Social decision making

Bullying can have a significant and negative impact on students' social and emotional development and other learning. An anxious, frightened, and withdrawn student has limited learning potential.

To reduce and ultimately prevent bullying it is important to focus on why most children and young people do not engage in bullying behavior. These individuals tend to display greater social and emotional competence than those who bully others. Children and adolescents who demonstrate social and emotional competence are also more likely to have positive relationships and social capabilities that reduce the likelihood of them being bullied. In addition, in the event that they are victimized or a bystander in a bullying incident, they are more aware of how to manage the bullying situation.

Bullying is more than an event between students who bully and students who are bullied. It is a social relationship involving group values and group standards of behavior, which means it requires consistent action across the school community to achieve positive change.

Chapter 5

How to Use the *Friendly Schools Plus* Teacher Resource Books

The teacher resource books include five focus areas, each representing one component of the social and emotional learning model.

1. Self-awareness
2. Self-management
3. Social awareness
4. Relationship skills
5. Social decision making

A table at the front of each focus area briefly describes the emphasis of each focus, and the outcomes the activities proposed will enable students to achieve. A comprehensive list of activities is also provided.

Teachers are encouraged to teach from each of the focus areas in the order presented, as each builds on the vocabulary, concepts, and skills covered in preceding focus areas.

Research clearly shows that the greater the dose of social and emotional learning, the better the outcomes for students. As such, the greater the number of learning activities completed in each focus area, the greater the likelihood students will achieve the social and emotional learning outcomes. Teachers are encouraged to determine the social and emotional learning needs of their students to ensure the activities chosen meet students' developmental levels, understandings, and competencies. It may also be important to consider the school's vision, priorities, and values in deciding which social and emotional learning activities to teach. With this knowledge, teachers can review the activities provided within the resource to decide which activities in each focus area they will implement.

Each focus is organized as follows.

- **Introducing key messages**—Sets the context for the activity and introduces the key messages to help students link previous social and emotional learning to new knowledge and skills
- **Developing key messages**—Provides students with opportunities to develop and practice key messages, relevant social and emotional understandings, and skills. Visit **go.solution-tree.com /behavior** for electronic copies of the student activity sheets linked to these learning activities.
- **Reflecting on key messages**—Encourages students to reflect and record their thoughts, feelings, and attitudes throughout the course of their social and emotional learning in their student journal. Teachers are also encouraged to reflect on the extent to which students have understood the key messages for each focus.

5.0 PLANNING TOOL: KEY UNDERSTANDINGS AND COMPETENCIES

Statement of Evidence for Key Understandings and Competencies

Schools that improve staff, student, and family understandings and competencies are more likely to effectively reduce bullying. Key understandings about bullying include nature, prevalence, and types of bullying as well as information about bystander roles. Key understandings are supported with skills or competencies needed to prevent, identify, and respond to bullying incidents effectively and consistently.

Review Action 5.1—Staff Professional Learning	Not yet initiated	In planning	Preparing staff	Partially in place	Fully in place	Sustained practice
5.1.1 All school staff (new and existing) are enabled and encouraged through ongoing, regular, evidence-based professional learning to actively support school action to reduce bullying.						
5.1.2 Specialized professional learning opportunities are provided for key counseling staff to effectively enable student behavior change.						
5.1.3 All school staff are informed of their legal responsibilities to protect students from bullying-related harm.						
5.1.4 Staff professional learning comprises a range of key understandings and skills:						
• What constitutes bullying (definition of bullying and cyberbullying)						
• How to identify bullying (including overt, covert, cyber)						
• The effects of bullying on all students						
• How to effectively respond to all forms of bullying behavior						
• Opportunities to learn about information and communication technologies (ICT) and their positive and negative uses						
• How to appropriately monitor and supervise students' online behavior						
• Referral to credible sources for further information and support about bullying and related issues, such as cyber safety resources and mental health support						

continued →

	Not yet initiated	In planning	Preparing staff	Partially in place	Fully in place	Sustained practice
• Ways to access current research on bullying and evidence-based approaches to reducing school bullying	Not yet initiated	In planning	Preparing staff	Partially in place	Fully in place	Sustained practice
5.1.5 School staff are provided with opportunities to promote their professional learning related to bullying prevention by networking with other schools and staff.						

Plan Action 5.1—Staff Professional Learning

What needs to be done?	Who is going to do it?	Timeline			What do we need?	Comments and reflections
		Status	Finish	Status		

Review Action 5.2—Explicit Student Learning Through the Curriculum

	Not yet initiated	In planning	Preparing staff	Partially in place	Fully in place	Sustained practice
5.2.1 A developmentally appropriate, comprehensive, and engaging social and emotional learning curriculum is taught across all grade levels.	Not yet initiated	In planning	Preparing staff	Partially in place	Fully in place	Sustained practice
5.2.2 Student curriculum comprises a range of key understandings and skills:	Not yet initiated	In planning	Preparing staff	Partially in place	Fully in place	Sustained practice
• What constitutes bullying (definition of bullying and cyberbullying)	Not yet initiated	In planning	Preparing staff	Partially in place	Fully in place	Sustained practice
• How to identify bullying (including overt, covert, cyber)	Not yet initiated	In planning	Preparing staff	Partially in place	Fully in place	Sustained practice
• The effects of bullying on all students	Not yet initiated	In planning	Preparing staff	Partially in place	Fully in place	Sustained practice
• Building skills to enhance positive, healthy relationships online and offline	Not yet initiated	In planning	Preparing staff	Partially in place	Fully in place	Sustained practice
• Building skills to effectively respond to bullying behavior online and offline (bystander behavior)	Not yet initiated	In planning	Preparing staff	Partially in place	Fully in place	Sustained practice
• Building skills to develop social responsibility online and offline	Not yet initiated	In planning	Preparing staff	Partially in place	Fully in place	Sustained practice
• Providing opportunities for self-reflection	Not yet initiated	In planning	Preparing staff	Partially in place	Fully in place	Sustained practice
• Providing "real-life" experiential activities to reinforce learning, such as role play, opportunities for positive online social interaction	Not yet initiated	In planning	Preparing staff	Partially in place	Fully in place	Sustained practice

Plan Action 5.2—Explicit Student Learning Through the Curriculum

What needs to be done?	Who is going to do it?	What do we need?	Timeline		Status	Comments and reflections
			Status	Finish		

continued →

Review Action 5.3—Effective Family Communication

	Not yet initiated	In planning	Preparing staff	Partially in place	Fully in place	Sustained practice
5.3.1 Multiple channels are used to communicate information and provide educational learning opportunities to families.	Not yet initiated	In planning	Preparing staff	Partially in place	Fully in place	Sustained practice
5.3.2 Parent information mirrors teacher knowledge and student learning to ensure common understandings and skills across a range of topics:	Not yet initiated	In planning	Preparing staff	Partially in place	Fully in place	Sustained practice
• What constitutes bullying (definition of bullying and cyberbullying)	Not yet initiated	In planning	Preparing staff	Partially in place	Fully in place	Sustained practice
• How to identify bullying (including overt, covert, cyber)	Not yet initiated	In planning	Preparing staff	Partially in place	Fully in place	Sustained practice
• The effects of bullying	Not yet initiated	In planning	Preparing staff	Partially in place	Fully in place	Sustained practice
• How to effectively communicate with their child about bullying	Not yet initiated	In planning	Preparing staff	Partially in place	Fully in place	Sustained practice
• How to appropriately monitor and supervise their child's online behavior	Not yet initiated	In planning	Preparing staff	Partially in place	Fully in place	Sustained practice
• Developmental stages of child and adolescent social and emotional learning	Not yet initiated	In planning	Preparing staff	Partially in place	Fully in place	Sustained practice
• Skills for parents to respond effectively to bullying (including specific strategies for overt, covert, and cyberbullying)	Not yet initiated	In planning	Preparing staff	Partially in place	Fully in place	Sustained practice
• Opportunities to learn about information and communication technologies (ICT), such as instant messaging, chat rooms, blogs, online gaming, mobile phones, and websites, and their positive and negative uses	Not yet initiated	In planning	Preparing staff	Partially in place	Fully in place	Sustained practice
• Skills for their child to build positive, healthy relationships	Not yet initiated	In planning	Preparing staff	Partially in place	Fully in place	Sustained practice
• Skills for their child to effectively respond to bullying behavior online and offline	Not yet initiated	In planning	Preparing staff	Partially in place	Fully in place	Sustained practice
• Skills for their child to develop social responsibility online and offline	Not yet initiated	In planning	Preparing staff	Partially in place	Fully in place	Sustained practice
• Referral to credible sources for further information and support about bullying and related issues, such as cyber safety resources and mental health support	Not yet initiated	In planning	Preparing staff	Partially in place	Fully in place	Sustained practice

Plan Action 5.3—Effective Family Communication

What needs to be done?	Who is going to do it?	Timeline			What do we need?	Comments and reflections
		Status	Finish	Status		

Chapter 6

Protective Physical Environment

A well-structured physical school environment helps promote learning and encourage positive social interactions among students and staff. These structures can be part of the school master plan or created by students. Student art, positive use of space, facilities, equipment, and activities that encourage cooperative behaviors can positively influence student behaviors.

WHILE THE PLAYGROUND DESIGN WAS CRITICISED BY MANY, IT DID REDUCE BULLYING DRAMATICALLY

Evidence for Building a Protective Physical Environment

A school's physical environment has long been regarded as simply the provision of play areas, buildings for classrooms, and well-maintained grounds. In 1995, the Health-Promoting Schools Framework (World Health Organization, 1996) identified the physical school environment as a central feature that can shape students' health behaviors and lead to improved opportunities for learning. Further, there is substantial theoretical evidence to suggest the environment in which we live greatly influences our behavior.

Only recently, however, have researchers begun investigating how the physical environment may influence students' academic and social outcomes. The school's environment can be conceptualized in three main areas: (1) the structural, (2) functional, and (3) built environment (Waters, Cross, & Runions, 2009). Structural features of a school include the school's size, students' socioeconomic status, functional features including the homeroom systems, guidance counseling programs and strategies, and built environment characteristics such as the presence of graffiti, the condition of the buildings, and equipment available for students. This comprehensive view of a school environment encapsulates more than just buildings and the schoolyard and identifies features of a school that can be modified without necessarily engaging in expensive building programs.

A Western Australian retrospective study (Waters, Cross, & Shaw, 2010) found the characteristics of secondary schools, such as a larger school size (represented by K–12 students on the campus), a higher socioeconomic status of students at the school, an elevated priority for guidance counseling, higher than average school-level reading, writing, and numeracy scores, no graffiti, and a well-established homeroom system, all predicted students' enhanced feelings of connectedness to their school and improved mental health outcomes compared with students at schools without these features. This research demonstrates how physical and intangible school structural characteristics can improve student outcomes, including students' feelings of connectedness and improved mental health.

This chapter discusses how the school's physical environment can actively promote connectedness and improve mental health to prevent and respond effectively to bullying in schools. The physical and structural characteristics of schools that need to be assessed and modified, where appropriate, to reduce bullying in schools include the physical attributes of the school and the supportive school facilities and activities.

Physical Attributes of the School

The school's physical environment is important to consider when managing bullying. The U.K. charity, Learning through Landscapes, provides funding for schools to modify their school grounds to improve learning and child development. After making improvements to the school environment, 64 percent of the 351 participating schools reported a reduction in bullying among other behavioral and learning outcomes (Learning through Landscapes, 2003). Similarly, a reduction in bullying was observed in Australian schools that implemented greener, more interesting and stimulating school grounds (Gould League, 2010).

> We argue that the obvious way to reduce aggressive behaviour and conflict on school grounds is to provide sufficient play activities with differing levels of complexity and variety that engage students and provide opportunities for cross-age interaction (Malone & Tranter, 2003).

The physical environment is an important aspect of school context that may foster students' feelings of connectedness to school (Waters et al., 2009). In particular, the absence of graffiti has the greatest impact on students' connectedness during their first year of secondary school (Waters et al., 2010).

Supportive School Facilities and Activities

A safe and supportive physical school environment includes the provision of facilities and equipment as well as structured activities for students to enjoy during break times. The relationship between structured activities in school and bullying is not clear; however, there may be an indirect link between participation and opportunities for increased connectedness to school and development of self-esteem and social skills. Physical education and sports have been suggested as avenues through which some disengaged students can be reached and their personal, social, and moral development enhanced (Holroyd & Armour, 2003). Sports activities involve teamwork and the use of sound communication skills, and teach physical and mental resilience; however, sports may foster competition rather than collaboration, and contact sports may bring about aggression (D'Escury & Dudink, 2009). Therefore, structured physical activities should be well organized, appropriately supervised by school staff, and inclusive of all students to ensure a social climate that does not alienate and marginalize students (Halas, 2002).

Given that much bullying occurs during break times, the availability of structured activities for students, including recreational activities other than physical activities and sports, is likely to be beneficial in reducing bullying. Students should also, for example, have well-supervised opportunities to access technology (Patchin & Hinduja, 2006), both for educational as well as social and recreational purposes. Providing meaningful structured activities during free-time periods in school may help reduce indirect aggression among girls in particular, as they have less time for gossip (Larson, Wilson, Brown, Furstenberg, & Verma, 2002; Owens, Shute, & Slee, 2000). Structured activities also provide students with the opportunity to belong, discouraging the need for students to exclude others in an effort to confirm their own acceptance (Adler & Adler, 1995). The provision of engaging and well-organized activities demonstrates a school's commitment to providing a safe and supportive school environment in which students' active participation and connectedness to the school are fostered.

Student supervision is another aspect of a school's context that may influence students' bullying behavior. Students tend to feel unsafe from bullying in locations where adult supervision is low (Vaillancourt et al., 2010). Common locations and times for bullying include the school grounds, hallways, and the school cafeteria during break times (Cross et al., 2009; Fekkes et al., 2005; Vaillancourt et al., 2010). Key program elements associated with a decrease in students bullying others were improving playground supervision (including training lunchtime supervisors) and identifying bullying problem areas (Smith & Sharp, 1994).

Actions for Building a Protective Physical Environment

Physical Attributes of the School

An attractive and well-maintained school environment suggests to students that their school values comfortable, friendly, and well-maintained surroundings. This can also impact students' feelings of safety and connection to members of their school community. Well-designed, planned, and constructed school environments are another learning environment that can improve social relationships among students and staff and promote positive attitudes. These environments also help reduce absenteeism and boost students' and staff self-esteem. All members of the school community can participate in efforts to modify their physical environment and also contribute to school connectedness by creating warm environments where staff and students feel their opinions and ideas are valued.

Schools can increase students' feelings of ownership, pride, and responsibility in maintaining their surroundings when they:

- Provide adequate space for activities during break times
- Organize seating structures to facilitate positive social interactions
- Conduct regular assessments of the school's physical environment
- Use these assessments to inform modifications
- Include students in the decision-making process

Strategies for Good Practice: Physical Attributes of the School

1. An assessment of the school's physical environment is conducted annually.
2. An attractive, friendly school environment is maintained.
3. The main entrance is well defined and welcoming to all members of the school community.

1 **An assessment of the school's physical environment is conducted annually.**

During free play or recess, students need a variety of play areas that are well supervised and areas they can go to if they feel unsafe or uncomfortable. The identification by students of areas where they feel less safe, and clear guidelines or policies regarding the use of these areas, will help schools to reduce the potential for bullying behavior.

An assessment of the school's physical environment can involve mapping and reviewing aspects of the environment that may enable or prevent bullying. For example, mapping these areas will allow the school to see overlapping supervision areas or areas that lack adequate supervision or safety. It is also important to consider access to facilities and equipment for all age groups.

The following are suggestions for reviewing the school's physical environment as well as procedures for reporting and recording school bullying incidents followed by questions that will help to evaluate the effectiveness of these methods.

Step 1: Mapping Your School's Physical Environment

Use a map of the school to identify:

- Outdoor and recreation areas (by grade level if applicable)
- Outdoor equipment
- Out-of-bounds areas
- Safest areas
- Supervision areas, including the number of staff assigned to each area, and time-out areas

An example of a student-friendly school map can be found in Protective Physical Environment toolkit 6.1, or readers may use existing maps of the school.

Step 2: Mapping Locations of Bullying Incidents

Using the map of the school's physical environment delineating the safest areas, supervision areas, boundaries, and so on, highlight the hot spots where bullying incidents are typically occurring using the school's records of bullying incidents. Consider supplying rough maps of the school (inside and out) or take photographs around the school, and ask students to highlight the places they believe bullying (including cyberbullying) takes place or where they feel unsafe. In a secondary setting, students can also be challenged by seeking submissions from students detailing their safer schoolyard designs, rationale, and recommendations. Compare these hot spots with the supervision boundaries, access to activities or equipment, and out-of-bounds areas.

Step 3: Review of the Physical Environment Map

Discuss the results of schoolyard mapping with all staff. Using the Protective Physical Environment toolkit 6.2 planning sheet, consider the potential problem areas and plan strategies for action. Consider the following questions while completing this review.

- **Are adequate areas provided for all students to play or spend time together?**
  Are there grassed, shaded, covered, and paved areas; sports and other equipment; and open spaces for students of all ages?

- **Are areas identified where students should not be spending time?**
  Are there areas that are unsafe, where supervision is limited, or where students are blocked from the view of duty teachers?
- **Are there some areas that are currently considered out-of-bounds that could become safer areas for students to spend time?**
  For example, the library provides a nonthreatening environment that is often seen by students as an area that has more teacher supervision and can, therefore, be safer from bullying than the schoolyard.
- **Are areas available during break times with higher levels of teacher supervision for students who may feel unsafe?**
  Areas supervised by empathic staff members should be provided within all school environments to enable students to seek refuge if they are bullied during break times.
- **Are time-out areas provided for students who display antisocial or bullying behaviors?**
  Asking students who are engaging in bullying or other antisocial behavior to take some time out from the situation provides an opportunity for them to cool down and reflect on their actions.
- **Are all outside areas supervised by teachers?**
  Recording the location and the types of activities students are engaging in allows the school to provide adequate levels of supervision.
- **Do all staff perceive it is their role to intervene in bullying incidents in the schoolyard?**
  Some staff can be reluctant to intervene in a bullying incident. Ensure staff are able to identify a bullying incident and respond in accordance with school procedures set out in school behavior policies.

Top tips for school improvement:

- Improve the coverage of teacher supervision of outdoor areas and bullying hot spots.
- Create safer areas for students to spend time during class breaks to avoid being bullied.
- Establish a time-out area for students who have behaved inappropriately to spend time during class breaks.
- Provide staff with skills and confidence to identify and respond effectively in bullying incidents.
- Create out-of-bounds areas in locations where teacher supervision is limited or bullying is prevalent.

 ## An attractive, friendly school environment is maintained.

Well-maintained, attractive school environments can have a positive impact on student attitude, behavior, motivation, and connectedness.

Some ways to make schools more attractive include:

- Removing graffiti as quickly as possible
- Providing forms for reporting school maintenance and improvements that are needed around the school and acting on them
- Regularly checking cleanliness and temperatures of all learning areas
- Creating garden beds using a variety of different plants
- Displaying student artwork and photographs around the school
- Acknowledging at assemblies and in newsletters or e-letters the commitment of the school community to maintaining school buildings and grounds

3 **The main entrance is well defined and welcoming to all members of the school community.**

A school whose main entrance is easy to locate and is warm and welcoming sends a strong and positive message to students and their families. It also promotes the school as a place committed to creating positive learning experiences. Many large companies and corporations invest significant amounts of money into how their main entrance looks to elicit a positive first impression from their customers and clients. While schools do not need to invest significant funding, a coat of paint, cultural symbols such as regional art, and student work can leave a lasting impression on parents, students, and visitors to the school.

Supportive School Facilities and Activities

Adequate facilities, such as seating within the school, help to ensure students enjoy their break times in constructive and engaging ways and participate in positive social interactions. Supportive school activities, such as semi-structured physical and nonphysical games, provide students with opportunities to develop an understanding of social rules. School leaders who expect appropriate behavior to be modeled at all times by all staff will notice an improvement in behaviors and attitudes of students. Schools that provide opportunities for responsible technology use demonstrate to students an awareness of the important role of technology in their lives and the potential benefits this can give to their social and educational development.

Strategies for Good Practice: Supportive School Facilities and Activities

1. Developmentally appropriate, competitive, and noncompetitive games and activities are provided during break times to assist students' skill development and understanding of social rules.
2. Students are encouraged to help younger students join in activities during break times.
3. Students are taught how to positively resolve conflicts and disagreements in games without requiring adult intervention.
4. Supervised opportunities are provided for students to positively use technology for academic and social purposes.
5. Outdoor areas, out-of-bounds areas, and "safer" areas are clearly identified to students, and students are encouraged to spend time in areas where adequate supervision is provided.
6. Health and other student support services are located in areas that encourage student access.
7. Competent supervision is provided by school staff.
8. Targeted professional learning is provided for duty teachers to identify and respond appropriately and effectively to bullying situations.

Chapter 6

1 **Developmentally appropriate, competitive, and noncompetitive games and activities are provided during break times to assist students' skill development and understanding of social rules.**

Break times can provide students with opportunities to socialize and engage in activities with their peers in a safe, supportive environment. When school members consistently model, encourage, and recognize appropriate social behaviors, they increase the likelihood of promoting positive behaviors and preventing bullying behaviors.

Schools can allow students to develop pro-social skills, extend key understandings about social rules, and practice behaving appropriately in both structured and semi-structured environments when they provide:

- A range of semi-structured indoor and outdoor activities
- Supervised activities for rainy days
- Recreational and hobby clubs
- Blogs managed by school staff

Ways schools can create more pro-social schoolyards include:

- Providing equipment that allows for different levels of challenging play
- Using attractive, age-appropriate outdoor equipment
- Facilitating greater use by students of available equipment

Step 1: Activity Review

Using Protective Physical Environment toolkit 6.3, list all the equipment (such as playground and sporting equipment) and activities (such as lunchtime concerts, teacher-led activities, and library access) that are available to students. Compile this list over several days involving as many staff as possible to ensure all activities and equipment available to students are captured.

For all equipment and activities, complete the "Who accesses?," "Could access be improved?," and "Comments" columns. Consider the following:

- What equipment and activities cater to developmental needs of students of all ages?
- How can this access be improved?
- Is there equity in the access to equipment and activities for all ages? If not, how can this be improved?
- Do students know in which areas they can spend their break times?
- Are students using these areas?
- Which groups of students would like to spend time in areas they are currently not allowed?
- Can provisions be made to accommodate these groups?

Step 2: Planning

Distribute the completed Protective Physical Environment toolkit 6.3 to staff, students, and parents to seek their input into the activities and equipment that are made available to students during break times to validate the initial list.

Using this information, work through Protective Physical Environment toolkit 6.4 to prioritize areas for improvement (for example, provision of new line markings on court areas and improved access to existing equipment and activities). This toolkit will help staff identify the areas of concern, suggest strategies to overcome these problem areas, and assign staff and a timeline for completing the changes.

 2 Students are encouraged to help younger students join in activities during break times.

Some students need support to join in activities in the schoolyard during break times. Engaging young people as leaders to facilitate activities during break times has many advantages.

Step 1: Engaging Students as Leaders

Students are powerful leaders in a school context and are largely underused by schools. To engage, train, and support student leaders, consider:

1. Choosing students who make good leaders and are already working toward leadership roles within the school or in the broader community
2. Identifying teacher mentors to manage the leadership programs and support and facilitate the student leader activities—The teacher mentor needs to have a good relationship with the students and be willing to support new and innovative ideas. It is important for the leaders to take ownership in initiating and directing ideas and activities.
3. Providing student leaders with time and space to meet to discuss their plans for the break time student-led activities
4. Allocating resources where necessary to implement their lunchtime activities
5. Providing ongoing support from the teacher mentor to the student leaders to develop and implement their activities

Step 2: Facilitating Interaction Between Leaders and Younger Students

To make the best use of volunteer leaders in both primary and secondary settings, encourage them to consult with staff and students to determine in what ways younger students need support. In a primary setting, leaders may be needed to keep a game going or to remind groups of the importance of following rules and the negotiation of any new rules. In the secondary setting, this may involve students mentoring new students, particularly at times of transition.

Chapter 6

By developing programs in the primary setting that train volunteer leaders to assist younger students with group games (for example, managing equipment and refereeing, teaching new games, and joining in games), schools can:

- Provide older students with the opportunity to develop their leadership skills
- Increase students' sense of social responsibility
- Allow students to learn new skills
- Form new friendship groups with strong positive role models

In the secondary setting, these programs will:

- Develop decision-making skills among volunteer leaders
- Provide positive role models for younger students
- Develop opportunities for volunteers to be more socially responsible
- Establish positive connections across age groups

Step 3: Review

Regularly review with the student leaders and the students they are working with to determine the use of, and student satisfaction with, the leadership program. The review could consider asking a sample of the younger students the following questions:

- Did you engage in lunchtime activities with student leaders?
- What did you like about these activities?
- What new skills did you learn?
- What could be improved or done differently?
- Would you like to see this program modified? If so, in what ways?
- What activities could be implemented next term?

3 **Students are taught how to positively resolve conflicts and disagreements in games without requiring adult intervention.**

When conflict resolution skills are explicitly taught within classroom curriculum, some students experience increased levels of confidence and feel better supported to transfer these skills to the schoolyard. Conflict resolution is more successful when the people involved in the conflict are the ones involved in finding a solution. Schools that develop a simple, well-defined process that is understood and adhered to by all students are usually more successful when resolving conflicts. A powerful component of this process involves encouraging students to consider points of view other than their own and to endeavor to resolve conflict by ensuring everyone gets a fair go.

The following is an example of a conflict resolution process as used in the Friendly Schools and Supportive Schools curriculum resources (see Key Understandings and Competencies toolkit 5.1).

- Respect each other.
- Think about the problem.
- Listen to the other person.
- Say what you feel.
- Brainstorm solutions.
- Stick to what you have decided.
- Talk again if the solution is not working.

4 **Supervised opportunities are provided for students to positively use technology for academic and social purposes.**

Cyberbullying is most likely to occur at home or during break times at school (Galen & Underwood, 1997) when young people are spending more time using technology for social purposes than academic purposes. While families need to be reminded of their responsibilities to support their children in cyberspace, young people and schools benefit from structured learning regarding the safer and effective use of technology for both academic and social purposes. As technology is constantly changing, the most effective learning is delivered in accordance with where they are spending time online. Teaching young people how to reduce their exposure to cyberbullying is important. School staff need to identify opportunities for young people to learn positive ways to use technology, especially to support someone who may have been cyberbullied. Many activities are provided in the Friendly Schools (primary) and Supportive Schools (secondary) classroom resources to increase student understandings and skills related to reducing harm from cyberbullying.

Opportunities to integrate teaching about positive technology use are included in the Friendly Schools and Supportive Schools curriculum resources, as described in Key Understandings and Competencies toolkit 5.1.

5 **Outdoor areas, out-of-bounds areas, and "safer" areas are clearly identified to students, and students are encouraged to spend time in areas where adequate supervision is provided.**

Students and their families need to be informed of the reasons behind some of the decisions regarding where students can and cannot spend break times. When there are consistent messages and clear understandings around the use of the schoolyard, students are more likely to understand and respect the boundaries.

Using Protective Physical Environment toolkit 6.1, as described earlier, provides a clear representation of which areas are available to students.

6 **Health and other student support services are located in areas that encourage student access.**

Some students feel uncomfortable accessing health and support services due to the stigma that can sometimes be associated with service use. There is the potential for this to be more pronounced in secondary settings given young people's increased vulnerability to being teased or ridiculed for seeking help. Several factors can be considered to maximize students' willingness to access health and support services:

- Locate these services with other facilities commonly used by students (such as those located near teachers with a leadership role).
- Ensure service staff are trained to be approachable and skilled to help.
- Actively promote the proactive nature of the school's support services so that students are encouraged to use them at all times, not just when they are feeling vulnerable.
- Reassure students about the confidentiality of their visit.
- Design the service environment to be comfortable and welcoming to young people.

Chapter 6

7 **Competent supervision is provided by school staff.**

Encouraging students to spend time in areas where the level of adult supervision is high will reduce the invisibility of bullying behavior. Schoolwide data collection on the prevalence of bullying, including where and when bullying occurs, can be used to inform the provision of well-organized supervision from trained staff to ensure:

- Signs and symptoms of bullying are identified
- Situations are responded to in a timely manner
- Students feel safe
- All areas of the school grounds that students may access are visible to duty staff
- Hot spots are identified
- Out-of-bounds areas are defined
- Improved use of the schoolyard by all students

Building Capacity toolkit 2.1 describes surveys that could be used to identify where and when bullying occurs.

Questions to review staff supervision during break times:

- **Is there a formal reporting process or system for bullying incidents in the schoolyard?**
  Establish if one exists and define the benefits for your school of having a formal reporting system. See chapter 4 for further information relating to the development of a reporting system.
- **To what extent are all staff, students, and parents aware of this reporting procedure?**
  Whole-school community awareness of the process of reporting incidents ensures effective and supported implementation across the school.
- **Is there a central register of all reported incidents in the schoolyard?**
  A central record system enables the effective recording, monitoring, and follow-up of bullying incidents.
- **Who maintains the record system, and what do they do with the information?**
  Assign the management of the central record system to a few key staff. The same key staff would ideally be trained in using the Shared Concern method and other restorative techniques to effectively respond to bullying incidents (see Proactive Policies and Practices toolkits 4.1, 4.2, and 4.3).
- **Is there a system to monitor reported incidents for emerging bullying behavior trends and repeat offenders?**
  Maintaining a central record system makes it easier for key staff to identify students who are repeatedly bullying others and those being bullied frequently as well as the locations where bullying is occurring. Monitoring reported incidents will also allow the school to identify bullying hot spots and modify schoolyard supervision accordingly.

Competent supervision across the school grounds is one of the most effective strategies to reduce bullying behavior. The following questions may help the school assess and refine its supervision strategies to help reduce and effectively manage bullying that occurs outside of the classroom.

- **Is there a coordinated and regularly updated supervision roster?**
  It is important that the on-duty staff and supervision roster are considered to be as important as staffing classrooms with appropriately trained staff. Supervision during break times must be consistent, supported by staff who are trained and know how to respond according to the school's behavior policies.

- **Are all staff trained to identify and respond effectively to bullying behavior?**
  Training staff in the school's preferred methods for reducing bullying incidents (from the behavior policies) before they conduct supervision duties at break times is important.
- **Are all staff trained in the school's system of recording incidents of bullying?**
  The whole-school community needs to be aware of the process of reporting incidents to ensure effective and supported implementation across the school.
- **Does the school use bright duty teacher vests to help students quickly and easily identify support staff?**
  Schools have found that having duty teachers clearly visible to other staff and students makes students feel safer. Students report it is also easier to identify a teacher when they need one.

8 **Targeted professional learning is provided for duty teachers to identify and respond appropriately and effectively to bullying situations.**

Duty teachers are often the first on the scene at a bullying incident and, therefore, need to know how to respond in a way consistent with the school's behavioral policies. As supervisors can include nonteaching staff and relief teachers, induction processes and professional learning opportunities need to be offered to all staff. This training should address the school's behavioral policies and response including:

- Identification of bullying incidents
- Ways to communicate with students to gain a better understanding of what has happened and who is involved
- Immediate responses to ensure the safety of all students
- Strategies to acknowledge positive bystander responses
- Methods of reporting that are consistent with the school policy
- Referral pathways and effective referral strategies
- Strategies for student support and follow-up

Summary

This chapter demonstrates the important role of the physical environment in facilitating or preventing engagement in bullying behaviors. To ensure a protective physical environment is provided, schools can consider the physical attributes as well as the facilities and activities available to students. Two school stories are provided in this chapter outlining how CHPRC research schools have enhanced their physical environment to reduce and prevent bullying and increased students' perceptions of safety.

Schools wishing to assess and modify their physical environment to determine perceptions of safety and connectedness will find the four toolkits in this chapter helpful.

- Protective Physical Environment toolkit 6.1 includes a mapping template for schools to assess their physical environment for safer zones, bullying hot spots, and areas of low and high supervision.
- Protective Physical Environment toolkit 6.2 is designed to be used in conjunction with Protective Physical Environment toolkit 6.1 to plan potential problem areas and ways to increase perceptions of safety in these zones.
- Protective Physical Environment toolkit 6.3 provides a template for schools to list the activities and equipment available to students at break times.

Chapter 6

- Protective Physical Environment toolkit 6.4 complements Protective Physical Environment toolkit 6.3 as a planning tool for schools to prioritize and assign resources to physical environment modifications for enhanced safety and efficient use of space.

School Stories

School Story 6.1

Brief background to school initiative:

While all staff at this school recognized that bullying was happening, they felt the students were less aware, as they didn't seem to understand what bullying was. A survey conducted by the school psychologist also supported these findings.

School profile:

- Public school
- 320 students
- Grades: K–7

Action

The principal and vice principal participated in schoolyard duty to keep in touch with what was happening in the school. The teachers on duty were very vigilant, and an upper-grades teacher was always rostered with a lower-grades teacher so all of the students were known to the teachers. There was a communication book for staff to write which students were potentially at risk and to monitor them more closely.

The play areas that were out of sight of staff were reduced or made off limits to the students. The school introduced nonaggressive recess activities at certain times of the year. In winter, students played soccer; when it became too rough, the staff introduced marbles. This was the only time of the year that students were allowed to bring marbles into the school. The library was also opened at various times through the year, and sometimes the table tennis equipment was set up. On occasion, a particular class was allowed to take their sports equipment out at recess (baseball bats, basketballs, soccer balls, and T-ball equipment).

Lunch and recess had been reduced from forty-five to forty minutes, as the school found that it was during the last five minutes that most behavioral problems would occur. This strategy worked particularly well. Students had ten minutes to eat, twenty-five minutes to play, and five minutes to get a drink and go to the restroom, which was still plenty of time.

What We Learned

Difficulties Encountered

Inexperienced staff who were busy planning and preparing their classroom often forgot to listen to what students were telling them. In the second year of implementation, it was found on the survey that bullying levels had increased, which concerned many parents.

Overcoming Difficulties

Through training and mentoring, new staff were able to quickly adjust to their new environment and concentrate on the needs of their students. An explanation of the survey results quickly assured parents, staff, and students that the increase in bullying reports was not due to a fault in the policy but was due to students having a better understanding of what bullying was and feeling more confident about reporting their experiences.

Recommendations for Other Schools

Use a whole-school approach because if one teacher isn't listening to student concerns, the whole program suffers.

More information about the strategies used by this school can be found in the following toolkits.

- Proactive Policies and Practices toolkit 4.7
- Protective Physical Environment toolkit 6.1
- Protective Physical Environment toolkit 6.2
- Protective Physical Environment toolkit 6.3
- Protective Physical Environment toolkit 6.4

School Story 6.2

Background to school initiative:

Parental expectations spurred the introduction of a new antibullying program.

School profile:

- Rural public school
- 140 students
- Grades: K–7
- This school is part of a community that is experiencing significant change. A large proportion of the community is no longer involved in farming.

Action

Students who engaged in bullying were put on a reward and contract system. Parents, the principal, and the student signed a contract that identified the rewards for appropriate behavior and the consequences of inappropriate behavior. Inappropriate behaviors were outlined. The school believed that this system would help to formalize behavior management strategies because all participants (teachers, parents, and students) were involved in the formulation of the contract.

To ensure the behavior management plan was followed by the school community, the school ensured that staff, students, and parents had a chance to provide input into the plan. Rewards and consequences were clearly identified to the students, and it was stressed that the plan had a positive focus with positive steps taken before punishment. The plan was regularly reviewed.

Chapter 6

The school formed a bullying prevention committee consisting of three parents, two seventh-grade students, and two staff members. The school wanted to encourage peer groups to be vigilant about bullying at the school, hence the involvement of the two seventh-grade students on the committee. The committee conducted a bullying survey, and from the results, it identified the strengths and weaknesses of the school's policy. Both younger and older students were asked a range of questions related to bullying and the school's approach. These included:

- "Where does bullying occur?"
- "How often does it occur?"
- "Do you feel safe?"
- "Do the teachers care about you?"

The data were collected, collated, and presented to the bullying committee for review. Parents were sent brochures informing them of the survey's results. These data indicated that the students generally felt safe but were able to identify areas where bullying did occur. The school believed that by raising awareness of bullying behavior, students were less likely to engage in it and more likely to stand up to bullying behavior by others.

Strategies suggested by the committee that the school believes worked well included developing the social skills of students, role-playing activities, and the development of assertive skills. In upper grades, the need to model positive behavior to other students was emphasized. Students were encouraged to enlist the support of their peers if they were being bullied. To reduce schoolyard bullying, staff reviewed the school plan and made some school areas off limits if they were difficult to monitor. Staff paid particular attention to areas where bullying occurred more often and ensured there was an even use of facilities so that there was less chance that students may become upset with each other. The school newsletter was used to keep parents informed of what was going on in the school.

What We Learned

Difficulties Encountered

Staff were worried that the introduction of a specific antibullying policy would be viewed as evidence of a bullying problem at the school and they would be labeled a bullying school. The school had a good reputation, and the staff didn't want to make it appear that the school had problems.

Overcoming Difficulties

The principal reassured staff that rather than being given a bad name, the school would be seen as being proactive and caring. Staff were provided with information about other schools that were introducing similar programs.

Changes to Make

In hindsight, the school would have made the survey instrument a little more specific to its needs, as the one it used was too general.

More information about the strategies used by this school can be found in the following toolkits.

- Proactive Policies and Practices toolkit 4.5
- Protective Physical Environment toolkit 6.1
- Protective Physical Environment toolkit 6.2

Toolkits for Action

6.1 Protective Physical Environment Toolkit 6.1

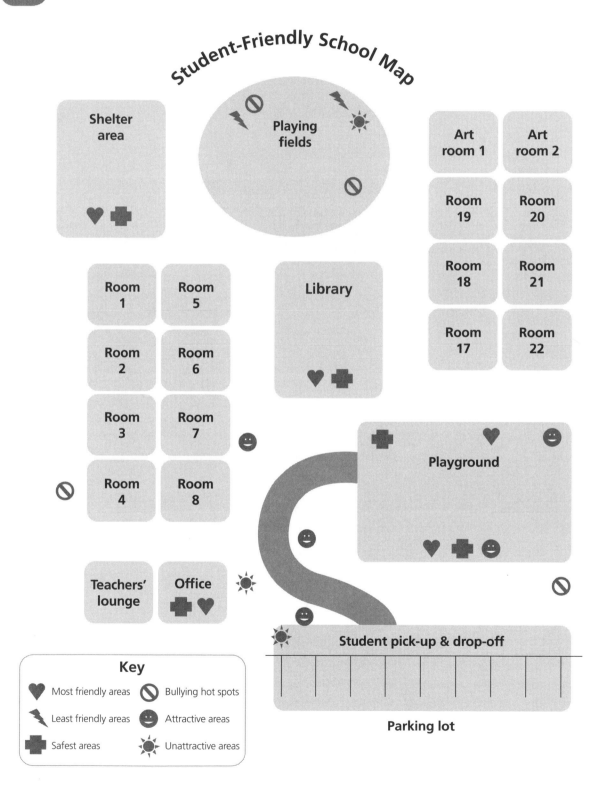

6.2 Protective Physical Environment Toolkit 6.2

Planning Sheet 1 Example:
Outdoors, Out-of-Bounds, Safer Areas, and Supervision Areas

Issues (Where and What)	Suggestions for Improvement	Staff Involved	Timeline for Implementation
Example: An area frequently used by students is blocked from the duty teachers' view by a bike shed. Antisocial and bullying behavior has been reported in this area.	Designate this as an off-limits area.	Principal	Insert date
	Relocate the bike shed.	Maintenance staff and parents	Insert date
	Allow students to continue playing in this area, and ensure the duty teacher frequently checks behind the shed.	Duty teachers	Immediate start and monitor
	Assign an extra duty teacher to supervise this area if the problem continues.	Duty teacher	Insert date

Planning Sheet 1: Outdoors, Out-of-Bounds, Safer Areas, and Supervision Areas

Issues (Where and What)	Suggestions for Improvement	Staff Involved	Timeline for Implementation
	1.		
	2.		
	3.		
	4.		
	5.		

6.3 Protective Physical Environment Toolkit 6.3

Review Sheet 1: Review of Equipment and Activities—What Is It, Who Is It Available To, and Could It Be Improved?

Equipment and Activities	Who Accesses?	Could Access Be Improved? (Yes/No)	Comments

6.4 Protective Physical Environment Toolkit 6.4

Planning Sheet 2: Physical Environment Strategies for Action

Issues (Where and What)	Suggestions for Improvement	Staff Involved	Timeline for Implementation

6.0 PLANNING TOOL: PROTECTIVE PHYSICAL ENVIRONMENT

Statement of Evidence for Protective Physical Environment

A well-maintained physical school environment helps promote learning and positive social interactions among students and staff. Attractive building design and location, adequate provision of space, and facilities and activities for recreation and learning (including through technology) can positively influence student behaviors.

Review Action 6.1—Physical Attributes of the School

	Not yet initiated	In planning	Preparing staff	Partially in place	Fully in place	Sustained practice
6.1.1 An assessment of the school's physical environment is conducted annually.						
6.1.2 An attractive, friendly school environment is maintained.						
6.1.3 The main entrance is well-defined and welcoming to all members of the school community.						
6.1.4 Modifications are made to the school's physical environment to facilitate positive social interactions among students and staff.						
6.1.5 The school recognizes that bullying or violence can be reduced in the school environment.						
6.1.6 Students are involved in the development and improvement of the school grounds.						

Plan Action 6.1—Physical Attributes of the School

What needs to be done?	Who is going to do it?	What do we need?	Status	Timeline		Comments and reflections
				Finish	Status	

Review Action 6.2—Supportive School Facilities and Activities

	Not yet initiated	In planning	Preparing staff	Partially in place	Fully in place	Sustained practice
6.2.1 Developmentally appropriate, competitive, and noncompetitive games and activities are provided during break times to assist students' skill development and understanding of social rules.	Not yet initiated	In planning	Preparing staff	Partially in place	Fully in place	Sustained practice
6.2.2 Students are encouraged to help younger students join in activities during break times.	Not yet initiated	In planning	Preparing staff	Partially in place	Fully in place	Sustained practice
6.2.3 Students are taught how to positively resolve conflicts and disagreements in games without requiring adult intervention.	Not yet initiated	In planning	Preparing staff	Partially in place	Fully in place	Sustained practice
6.2.4 Supervised opportunities are provided for students to positively use technology for academic and social purposes.	Not yet initiated	In planning	Preparing staff	Partially in place	Fully in place	Sustained practice
6.2.5 Outdoor areas, off-limits areas, and "safer" areas are clearly identified to students, and students are encouraged to spend time in areas where adequate supervision is provided.	Not yet initiated	In planning	Preparing staff	Partially in place	Fully in place	Sustained practice
6.2.6 Health and student support services are located in areas that encourage student access.	Not yet initiated	In planning	Preparing staff	Partially in place	Fully in place	Sustained practice
6.2.7 Competent supervision is provided by school staff.	Not yet initiated	In planning	Preparing staff	Partially in place	Fully in place	Sustained practice
6.2.8 Targeted professional learning is provided for duty teachers to identify and respond appropriately and effectively to bullying situations.	Not yet initiated	In planning	Preparing staff	Partially in place	Fully in place	Sustained practice

Action Plan 6.2—Supportive School Facilities and Activities

What needs to be done?	Who is going to do it?	Status	Timeline		What do we need?	Comments and reflections
			Status	Finish		

School–Family–Community Partnerships

Schools that encourage active participation of students' families and community services providers recognize that addressing bullying is the responsibility of the whole-school community. Creating links with relevant health, educational, and community agencies that provide services to students and their families will foster vital support for school action to reduce bullying.

IN A DESPERATE ATTEMPT TO TACKLE BULLYING THE PRINCIPAL REACHED OUT TO THE PARENTS

Evidence for Strengthening School–Family–Community Partnerships

The key link between actions and messages implemented in the school setting and those applied in family and community environments is recognized in the Health-Promoting Schools model as a way to reinforce learning and behaviors. In addition, the Social Ecological model described by

Bronfenbrenner (1977) acknowledges the key role of both the school and families and communities in influencing child and adolescent development. In both models, children and adolescents are exposed to adult role models who can help shape their knowledge, attitudes, and behaviors. It is important to present consistent messages to children and adolescents to encourage uptake of positive and prosocial behaviors and attitudes that they implement in all settings.

Research shows collaborative partnerships are beneficial in fostering school action to reduce bullying. These key partnerships can be between:

- The school and students' parents or caregivers and families
- The school and relevant service providers in the community

In this chapter, the importance of links between schools, families, and community organizations is discussed as ways to promote this consistent approach as well as an opportunity to work within resource limitations and expertise.

Strengthening Family Links

Bullying is not just a school issue. According to a socioecological perspective, the occurrence of bullying can be enabled and maintained over time by complex interactions between factors, both within and outside the individual (Espelage & Swearer, 2003). Individual characteristics such as self-esteem and empathy influence, and are influenced by, factors in the wider context in which the individual is embedded, including the influence of peers, teachers, schools, families, and communities (Espelage & Swearer, 2003). The links between the major settings in which a student participates are also important, as is the congruency between these environments regarding bullying prevention strategies (Bronfenbrenner, 1977; Espelage & Swearer, 2004).

It is vital for schools to work with families to foster strong links that will facilitate a coordinated response to reducing bullying and the promotion of consistent messages about bullying. Positive teacher communication with parents has a beneficial influence on the development of a positive school climate (Lee, 2010). Similarly, parental involvement, including parents taking an interest in their child's school work, is associated with less bullying behavior among adolescents (Flouri & Buchanan, 2003).

As discussed in chapter 5, Key Understandings and Competencies, information provision and skill development for parents are necessary to reduce bullying behavior (Antonovsky, 1996). It is likely that the beneficial effect of such information and training lies not only in the actual content but also in the communicative mechanisms through which it is delivered to parents. This strengthens links between students' school and home and demonstrates a collaborative effort by schools and families to reduce bullying.

In Farrington and Ttofi's (2009) meta-analysis, information for parents (for example, information about the bullying prevention initiatives at the school or general tips about bullying) was identified as an important program element related to a decrease in students bullying others. Parent training (information nights, parent-teacher meetings) was significantly associated with both a decrease in bullying and being bullied. Given that cyberbullying has generally been found to occur more outside school hours rather than during school (Slonje & Smith, 2008; Smith et al., 2008), developing parent awareness about cyberbullying is crucial and can assist in preventing and responding to cyberbullying.

Many students who are frequently bullied do not report the bullying (Bradshaw, Sawyer, & O'Brennan, 2007; Cowie & Olafsson, 2000; Rigby, 1997; Whitney & Smith, 1993) and report that they would receive greater support from talking to a peer about bullying compared to speaking with an adult (Rigby, 1997; Smith & Shu, 2000). Parents may be unaware of their child's experiences of bullying (Stockdale, Hangaduambo, Duys, Larson, & Sarvela, 2002), and similarly, teachers have been found to underestimate the prevalence of bullying reported by students within their school (Bradshaw et al., 2007). Adequate recognition of the signs and symptoms of bullying, through regular communication between students' families and the school, will facilitate timely resolution of bullying incidents and provide support for students involved in bullying situations.

Students who perpetrate potentially offensive Internet and mobile phone practices usually have parents who are less involved with their computer and Internet use (Vandebosch & Van Cleemput, 2009). Cyberbullies are also more likely to report a poor emotional bond with their parents or caregivers as well as more frequent discipline and more infrequent monitoring on the part of their caregiver (Ybarra & Mitchell, 2004). These findings suggest there is a need to communicate with parents to encourage them to employ strategies to effectively monitor and communicate with their child about cyberbullying.

Being cyberbullied is also associated with a family composition other than living with two biological parents (for example, single, remarried, adoptive parents, grandparents, foster care) (Sourander et al., 2010). Schools can help reduce the likelihood of students being cyberbullied or help them to respond to cyberbullying more effectively by providing targeted information to all caregivers at times and in locations that maximize attendance and understanding.

Working Collaboratively With Health, Education, and Community Services Providers

Working to create and strengthen links with relevant health, education, and community agencies will help support the school's action to reduce bullying. In Farrington and Ttofi's (2009) meta-analysis, one of the program components associated with a decrease in being bullied was cooperative group work among different professionals (such as teachers and other professionals) in working with students involved in bullying. Involvement in bullying has been associated with anxiety, depression, low self-esteem, suicidality, poor academic achievement, poorer relationships with peers, increased loneliness, and poorer physical health (Jankauskiene et al., 2008; Kaltiala-Heino, Rimpelä, Marttunen, Rimpelä, & Rantanen, 1999; Kaltiala-Heino et al., 2000; Kaukiainen et al., 1999; Nansel et al., 2001; Wolke et al., 2001). Given this range of factors linked to bullying, it is crucial to form partnerships with professionals such as psychologists, counselors, general practitioners, social workers, youth workers, and education support services to provide additional assistance to students who are involved in bullying and also to identify those students who may be at increased risk of involvement in bullying situations.

Chapter 7

Actions for Strengthening School–Family–Community Partnerships

Strengthening Family Links

Involving students and families in the school's strategies to address bullying will increase the chance of achieving lasting behavior change in students. Some ways to achieve this include:

- Involving students' families in the school's operations where practical and appropriate
- Creating opportunities for input into school planning and policy
- Planning activities to ensure regular positive communication
- Using numerous channels of communication to reach all families
- Cooperating closely with families to ensure early recognition of the signs and symptoms of bullying and determining those students who may be at increased risk of involvement in bullying
- Collaborating with families to resolve specific instances of bullying and provide targeted support to the student involved in bullying and his or her family
- Acknowledging differences in family, parent, and community priorities

Strategies for Good Practice: Strengthening Family Links

1. Schools provide regular, positive communication to engage families and encourage their involvement.
2. Students invite families to school events and activities.
3. The school's response to reducing bullying is developed in collaboration with families.
4. There is close cooperation between staff and families in responding to specific bullying situations that arise.
5. Families and the community are encouraged to consistently demonstrate an intolerance of bullying behavior.

1 **Schools provide regular, positive communication to engage families and encourage their involvement.**

Establishing and maintaining open channels of regular, positive communication with families leads to the development of a school culture that values their important contribution. Leaders that recognize diverse cultures in their school community will make use of multiple communication channels, including the translation of written materials to reach the whole-school community. This is particularly important prior to and following student transition from primary to secondary school. Families are also becoming more open to using electronic communication via email or school portals where regular information and active links to resources can be provided to families.

Regular communication with families:

- Ensures they are continually updated with current information on policy development and organization

- Encourages conversations across school and home
- Fosters curiosity for schools and families to learn about each other
- Helps them feel valued and respected as real partners who can help solve problems
- Increases their willingness to become involved on a number of levels, bringing their many and varied skills into the school
- Builds positive relationships
- Makes parents feel welcome at school
- Cements common understandings related to school, family, and community priorities and actions to reduce bullying

Use the School–Family–Community Partnerships toolkit 7.1 to survey families to determine how welcome they feel at the school. Try to accommodate, where possible, families who do not speak English as a first language. Collate the results and appoint a committee comprised of parent, principal, and teacher representatives to decide how best to use the information. Formulate and implement recommendations to help parents feel more welcome in the school. This set of questions could be used in conjunction with whole-school assessment strategies described in Building Capacity toolkit 2.1.

Family communication sheets can provide the impetus for family discussion about school matters, including increasing communication and reducing bullying. School–Family–Community Partnerships toolkits 7.2 and 7.3 include two family communication sheets that can be included in the school's newsletter, which can be enlarged to create posters displayed in areas of the school used by families, or distributed to families in need of support regarding communication strategies and bullying behavior. In addition, Supportive School Culture toolkits 3.1 and 3.2 provide further examples of ways to communicate with parents through newsletter and assembly items.

 ## Students invite families to school events and activities.

Many parents comment that the only time they are invited to the school, especially in secondary schools, is when their child is behaving inappropriately or there is some other problem. It can be valuable to ask families how they want to be involved with the school, find out which days and times suit them better, and ask how they would like to receive communications.

Inviting families to special activities, in addition to assemblies, that provide positive experiences, will help them feel more comfortable and welcome in the school and more inclined to make return visits. This is particularly beneficial following the transition to secondary school when students may feel disconnected to their new school. Invite families to events using the natural groupings that occur within the school, for example, send invitations to a meet-and-greet through student pastoral care/tutor groups, so families feel they have a group to which they can belong, especially if the tutor group remains together for a number of years. Attendance by parents is always better when their children are performing, when children personally invite their parents via a letter or something similar, and when child care is provided.

Some activities used effectively by schools include:

- Family sports days
- Special assemblies (for example, grandparents' day)
- ICT information or social media workshops with students and families (these work well when students are involved in or lead the presentations)
- Expert guest speaker presentations discussing topics with families such as cyberbullying and cyber safety

When families feel strong connections to schools, they are more confident and willing to work in partnership with schools to support their children's learning. In addition to traditional school-home communication opportunities, the *Friendly Schools and Families* project distributed family communication and activity sheets that focused on family and school connectedness, parent-child engagement, and communication pointers. The aim of these sheets was to increase the level and quality of communication between parents and their children, such that parents were more receptive to school communication and thus were more informed of and attended more school events.

One way to engage families in the development of a supportive school culture is to host a family friendship carnival, as described in School–Family–Community Partnerships toolkit 7.5. The aim of the carnival is to involve staff, students, and parents in activities designed to encourage all school community members to practice and enhance social skills in a fun and nonthreatening environment.

3   The school's response to reducing bullying is developed in collaboration with families.

Many parents are concerned about the effects of bullying on their children; however, they are often unsure how to help their children prevent bullying and respond effectively, especially when the bullying is perpetrated via technology, as with cyberbullying. By involving parents in the development of behavior policies (see Proactive Policies and Practices toolkit 4.5) that relate to bullying (and other issues), schools can strengthen the likely impact of these policies on student behavior. By working together, the whole-school community can:

- Foster positive attitudes and friendlier schools
- Develop a safe and happy environment for children
- Encourage children and adults to talk about bullying
- Let children know that bullying is unacceptable behavior anywhere in the community

Schools can create links with families and communities by providing targeted information sessions that educate families about how to:

- Work in collaboration with schools to develop students' social skills
- Help their children initiate and maintain positive friendships, both online and offline
- Respond effectively if their child is being bullied either online or offline
- Respond effectively if their child is bullying others (including siblings)
- Use social media in positive ways

These strategies demonstrate to parents the strong commitment of school leaders to establishing a positive school culture where all members feel safe, valued, and supported. It is important for students to see their parents and the school working together with a common desire to help them feel safer, happier, and supported at school. This partnership will be most effective when parents:

- Encourage children to talk about online and offline bullying, both at school and at home
- Cooperate with class teachers to share valuable information about how their children are feeling
- Talk and work with their children's school to help achieve the most positive outcome for their children
- Become familiar with their school's bullying and cyberbullying policy, which should outline how the school plans to respond to these behaviors

In Supportive School Culture toolkit 3.4, the role of bystanders is discussed and could be shared with parents to help them understand how their children can help reduce bullying behavior. In addition, Supportive School Culture toolkit 4.5 provides information about the development of assertiveness skills in students to increase self-esteem and confidence.

4   **There is close cooperation between staff and families in responding to specific bullying situations that arise.**

When schools and families cooperate in responding to specific bullying incidents, a positive outcome is more likely. This demonstrates the school's commitment to resolving the problem collaboratively, in a transparent and consistent manner. Chapter 4, which includes Proactive Policies and Practices toolkit 4.5, and chapter 7 describe ways that parents and caregivers of the bullying target or targets, the perpetrators, and the bystanders can be effectively involved in the school's response to a bullying incident, especially if the incident is severe.

Parents can:

- Discuss with their children positive ways to develop and maintain friendships
- Encourage children to think about how bullying behavior makes others feel
- Explain the concepts of respect, cooperation, and negotiation

Parents can be encouraged to use the following questions when specific bullying situations arise:

- If you saw your friend being teased, how would you feel? What could you do?
- If your friend asked you to help bully another child, how would this make you feel? What could you do?
- Who would you talk to if you were bullied?
- What would you do if you were bullied?

When a bullying situation arises, it is important to separate the child and the behavior and that students are not labeled as bullies. By doing so, the message students receive is that bullying is a bad behavior, not that a student who bullies is a bad person. It is easy to focus on "busting" the bullies; however, a strategy like the Shared Concern method, which promotes and demonstrates how to solve problems and find positive solutions, is usually more effective and likely to lead to longer-term positive behavior change.

Restorative techniques such as the Support Group method and Shared Concern method are beneficial if parents understand their purpose and expected outcomes. School–Family–Community Partnerships toolkit 7.4 describes the Shared Concern method in a format suitable for families and school staff and contains an additional family activity that may assist in reinforcing the process followed in this technique to resolve relationship conflicts. Proactive Policies and Practices toolkits 4.1 and 4.2 provide information about these techniques in more detail for school staff.

When children are bullied, parents can assist their children and the school by supporting the identification of a group of people (support group) their child feels comfortable talking with and turning to for help. Role-playing what they would say if they approached these people about a bullying situation will help students feel more comfortable seeking support and reassure parents their children have the skills to ask for help if they need it. This group generally includes:

- Parents
- Classroom teacher
- Teachers on duty at recess or lunchtime
- Other school staff members
- School friends
- Family friends

CHPRC research found that it was valuable for the school to always advise parents if a bullying incident occurred that involved their children, similar to the process a school would use if a student was to visit the school health center for an illness or injury during the day. Depending on the severity of the incident it may not be necessary for the parents to visit the school, but they should at least be apprised of the school's action in response to the incident. This communication allows parents to be well aware of incidents and the actions by the school, and also helps parents talk with their children following these incidents.

5 Families and the community are encouraged to consistently demonstrate an intolerance of bullying behavior.

To change behavior, bullying reduction strategies need to focus not only on the school environment but also include the home and community. Parents can:

- Encourage children to talk about bullying both at school and at home
- Cooperate with class teachers to share valuable information about how their children are feeling
- Talk and work with the school to help achieve the most positive outcome for their child
- Become familiar with the school's bullying policy

Building a consistent, positive community response that actively discourages bullying behavior may require a shift in attitudes and knowledge about the harms associated with this behavior for both the target and the perpetrator. To achieve this normative change, teachers, families, and the wider community need to be aware of what behaviors constitute bullying, especially covert bullying such as social exclusion, rumor spreading, and cyberbullying. They also need to know what action to take if they see a bullying incident and to be aware of what young people perceive if adults take no action when bullying occurs. If an adult observes bullying behavior or other forms of aggression and takes no action, there is a likelihood this behavior will continue and may intensify compared to a situation where there is no adult present. This has important implications for the whole-school community, which may be seen by students to be condoning bullying through their inaction when the behavior occurs in their presence.

The whole-school community can send a strong, consistent message about bullying, when stakeholders are provided with:

- Current evidence-based information about bullying behavior
- Open and encouraging invitations to attend meetings to discuss bullying behavior and engage in decision making regarding possible school actions
- Ongoing information about school action, progress, and policy

Working Collaboratively With Health, Education, and Community Services Providers

Due to the social, psychological, emotional, physical, and academic harms linked with bullying, it is imperative to build and maintain strong partnerships with relevant professionals both within the school, such as student services teams, and external to the school, for example, social workers, youth workers, clinical psychologists, and mental health agencies. This ensures students experiencing difficulties related to bullying (and other issues), who are not able to be supported by trained school staff, can be efficiently referred to these services to receive appropriate support. Engaging the expertise of these professionals in the development of school planning and policy to reduce bullying allows this behavior to be considered within a broader health and education context. This has particular relevance in relation to use of technology on and off school grounds and the impact of cyberbullying and other types of social media behaviors. External service providers for school activities such as extracurricular activities, for example, also need to be aware of school policies related to bullying and other responsibilities related to student care and need to be well briefed on actions they are required to take based on the school policy when teaching students from the school. Local community groups can also be engaged to assist in providing resources to support school action to reduce bullying, such as libraries, clubs, and other recreation venues for extracurricular activities.

Forming partnerships with IT professionals is also useful to help inform school action to address cyberbullying and other inappropriate online behaviors. This can help schools, students, and families keep apprised of technological developments and the implications of this for online behavior. Partnerships can also be formed with police to investigate the legal issues around bullying and particularly around cyberbullying due to its potential to escalate within a short period of time.

Strategies for Good Practice: Working Collaboratively With Health, Education, and Community Services Providers

1. School action to reduce bullying involves the support of the student services teams.
2. The school invites, encourages, and values the participation of the community to reduce bullying behavior.
3. Partnerships are established with local community organizations engaged with the school to provide resources and expertise to support specific efforts to reduce bullying behavior.
4. The school consults and works with community, health, and education support services to respond to specific instances of bullying as appropriate.
5. The school identifies opportunities for students and families to link with other professionals when further support is required.

 School action to reduce bullying involves the support of the student services teams.

Student services teams typically refer to school staff associated with the care of students, including the school psychologist, social worker, school nurse, and school-based police officers. School leaders who actively engage student services teams and seek their input and advice on school policy and practice as part of the whole-school effort to reducing bullying behavior develop and sustain a positive school culture that supports all students. Student services teams can provide families with:

- Support around student issues
- Support services
- Links to, and assistance in, accessing support services beyond the school for students experiencing difficulties
- Information about new approaches to discipline, communication, and positive interactions with their children

Some families may feel more comfortable speaking with staff from support services than other staff and may also be more open to discussing the issues they are facing and the help they need with these trained professionals. School staff who are not trained psychologists may occasionally be put in situations in which they are being asked to provide support to students that is beyond their training and expertise. It is important to provide a structure for staff to recognize their limitations and know who to refer students to in order to ensure they meet the responsibilities they have to students. However, all staff can be trained to provide initial support to students such as was identified in the KIT+ research conducted by the CHPRC. In this study, it was found that the Co-LATE model (see Proactive Policies and Practices toolkit 4.7) was an effective discussion framework for staff to demonstrate to students that staff are supportive and want to help when they can.

2 The school invites, encourages, and values the participation of the community to reduce bullying behavior.

When schools ensure that professional assistance from the community is available and accessible, they are more likely to experience greater support from families, as they are seen to have a strong commitment to reducing bullying behavior. Engaging the community strongly communicates that the school is not prepared to ignore bullying behavior and will seek support from external organizations to assist with their approach to this issue. Many outside agencies, such as local police, welcome invitations from schools to meet with leaders, staff, and parents to discuss and plan how all sectors can effectively help each other ensure that consistent messages are communicated about bullying behavior.

3 Partnerships are established with local community organizations engaged with the school to provide resources and expertise to support specific efforts to reduce bullying behavior.

A key part of developing a positive school culture is to encourage student commitment to community projects and clubs. Many students, particularly secondary school students, spend time engaged in the local community. While some students have families who support and encourage this engagement, others need to rely on school leaders and staff to raise awareness and help them take advantage of what the community has to offer. Community organizations also want to reduce bullying and are likely to be receptive to partnership opportunities with interested schools. When community organizations and schools work together for a common goal, opportunities and capacity to build a wider culture of disapproval of bullying are increased.

4 **The school consults and works with community, health, and education support services to respond to specific instances of bullying as appropriate.**

Designing a plan that provides a step-by-step approach to preventing and effectively responding to bullying behavior and that is clearly understood by all members of the whole-school community provides a consistent response. This plan allows for responses to incidences of varying severity and enables individuals to understand their role in implementing the plan.

Consulting community, health, and education support services about the school's response plan increases awareness of the school's efforts to reduce bullying behavior and opens communication channels between schools and external support agencies. Community, health, and education support services could assist school staff to:

- Increase their capacity and confidence to identify bullying behaviors and symptoms of bullying
- Increase their capacity and confidence to respond to different levels of severity and types of bullying situations
- Identify the nature and severity of bullying situations and make decisions about appropriate and protective responses
- Increase their knowledge of how to effectively refer students when they need additional support services

5 **The school identifies opportunities for students and families to link with other professionals when further support is required.**

Schools can increase their capacity to support students and families by providing current information about external student support agencies that can assist students with needs beyond the capacity of schools. While many parents will be receptive to working with the school to reduce bullying behavior, they may not know where to go for help and support if the involvement of external professionals is recommended. The student support team can compile and disseminate information about external professionals or agencies and ensure effective and sensitive referral of students and families.

School staff knowing and using the appropriate protocol and procedures for referring students and their families to other professionals makes it more likely that appropriate services will be obtained. More than just knowing the protocol for referral, it is often helpful if school staff have some awareness of the services to which they refer students. Questions for consideration include:

- Is the service located close to the students' homes or accessible by transportation services?
- Is there a cost for attending?
- Does the service cater to, and are the staff trained to effectively deal with, school-age children?
- Is the service located somewhere accessible to students?
- Does the service operate during hours that are accessible to students?

Chapter 7

Summary

As demonstrated in theoretical models such as the Health-Promoting Schools model (World Health Organization, 1996) and the Social Ecological model (Bronfenbrenner, 1977), students' families and communities influence and have a role to play in their development of positive, prosocial behaviors. Moreover, bullying is not just an issue for schools to respond to, especially with the opportunities for bullying via technology (cyberbullying), which often occurs outside school grounds and hours. Hence, schools that encourage active participation of students' families and community services providers recognize that addressing bullying is the responsibility of the whole school and its wider community.

Two school stories are provided in this chapter to illustrate ways CHPRC research schools have implemented strategies to foster student–family–community partnerships. Schools wishing to implement these and the strategies outlined in this chapter may refer to the five school–family–community toolkits provided.

- School–Family–Community Partnerships toolkit 7.1 provides an example of how to evaluate the extent to which parents feel welcome in the school.
- Two family communication sheets are included in School–Family–Community Partnerships toolkits 7.2 and 7.3 as examples of ways to engage parents and promote common understandings across the whole-school community.
- School–Family–Community Partnerships toolkit 7.4 describes the Shared Concern method (which the school may choose to implement) for parents. A version for staff is included in Proactive Policies and Practices toolkit 4.1.
- School–Family–Community Partnerships toolkit 7.5 provides an example of a family engagement strategy—a family friendship carnival—to engage parents and promote consistent messages between the school and families regarding social skill development and interpersonal relationship skills.

Several other toolkits included in this book are identified in this chapter. While the principles discussed in this chapter are particularly relevant for the involvement of families and communities in school action against bullying behavior, it is important to involve both groups at all opportunities to ensure a consistent approach.

School Stories

School Story 7.1

Brief background to school initiative:

This school made changes to encourage parents to think in positive ways about the school. Often these parents had bad experiences in school themselves. The school attempted to enable parents to be a proactive influence in their child's education.

School profile:

- Metropolitan public school
- 1,020 students
- Grades: K–7
- This is a multicultural school with a transient community. The school felt there was only a limited amount of parental support.

Action

The school believed parents were becoming alienated and wanted to engage parents more fully. The school staff established programs and strategies to involve parents including the four-week Parents as Partners program, a course that taught parents how to help with reading, writing, and language activities in class. The school attempted to minimize the number of students per parent and increase the one-on-one interaction during the scheduled activity. This program was offered to first- through third-grade parents. The student services manager made himself available for daily contact. The school held meetings every two weeks between parents and the principal to discuss important issues.

Conference sessions were conducted with students being bullied, the students engaging in bullying behavior, and their families. The tone of these sessions was informal with refreshments provided. They were designed to facilitate discussion of bullying issues and potential solutions. Strategies that could be used at home were made available to parents by the student services manager, school psychologist, teachers, and school nurse.

What We Learned

Difficulties Encountered

Initially, parents did not want to talk about personal problems that may have affected their child's behavior. Many were, therefore, unwilling to come to meetings to discuss their child's behavior and possible solutions. From a logistics point of view, there were also problems with finding a conference time to suit the part-time school psychologist or nurse as well as fitting meetings in with teachers' nonteaching time and parents' schedules.

Chapter 7

Overcoming Difficulties

The conferences were set in an environment conducive to discussion. Armchairs were provided as well as tea, coffee, and pastries. As few participants as possible were involved in the conference to ensure parents weren't embarrassed to talk about sensitive issues. Early morning or late afternoon meetings were scheduled, when appropriate, to ensure all parties could attend, with particular emphasis on participation from fathers when possible.

More information about the strategies used by this school can be found in the following toolkit.

- School–Family–Community Partnerships toolkit 7.4

School Story 7.2

Brief background to school initiative:

This school identified a need to increase parent involvement in behavior modification strategies.

School profile:

- Metropolitan public school
- 781 students
- Grades: K–6

Action

The school engaged in strategies that did not at first appear to address bullying; however, over time, staff came together to reduce and prevent bullying. The eight steps used to promote antibullying messages, strategies, and activities at the school included:

1. Establishing and consistently applying a behavior management policy
2. Having staff ratify and review the behavior management policy
3. Ensuring that parents were contacted in cases of student absenteeism and reporting nonsupported absenteeism to welfare
4. Recording incidents on a computer database to facilitate immediate follow-up
5. Gradually encouraging parent support (parents were originally aggressive)
6. Providing useful hints for parents in newsletters
7. Including a group of students with severe behavioral problems in the Exploring Together program
8. Inviting offending students and their parents to a ten-week course run by four facilitators (two for parents, two for the children), where parents and children would meet separately for one hour and then regroup for the last half hour

The Exploring Together program provided students with frameworks for social interaction and problem solving to resolve issues and conflict without violence. Problem-solving skills were taught to students so that they were able to deal with incidents themselves. The program taught students to look at how other people felt and choose a win-win solution.

The Exploring Together program aimed to build better relationships between parents and children. Two courses were run per year. Up to eight students per course could attend. The resources and facilitators for this program were provided by the local Community Center. The program targeted students who were involved in repeated incidents of inappropriate behavior. Students were identified by classroom teachers and through computer-database records of inappropriate behavior. The program involved the students, their parents, and teachers and focused on the development of social skills, parenting practices, and the strengthening of family units. There was a student group, a parent group, and meetings for partners and teachers. In promoting positive social relations, the school believed that consistency, role modeling, interaction with parents, and the belief that things could be improved were essential.

To achieve cooperation between parent groups and school staff regarding behavior management, the school believed that stability of staffing, communication, and staff role modeling for parents were essential. Communication occurred through a formalized procedure of follow-up with parents after incidents, newsletter articles (social skills snippets), and casual discussion in the schoolyard. Students were encouraged to share what they learned at school with their parents.

The school recently built a new playground for younger students. This initiative was partially funded by the local community. The parent body helped raise additional funds and build the actual playground. This new playground has provided the younger students with constructive play opportunities. Furthermore, it has provided them with a separate play area from the older students and thus has reduced the potential for bullying.

What We Learned

Difficulties Encountered

At the start of the program, parents were resistant to the Exploring Together program, as they did not see behavior problems with their children at home. Many parents did not understand that their children sometimes behaved differently at home and at school.

Overcoming Difficulties

Meetings held with the parents to discuss the problems and the program allowed parents to understand the program before they joined up. It was also found that after the first program was run, the response from parents was positive, and through word of mouth, others wanted to join.

More information about the strategies used by this school can be found in the following toolkits.

- Supportive School Culture toolkit 3.1
- Proactive Policies and Practices toolkit 4.5
- School–Family–Community Partnerships toolkit 6.2
- School–Family–Community Partnerships toolkit 6.3
- School–Family–Community Partnerships toolkit 6.4

Toolkits for Action

 **Family Links Toolkit 7.1**

How Welcome Do Families Feel in Our School?

Dear Parent,

Please take a few minutes to fill out the following brief survey to tell us how you feel when you visit our school. Be honest, as answers are anonymous—there is no need to write your name on the sheet.

	Strongly Agree	Agree	Disagree	Strongly Disagree	Unsure
I am greeted in a friendly, courteous way when I contact the school.	1	2	3	4	5
The school provides a valuable orientation program.	1	2	3	4	5
The school provides informal opportunities for staff and parents to get to know each other during the school year.	1	2	3	4	5
The principal makes time for students and their families.	1	2	3	4	5
The school encourages students and families to share their ideas on ways to improve our school.	1	2	3	4	5
The school implements relevant suggestions made by students and parents.	1	2	3	4	5
The school encourages positive parent-teacher communication.	1	2	3	4	5
The school caters to families for whom English is their second language.	1	2	3	4	5
The school communicates important information in an effective way.	1	2	3	4	5

Please write any other comments or suggestions here:

7.2 Family Links Toolkit 7.2
Family Communication Sheet 1

Communicating With Your Children

Talking with your children regularly about everyday topics will increase the chances of them talking to you about more difficult issues such as bullying. When your children talk to you, consider the following.

- Stop what you are doing, look at them, and listen.
- Be supportive, and encourage them to talk.
- Show your children you enjoy talking with them.
- Let your children know you are always interested in what is going on in their lives, not only when they are in trouble or having problems.
- Arrange opportunities to share time with your children when you can talk while doing an activity together, for example, cooking, crafts, going to a football game, family meal times, or family meetings.
- Ask your children their opinion on events, issues, and general daily proceedings so they feel their opinion is valued.
- *Praise* your children. Not just when they have had success but also when they have tried.
- Encourage and model positive language, for example: *I really like the way you asked your brother if you could borrow his bike.*
- "Catch" your children doing good things, and congratulate them in as many creative ways as you can.
- During dinner, ask everyone to share his or her favorite part of the day or what he or she hopes to achieve tomorrow.
- Sit beside your child while he or she is on the computer, and ask him or her to *explain* to you how what he or she is using works.
- Ask lots of open-ended questions that require a sentence answer, like: *"What happened today? Who did you spend time with at lunch today? How can we make things better? It sounds like you are pretty unhappy; what has been going on?"*
- Allow for cooling off time if you or your child are feeling upset or angry.
- Check that you have understood what your child is trying to tell you.

Stay in Touch

Consider using the following questions to get up to date with your children, and encourage them to ask you questions too.

- What is your favorite game?
- Who are your friends, and why do you like them?
- What makes you laugh?
- Who is your favorite band?
- What do you like doing most at school?
- What are you most afraid of?

- What is your favorite website?
- What is your favorite television show?
- What are the best things we do together as a family?
- What would you like us to do more of as a family?

7.3 Family Links Toolkit 7.3
Family Communication Sheet 2

Discussing Bullying

What is bullying?

Bullying is when a person or a group of people offline or online (mobile phone or Internet):

Make fun of and tease someone in a mean and hurtful way

Tell lies or spread nasty rumors about someone to try to make others not like him or her

Leave someone out on purpose or not allow him or her to join in

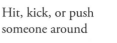

Hit, kick, or push someone around

Deliberately damage, destroy, or steal someone's things

Threaten or make someone feel afraid of getting hurt

It is NOT bullying when:

Teasing is done in a friendly, playful way

Two people who are as strong as each other argue or fight

Cyberbullying is when a person:

- Sends nasty or threatening emails or messages on the Internet or via a mobile phone
- Posts mean or nasty comments or pictures about others to websites such as Myspace or Facebook or sends them to other students' mobile phones
- Deliberately ignores or leaves others out over the Internet
- Pretends to be someone else online to hurt that person or make him or her look foolish

Cyberbullying can happen when things such as hurtful text messages, pictures, video clips, and emails are being sent to you. It can also happen when these things are sent to others about you.

Why do children bully?

- To get what they want
- They are afraid of being the one left out
- They are unhappy, so they take it out on others
- They are jealous of others
- It seems like fun
- They are bored
- They enjoy the sense of power
- Their significant role models bully
- Because they are being bullied themselves
- To try to be popular and to get friends at school

Possible signs your child is being bullied:

- Decreased interest in school
- Reluctance to attend school or absenteeism
- Below-average academic performance
- Complaints of headaches or stomachaches
- Request to change schools
- Frequent damage to or loss of personal items
- Frequent injuries such as bruises or cuts
- Lack of friends and socially withdrawn behavior
- Interrupted sleep patterns
- Unhappy, miserable, moody, or irritable
- Threats or attempts to harm himself or herself

When discussing bullying, it is helpful as a parent to:

- Listen and react in a calm, helpful, and supportive manner and show you understand your child is upset by the bullying
- Encourage your children to explain what happened and how they feel about it
- Consider there may be factors you are not aware of, such as the involvement of others or previous events
- Ensure your children know what support services are available at school
- Highlight the importance of having more than one good friend, as this reduces the impact of bullying
- Support your children to plan safe actions they can take to improve the situation
- Help your children identify trusted people they can talk to, including school staff, friends, and other family members
- Tell your children bullying is wrong and they have the right to feel safe and happy

Chapter 7

Helpful Parent Responses

If your child tells you about being bullied:

- Believe your child so he or she feels confident to talk to you about problems
- Take the child's concerns seriously without being overprotective
- Listen to your child and show you understand that he or she is upset by the bullying
- Encourage your child to talk about the situation
- Tell your child that bullying is wrong, and remind him or her that he or she has the right to feel safe and happy
- Keep in mind that there may be other factors involved in the situation that you may not be aware of, such as other people who are involved or other things that have happened in the past
- Be aware of your own responses, and react in a calm, helpful, and supportive manner
- Make sure your child knows how to get help and support at school
- Help your child enhance his or her friendship skills (having more than one good friend has been shown to reduce the likelihood or impact of bullying)
- Encourage your child to participate in activities other than those related to the school so he or she has other friendship groups
- Help your child reflect on what has been done to resolve the situation so far
- Help your child work out a plan of what he or she could do to help make the situation better

What Can I Tell My Child to Do If He or She Is Bullied?

Like most complex problems, there is not a single strategy that will stop all bullying. As a first step, it is usually best to encourage your child to talk about what has happened.

Planning Tool for Children

When I have a problem, I can:

- Try to stand up for myself in a positive way
- Walk away and ignore the person completely
- Try to talk to the person I am having a problem with
- Get help from someone in my support group
- Try coming to an agreement with the other person
- Ignore the situation and keep playing or working
- Talk to a friend to get some ideas to help me make a decision

Figure 23: Action plan for children.

Family Links Toolkit 7.4

The Shared Concern Method

The key to stopping bullying is getting those involved to acknowledge there is a problem affecting them and encouraging them to decide on some ways to positively change the situations that are supporting the bullying behaviors. Bullying involves the misuse of power and tends to occur where power is not equal. This is why much of the bullying we see in schools and our communities involves more powerful groups of people bullying individuals or smaller or weaker groups. One approach that is used in schools to respond to this bullying is the Shared Concern method. The Shared Concern method helps to equalize power imbalances, reduces a group's ability to bully others, and helps the students involved address any problems that may have caused the bullying to start in the first place.

The Shared Concern method enables all of the students involved in the bullying to find solutions to the problems and situations supporting the bullying. The Shared Concern method aims to change the causes of the behavior of students involved in bullying incidents and improve the situation for all, particularly those being bullied. It helps the students bullying others develop empathy and concern for the individuals being bullied. It then provides the students, including the bullied student or students, with a process that will enable them to generate positive responses for the social problems affecting them, increase their acceptance of each other, and promote skills for peaceful coexistence.

Practical Steps of the Shared Concern Method

All students who are involved in the bullying incident or incidents are asked to meet and talk with a designated staff member. The process begins with individual interviews with each of the students who are believed to be perpetrating bullying. Clear steps are used to reach the point where each student agrees that there is a problem for the targets of the bullying and has contributed some ideas that they will act on to help improve the situation for the targets. Consider the following five steps.

1. The individuals involved in the bullying situation are identified, and individual meetings are held with each of these students (the students believed to be carrying out the bullying, the student or students reportedly being bullied, and any significant bystanders who may be able to assist the students involved—it is optional to include bystanders).

2. Each student believed to be perpetrating the bullying is asked about the problem affecting the target and to suggest ways in which he or she personally could help improve the situation. This does not involve forcing the students to admit guilt, to apologize, or to set a consequence for any behaviors believed to have occurred. This step is designed to encourage the students involved in the bullying to have empathy for the bullied student's situation and to really want to do something about it. Empathy reduces the attitudes that support bullying behaviors. Thinking of something they could do to improve the situation encourages the alleged perpetrator to take on a more positive attitude toward the problems. The staff member follows these same steps with any bystanders included in the process.

3. The target of the bullying is also given an opportunity for a one-on-one meeting with the staff member to discuss what is happening to him or her and encouraged to think of ways the situation could be improved. The student is encouraged to look for improvements from the students who were believed to have previously been bullied and asked to consider eventually meeting with these other students once improvements have started to occur.

Chapter 7

4. Follow-up meetings with the individuals involved are necessary to support their progress in improving the situation. However, the next major step is for the staff member to meet the students who were believed to have been bullying and the bystanders, as a whole group. The staff member encourages them, in front of each other, to report the good outcomes of their individual actions in attempting to improve the situation for the student or students who had been bullied. The staff member acknowledges each effort and encourages the group to feel positive about the efforts of each member. This process enhances the development of more positive attitudes to the situation and to each other. These positive attitudes and increasing empathy for the bullied student or students significantly reduce the risk of the group continuing to bully others as a group, the power imbalance, and the bully's misuse of that power, which supported the bullying.

5. The final step involves the staff member bringing all the students involved together, including the student or students who were targeted by the bullying, if appropriate. In this meeting, the staff member encourages all students to report their positive observations and outcomes. Any problems can be shared and new ideas generated to solve them. Then the whole group discusses and agrees on ways to talk to each other and what to do if the problems begin again.

All school staff can adopt a Shared Concern attitude when they see bullying behavior occurring by expressing their own concern for the target student or students to the group or individual doing the bullying. For example, the teacher could say, "I can see that X is having a hard time; he looks sad," and even asking the bullying student or students if there is something they can think of that could help X (if they show empathy or concern, that is, they agree that X is having a hard time). Schools that have used this method have reported excellent results in reducing bullying behavior.

How Can Parents Support This Method?

Schools need to encourage parents to talk with staff if their child is experiencing a problem, as parents often find out about bullying before the school does. The focus should always be on making sure children feel safe and happy at school.

Parents and caregivers need to be encouraged (via the school website or newsletter, and so on) to take the following actions if they feel their child is experiencing a problem.

- Talk to and listen to their child to help him or her develop some strategies to:
  - Respond to bullying that is happening to him or her
  - Respond to bullying he or she is witnessing (bystander)
  - Change his or her own behavior if he or she is taking part in the bullying of others
- Talk to their child's teacher about the situation, and decide what will be done. Arrange for a follow-up meeting to discuss outcomes.
- Once they have worked with the teacher and talked with their child, reinforce recommended strategies at home.
- Keep in contact with the school, even if the situation has improved, to ensure the changes are maintained.

Encourage parents to recognize that the key to stopping bullying is helping the children involved talk about what is happening and decide what to do to solve any problems. Direct parents to the school's whole-school plan addressing student behavior, which includes bullying behaviors. Help parents to see how this plan provides students, staff, and parents with information about the school's processes for managing and preventing bullying behaviors at school.

Help parents adopt a Shared Concern attitude when they come across bullying or when bullying is reported to them by:

- Responding calmly
- Showing concern for the situation affecting the bullied child or children
- Empowering and supporting the child to develop responses he or she feels will help him or her
- Demonstrating a positive belief that by working together the situation can be improved
- Encouraging others to take positive steps to improve the situation

Discuss with parents how they can deal with a bullying situation between siblings at home using the following social problem-solving steps.

For example, a situation in which an older brother is often teasing and putting down a younger sibling who retaliates by hiding his things could be addressed by parents using the following steps.

Step 1
Agree to solve the problem together.

Step 2
Make a time to meet when the situation is calm.

Step 3
Set ground rules about how the problem will be discussed.
- Each person has a turn.
- Each person listens to the other person and acknowledges what he or she said.
- Talk about the problem, not the person (no put-downs).

Step 4
Discuss what the problem is.
- Each sibling states the issue and how it makes him or her feel.

Step 5
Each person suggests a solution.
- Explore the effect of each solution.

Step 6
Decide on the best combined solution, with a timeline and time to meet again.
- How will you know if it is working?
- What will it look like, sound like, and feel like?

Step 7
Meet again.
- What worked? What would make it work better?
- The parent acknowledges all positive efforts.

Family Links Toolkit 7.5

The Family Friendship Carnival

Why?	Evidence suggests that enhancing social skills within the school community promotes a positive social environment where bullying may be reduced and student learning improved.
Who?	The carnival could involve students, staff, and most importantly, families.
What?	The carnival may be structured similar to a field day in which staff, students, and families work together in cooperative activities to achieve a common goal.
When?	The theme of this carnival is to promote friendship, cooperation, teamwork, sharing, and other social skills within your school community.

Planning Your Family Friendship Carnival

- Choose an appropriate time for your school to host the carnival. Consider planning the carnival to coincide with International Friendship Day (the first Sunday in August).
- Choose whether your family friendship carnival will be a full-day or half-day event.
- Choose games that promote social skill development and are fun to participate in.
- Decide on the structure of the day.
  - Number of stations
  - How long each group will spend at each station
  - How long students will be grouped (mixed-age groups or in grade levels)
  - How parents will be involved (as officials or part of each group)
  - How staff will be involved (as officials or part of each group)
- Decide on the most effective ways to promote the carnival within the school community.

Promotion

This is the most important component in building anticipation of the family friendship carnival. Students, staff, and parents should be targeted in the specific promotion of this event.

Staff:

- Keep staff informed of the plans for the carnival.
- Provide clear instructions to all staff regarding starting and finishing times, activities planned, agenda for the day, and each staff member's role for the day.
- Communicate all aspects of the promotion of the carnival to staff so they are aware of what information is being sent home.
- Ask staff to promote the carnival to their students and set aside time for students to write a personal letter or invitation to their parents.

Students:

- Inform all students of the upcoming carnival at assemblies and encourage them to talk about the carnival with their family.
- Involve students in the promotion of the day.
- Have a general discussion in class about the carnival.
- Involve students in selecting cooperative, friendly games for the carnival.

Parents:

- Inform parents of the family friendship carnival as soon as you have set the date.
- Ask students to send a personal invitation home to invite their parents to participate in the carnival.
- Invite parents to be a part of the carnival as participants with their children or as officials on the day.
- Place regular reminders on your school's website or newsletter reminding parents of the carnival.
- Use assemblies to regularly discuss the carnival with parents, staff, and students.
- Involve the school PTA in suggesting ways to involve families and ways in which the carnival could be promoted to them.

Running the Day

Your school's family friendship carnival can be conducted in whatever way is most suitable to your school community. Some suggestions to consider during the day are as follows:

- Prepare an agenda or timetable for the day.
- Consider whether you will assign an official to each station or to each group. Some schools have found both methods effective. Assigning a teacher or parent as the official to each station provides an opportunity for staff to interact with all students and parents.
- Consider having a scoring system to award prizes to the winning groups. If you do have a scoring system, consider using staff to monitor scoring and judging. Also consider how each activity can be scored.
- Provide plenty of shade, water, and sunscreen.

Activities

It is important to choose activities with the aim of the carnival in mind—to involve the whole-school community in activities that promote friendship, cooperation, and other social skills to achieve a common goal. Ideally, the activities should last no more than fifteen to twenty minutes; however, this can be altered if there is a wide variety of activities that are of a short duration. Some key elements to look for in potential activities for the school's family friendship carnival are:

- To involve group work and team building
- Suitability for all age groups from students to adults
- Simple to explain and conduct
- To encourage cooperation and sharing
- To allow for scoring or counting (if desired)

Chapter 7

7.0 PLANNING TOOL: SCHOOL–FAMILY–COMMUNITY PARTNERSHIPS

Statement of Evidence for School–Family–Community Partnerships

Schools that encourage active participation of students' families and community services providers recognize that addressing bullying is the responsibility of the whole-school community. Creating linkages with relevant health, educational, and community agencies that provide services to students and their families will foster vital support for school action to reduce bullying.

Review Action 7.1—Strengthening Family Links

	Not yet initiated	In planning	Preparing staff	Partially in place	Fully in place	Sustained practice
7.1.1 School provides regular, positive communication to engage families and encourage their involvement.						
7.1.2 Students invite families to school events and activities.						
7.1.3 The school's response to reducing bullying is developed in collaboration with families.						
7.1.4 There is close cooperation between staff and families in responding to specific bullying situations that arise.						
7.1.5 Families and the community are encouraged to consistently demonstrate an intolerance of bullying behavior.						

Plan Action 7.1—Strengthening Family Links

What needs to be done?	Who is going to do it?	Timeline		Status	What do we need?	Comments and reflections
		Status	Finish			

Review Action 7.2—Working Collaboratively With Health, Education, and Community Services Providers

	Not yet initiated	In planning	Preparing staff	Partially in place	Fully in place	Sustained practice
7.2.1 School action to reduce bullying involves the support of the student services teams.						
7.2.2 The school invites, encourages, and values the participation of the community to reduce bullying behavior.						
7.2.3 Partnerships are established with organizations engaged with the school to provide resources and expertise to support specific efforts to reduce bullying behavior.						
7.2.4 The school consults and works with community, health, and education support services to respond to specific instances of bullying as appropriate.						
7.2.5 The school identifies opportunities for students and families to link with other professionals when further support is required.						

Plan Action 7.2—Working Collaboratively With Health, Education, and Community Services Providers

What needs to be done?	Who is going to do it?	Timeline Status	Finish	Status	What do we need? Comments and reflections

References and Resources

Adamson, G., McAleavy, G., Donegan, T., & Shevlin, M. (2006). Teachers' perception of health education practice in Northern Ireland: Reported differences between policy and non-policy holding schools. *Health Promotion International, 21*(2), 113–120.

Adler, P. A., & Adler, P. (1995). Dynamics of inclusion and exclusion in preadolescent cliques. *Social Psychology Quarterly, 58*(3), 145–162.

Agatston, P. W., Kowalski, R., & Limber, S. (2007). Students' perspectives on cyber bullying. *Journal of Adolescent Health, 41*(6), S59–S60.

Aman-Back, S., & Björkqvist, K. (2007). Relationship between home and school adjustment: Children's experiences at ages 10 and 14. *Perceptual and Motor Skills, 104*(3), 965–974.

Anderson, C., & Dill, K. (2000). Video games and aggressive thoughts, feelings and behavior in the laboratory and in life. *Journal of Personality and Social Psychology, 78*(4), 772–790.

Anderson, C. A., & Bushman, B. J. (2001). Media violence and the American public: Scientific facts versus media misinformation. *American Psychologist, 56*(5–6), 477–489.

Andreou, E., & Metallidou, P. (2004). The relationship of academic and social cognition to behaviour in bullying situations among Greek primary school children. *Educational Psychology, 24*(1), 27–41.

Antonovsky, A. (1996). The salutogenic model as a theory to guide health promotion. *Health Promotion International, 11*(1), 11–18.

Arseneault, L., Bowes, L., & Shakoor, S. (2010). Bullying victimization in youths and mental health problems: 'Much ado about nothing'? *Psychological Medicine, 40*(5), 717–729.

Ary, D. V., Duncan, T. E., Biglan, A., Metzler, C. W., Noell, J. W., & Smolkowski, K. (1999). Development of adolescent problem behavior. *Journal of Abnormal Child Psychology, 27*(2), 141–150.

Atlas, R. S., & Pepler, D. J. (1998). Observations of bullying in the classroom. *The Journal of Educational Research, 92*(2), 86–99.

Australian Communications and Media Authority. (2008). *Cybersmart—Hints and tips.* Sydney, Australia: Author.

Australian Curriculum, Assessment and Reporting Authority. (2012, January 23). *Australian curriculum V3.0.* Accessed at www.australiancurriculum.edu.au on January 15, 2014.

Bacchini, D., Esposito, G., & Affuso, G. (2009). Social experience and school bullying. *Journal of Community and Applied Social Psychology, 19*(1), 17–32.

Baldry, A. C. (2003). Bullying in schools and exposure to domestic violence. *Child Abuse and Neglect, 27*(7), 713–732.

Baldry, A. C., & Farrington, D. P. (2007). Effectiveness of programs to prevent school bullying. *Victims and Offenders, 2*(2), 183–204.

Bandura, A. (1973). *Aggression: A social learning analysis.* Englewood Cliffs, NJ: Prentice Hall.

Bandura, A. (1978). The self system in reciprocal determinism. *American Psychologist, 33*(4), 344–358.

Bandura, A. (1983). Self-efficacy determinants of anticipated fears and calamities. *Journal of Personality and Social Psychology, 45*(2), 464–469.

Batsche, G. M., & Knoff, H. M. (1994). Bullies and their victims: Understanding a pervasive problem in the schools. *School Psychology Review, 23*(2), 165–174.

Bauman, S., & Del Rio, A. (2006). Preservice teachers' responses to bullying scenarios: Comparing physical, verbal, and relational bullying. *Journal of Educational Psychology, 98*(1), 219–231.

Bhat, C. S. (2008). Cyber bullying: Overview and strategies for school counsellors, guidance officers, and all school personnel. *Australian Journal of Guidance and Counselling, 18*(1), 53–66.

Blair, J. (2003). New breed of bullies torment their peers on the Internet. *Education Week, 22*(1), 6–7.

Boivin, M., & Vitaro, F. (1995). The impact of peer relationships on aggression in childhood: Inhibition through coercion and or promotion through peer support. In J. McCord (Ed.), *Coercion and punishment in long-term perspectives* (pp. 183–197). New York: Cambridge University Press.

Bond, L., Butler, H., Thomas, L., Carlin, J., Glover, S., Bowes, G., et al. (2007). Social and school connectedness in early secondary school as predictors of late teenage substance use, mental health, and academic outcomes. *Journal of Adolescent Health, 40*(4), 357.e9–357.e18.

Booth, M. L. (1997). Health-promoting schools in Australia: Models and measurement. *Australian and New Zealand Journal of Public Health, 21*(4), 365–370.

Bosworth, K., Gingiss, P. M., Potthoff, S., & Roberts-Gray, C. (1999). A Bayesian model to predict the success of the implementation of health and education innovations in school-centered programs. *Evaluation and Program Planning, 22*(1), 1–11.

Boulton, M. (2008). Pupils' perceptions of bullying and disruptions to concentration and attention to school work. *Pastoral Care in Education: An International Journal of Personal, Social and Emotional Development, 26*(2), 83–89.

Boulton, M. J., Trueman, M., & Murray, L. (2008). Associations between peer victimization, fear of future victimization and disrupted concentration on class work among junior school pupils. *British Journal of Educational Psychology, 78*(3), 473–489.

Bradshaw, C. P., O'Brennan, L. M., & Sawyer, A. L. (2008). Examining variation in attitudes toward aggressive retaliation and perceptions of safety among bullies, victims, and bully/victims. *Professional School Counseling, 12*(1), 10–21.

Bradshaw, C. P., Sawyer, A. L., & O'Brennan, L. M. (2007). Bullying and peer victimization at school: Perceptual differences between students and school staff. *School Psychology Review, 36*(3), 361–382.

Brendgen, M., Markiewicz, D., Doyle, A. B., & Bukowski, W. M. (2001). The relations between friendship quality, ranked-friendship preference, and adolescents' behavior with their friends. *Merrill-Palmer Quarterly, 47*(3), 395–415.

Bronfenbrenner, U. (1977). Toward an experimental ecology of human development. *American Psychologist, 32*(7), 513–531.

Burns, S., Cross, D., Alfonso, H., & Maycock, B. (2008). Predictors of bullying among 10 to 11 year old school students in Australia. *Advances in School Mental Health Promotion, 1*(2), 49–60.

Burns, S., Cross, D., & Maycock, B. (2010). "That could be me squishing chips on someone's car." How friends can positively influence bullying behaviors. *Journal of Primary Prevention, 31*(4), 209–222.

Burns, S., Maycock, B., Cross, D., & Brown, G. (2008). The power of peers: Why some students bully others to conform. *Qualitative Health Research, 18*(12), 1704–1716.

Camodeca, M., & Goossens, F. A. (2005). Aggression, social cognitions, anger and sadness in bullies and victims. *Journal of Child Psychology and Psychiatry, 46*(2), 186–197.

Camodeca, M., Goossens, F. A., Terwogt, M. M., & Schuengel, C. (2002). Bullying and victimization among school-age children: Stability and links to proactive and reactive aggression. *Social Development, 11*(3), 332–345.

Campbell, M. (2005). Cyber bullying: An old problem in a new guise? *Australian Journal of Guidance and Counselling, 15*(1), 68–76.

Campbell, M., Cross, D., Spears, B., & Slee, P. (2010). *Cyberbullying: Legal implications for schools* (Occasional Papers OP118). Melbourne, Australia: Centre for Strategic Education.

Campbell, M., Spears, B., Cross, D., & Slee, P. (2011). Cyberbullying in Australia. In J. A. Mora-Merchán & T. Jäger (Eds.), *Cyberbullying: A cross-national comparison* (pp. 232–244). Landau, Germany: Verlag Empirische Pädagogik.

Campbell, M. A., & Gardner, S. (2005). A pilot study to assess the effects of life coaching with Year 12 students. In M. Cavanagh, A. Grant, & T. Kemp (Eds.), *Evidence-based coaching* (pp. 159–170). Bowen Hills, Queensland, Australia: Australian Academic Press.

Casey-Cannon, S., Hayward, C., & Gowen, K. (2001). Middle-school girls' reports of peer victimization: Concerns, consequences, and implications. *Professional School Counseling, 5*(2), 138–147.

Channon, S., & Crawford, S. (2000). The effects of anterior lesions on performance on a story comprehension test: Left anterior impairment on a theory of mind-type task. *Neuropsychologia, 38*(7), 1007–1017.

Chesney-Lind, M., Morash, M., & Irwin, K. (2007). Policing girlhood? Relational aggression and violence prevention. *Youth Violence and Juvenile Justice, 5*(3), 328–345.

Child Health Promotion Research Centre. (2010). *An empirical intervention to reduce cyber bullying in adolescents: Annual report to Healthway.* Perth, Australia: Author.

Coffin, J., Cross, D., & Larson, A. (2010). Bullying in an Aboriginal context. *The Australian Journal of Indigenous Education, 39,* 77–87.

Coie, J. D., Terry, R., Zakriski, A., & Lochman, J. (1995). Early adolescent social influences on delinquent behavior. In J. McCord (Ed.), *Coercion and punishment in long-term perspectives* (pp. 229–244). New York: Cambridge University Press.

Collaborative for Academic, Social, and Emotional Learning. (2003). *Safe and sound: An educational leader's guide to evidence-based social and emotional learning (SEL) programs.* Chicago: Author.

Collaborative for Academic, Social, and Emotional Learning. (2011). *Illinois Social Emotional Learning Standards.* Accessed at http://casel.org/wp-content/uploads/2011/04/Illinois-SEL-Standards.pdf.

Conners-Burrow, N. A., Johnson, D. L., Whiteside-Mansell, L., McKelvey, L., & Gargus, R. A. (2009). Adults matter: Protecting children from the negative impacts of bullying. *Psychology in the Schools, 46*(7), 593–604.

Connor, D. F., Steingard, R. J., Cunningham, J. A., Melloni, R. H., Jr., & Anderson, J. J. (2004). Proactive and reactive aggression in referred children and adolescents. *American Journal of Orthopsychiatry, 74*(2), 129–136.

Cowie, H., & Olafsson, R. (2000). The role of peer support in helping the victims of bullying in a school with high levels of aggression. *School Psychology International, 21*(1), 79–95.

Craig, W. M., & Harel, Y. (2004). Bullying, physical fighting and victimization. In C. Currie, C. Roberts, A. Morgan, R. Smith, W. Settertobulte, O. Samdal, et al. (Eds.), *Young people's health in context: Health Behavior in School-Aged Children Study (HBSC)—International study from the 2001/2002 survey (Health Policy for Children and Adolescents,* No. 4; pp. 133–144). Copenhagen, Denmark: World Health Organization.

Craig, W. M., & Pepler, D. J. (1998). Observations of bullying and victimization in the school yard. *Canadian Journal of School Psychology, 13*(2), 41–59.

Craig, W. M., Pepler, D., & Atlas, R. (2000). Observations of bullying in the playground and in the classroom. *School Psychology International, 21*(1), 22–36.

Craig, W. M., Pepler, D., & Blais, J. (2007). Responding to bullying: What works? *School Psychology International, 28*(4), 465–477.

Crick, N. R., & Bigbee, M. A. (1998). Relational and overt forms of peer victimization: A multiinformant approach. *Journal of Consulting and Clinical Psychology, 66*(2), 337–347.

Crick, N. R., & Dodge, K. A. (1994). A review and reformulation of social information processing mechanisms in children's adjustment. *Psychological Bulletin, 115*(1), 74–101.

Crick, N. R., & Dodge, K. A. (1996). Social information-processing mechanisms in reactive and proactive aggression. *Child Development, 67*(3), 993–1002.

Crick, N. R., & Grotpeter, J. K. (1995). Relational aggression, gender, and social-psychological adjustment. *Child Development, 66*(3), 710–722.

Cross, D., Epstein, M., Hearn, L., Slee, P., Shaw, T., & Monks, H. (2011). National Safe Schools Framework: Policy and practice to reduce bullying in Australian schools. *International Journal of Behavioral Development, 35*(5), 398–404.

Cross, D., Hall, M., Hamilton, G., Pintabona, Y., & Erceg, E. (2008). Australia: The Friendly Schools project. In P. K. Smith, D. Pepler, & K. Rigby (Eds.), *Bullying in schools: How successful can interventions be?* (pp. 187–210). Cambridge, United Kingdom: Cambridge University Press.

Cross, D., Hall, M., Waters, S., & Hamilton, G. (2008). *A randomised control trial to reduce bullying and other aggressive behaviours in secondary schools* (Healthway Final Report). Perth, Australia: Child Health Promotion Research Centre, Edith Cowan University.

Cross, D., Li, Q., Smith, P. K., & Monks, H. (2011). Understanding and preventing cyberbullying: Where have we been and where should we be going? In Q. Li, D. Cross, & P. Smith (Eds.), *Cyberbullying in the global playground: Research from international perspectives* (pp. 287–305). Chichester, United Kingdom: Wiley-Blackwell.

Cross, D., Monks, H., Campbell, M., Spears, B., & Slee, P. (2011). *School-based strategies to address cyberbullying.* (Occasional Papers OP119). Melbourne, Australia: Centre for Strategic Education.

Cross, D., Monks, H., Hall, M., Shaw, T., Pintabona, Y., Erceg, E., et al. (2011). Three-year results of the Friendly Schools whole-of-school intervention on children's bullying behaviour. *British Educational Research Journal, 37*(1), 105–129.

Cross, D., Pintabona, Y., Hall, M., Hamilton, G., & Erceg, E. (2004). Validated guidelines for school-based bullying prevention and management. *International Journal of Mental Health Promotion, 6*(3), 34–42.

Cross, D., Shaw, T., Epstein, M., Monks, H., Dooley, J., & Hearn, L. (2011). Cyberbullying in Australia: Is school context related to cyberbullying behavior? In Q. Li, D. Cross, & P. Smith (Eds.), *Cyberbullying in the global playground: Research from International Perspectives* (pp. 75–98). Chichester, United Kingdom: Wiley-Blackwell.

Cross, D., Shaw, T., Hearn, L., Epstein, M., Monks, H., Lester, L., et al. (2009). *Australian Covert Bullying Prevalence Study (ACBPS).* Perth, Australia: Child Health Promotion Research Centre, Edith Cowan University.

Cross, D., Shaw, T., Monks, H., Waters, S., & Lester, L. (2013). Using evidence to reduce the bullying behavior experienced by girls. In D. Pepler & H. B. Ferguson (Eds.), *Understanding and addressing girls' aggressive behaviour problems* (pp. 97–113). Waterloo, Canada: Wilfrid Laurier University Press.

Cross, D., Shaw, T., Pearce, N., Erceg, E., Waters, S., Pintabona, Y., et al. (2008). School-based intervention research to reduce bullying in Australia 1999–2007: What works, what doesn't, and what's promising? In D. Pepler & W. Craig (Eds.), *Understanding and addressing bullying: An international perspective* (pp. 289–310). Bloomington, IN: AuthorHouse.

Cross, D., Shaw, T., Pintabona, Y., Hall, M., Hamilton, G., Erceg, E., et al. (n.d.). *Social, attitudinal, psychological and school adjustment factors associated with bullying behaviour in Australian primary school students.* Manuscript submitted for publication.

Cross, D., Waters, S., Pearce, N., Shaw, T., Hall, M., Erceg, E., et al. (2012). The Friendly Schools Friendly Families programme: Three-year bullying behaviour outcomes in primary school children. *International Journal of Educational Research, 53*, 394–406.

Cunningham, C. E., Vaillancourt, T., Rimas, H., Deal, K., Cunningham, L., Short, K., et al. (2009). Modeling the bullying prevention program preferences of educators: A discrete choice conjoint experiment. *Journal of Abnormal Child Psychology, 37*(7), 929–943.

Cunningham, P. B., & Henggeler, S. W. (2001). Implementation of an empirically based drug and violence prevention and intervention program in public school settings. *Journal of Clinical Child and Adolescent Psychology, 30*(2), 221–232.

Damschroder, L. J., Aron, D. C., Keith, R. E., Kirsh, S. R., Alexander, J. A., & Lowery, J. C. (2009). Fostering implementation of health services research findings into practice: A consolidated framework for advancing implementation science. *Implementation Science, 4*(50).

Darley, J. M., & Latane, B. (1968). Bystander intervention in emergencies: Diffusion of responsibility. *Journal of Personality and Social Psychology, 8*(4), 377–383.

Davis, S., & Nixon, C. (2010). *The Youth Voice Project.* Accessed at www.youthvoiceproject.com on January 23, 2014.

D'Escury, A. L. C., & Dudink, A. C. M. (2009). Bullying beyond the school: Examining the role of sports. In S. R. Jimerson, S. M. Swearer, & D. L. Espelage (Eds.), *Handbook of bullying in schools: An international perspective* (pp. 235–248). New York: Routledge.

Dodge, K. A., & Coie, J. D. (1987). Social information processing factors in reactive and proactive aggression in children's peer groups. *Journal of Personality and Social Psychology, 53*(6), 1146–1158.

Dodge, K. A., Lochman, J. E., Harnish, J. D., Bates, J. E., & Pettit, G. S. (1997). Reactive and proactive aggression in school children and psychiatrically-impaired chronically assaultive youth. *Journal of Abnormal Psychology, 106*(1), 37–51.

Dooley, J. J., Cross., D., Hearn, L., & Treyvaud, R. (2009). *Review of existing Australian and international cyber-safety research.* Perth, Australia: Child Health Promotion Research Centre, Edith Cowan University.

Dooley, J. J., Gradinger, P., Strohmeier, D., Cross, D., & Spiel, C. (2010). Cyber-victimisation: The association between help-seeking behaviours and self-reported emotional symptoms in Australia and Austria. *Australian Journal of Guidance and Counselling, 20*(2), 194–209.

Dooley, J. J., Pyzalski, J., & Cross, D. (2009). Cyberbullying versus face-to-face bullying: A theoretical and conceptual review. *Journal of Psychology, 217*(4), 182–188.

Due, P., Holstem, B. E., Lynch, J., Diderichsen, F., NicGabhain, S., Scheidt, P., et al. (2005). Bullying and symptoms among school aged children: International comparative cross sectional study in 28 countries. *European Journal of Public Health, 15,* 128–132.

Duncan, A. (1996). The shared concern method for resolving group bullying in schools. *Educational Psychology in Practice, 12*(2), 94–98.

Durlak, J. A., & DuPre, E. P. (2008). Implementation matters: A review of research on the influence of implementation on program outcomes and the factors affecting implementation. *American Journal of Community Psychology, 41*(1–2), 327–350.

Dusenbury, L., Falco, M., Lakem, A., Brannigan, R., & Bosworth, K. (1997). Nine critical elements of promising violence prevention programs. *Journal of School Health, 67*(10), 409–414.

Dwyer, K. P., Osher, D., & Hoffman, C. C. (2000). Creating responsive schools: Contextualizing early warning, timely response. *Exceptional Children, 66*(3), 347–365.

Eisenberg, M., & Neumark-Sztainer, D. (2008). Peer harassment and disordered eating. *International Journal of Adolescent Medicine and Health, 20*(2), 155–164.

Eisenberg, M. E., Neumark-Sztainer, D., & Perry, C. L. (2003). Peer harassment, school connectedness, and academic achievement. *Journal of School Health, 73*(8), 311–316.

Elias, M. J., & Weissberg, R. P. (2000). Primary prevention: Educational approaches to enhance social and emotional learning. *Journal of School Health, 70*(5), 186–190.

Emmer, E. T., & Stough, L. M. (2001). Classroom management: A critical part of educational psychology, with implications for teacher education. *Educational Psychologist, 36*(2), 103–112.

Espelage, D. L., Bosworth, K., & Simon, T. R. (2000). Examining the social context of bullying behaviors in early adolescence. *Journal of Counseling and Development, 78*(3), 326–333.

Espelage, D. L., Mebane, S. E., & Adams, R. S. (2004). Empathy, caring, and bullying: Toward an understanding of complex associations. In D. L. Espelage & S. M. Swearer (Eds.), *Bullying in American schools: A social-ecological perspective on prevention and intervention* (pp. 37–61). Mahwah, NJ: Erlbaum.

Espelage, D. L., & Swearer, S. M. (2003). Research on school bullying and victimization: What have we learned and where do we go from here? *School Psychology Review, 32*(3), 365–383.

Espelage, D. L., & Swearer, S. M. (Eds.). (2004). *Bullying in American schools: A social-ecological perspective on prevention and intervention.* Mahwah, NJ: Erlbaum.

Farrington, D. P., & Ttofi, M. M. (2009). School-based programs to reduce bullying and victimization. *Campbell Systematic Reviews, 6.*

Farrington, D. P., & Ttofi, M. M. (2011). Bullying as a predictor of offending, violence and later life outcomes. *Criminal Behaviour and Mental Health, 21*(2), 90–98.

Fekkes, M., Pijpers, F. I. M., & Verloove-Vanhorick, S. P. (2005). Bullying: Who does what, when and where? Involvement of children, teachers and parents in bullying behavior. *Health Education Research, 20*(1), 81–91.

Fekkes, M., Pijpers, F. I. M., & Verloove-Vanhorick, S. P. (2006). Effects of antibullying school program on bullying and heath complaints. *Archives of Pediatrics and Adolescent Medicine, 160*(6), 638–644.

Ferguson, C. J., San Miguel, C., Kilburn, J. C., Jr., & Sanchez, P. (2007). The effectiveness of school-based anti-bullying programs: A meta-analytic review. *Criminal Justice Review, 32*(4), 401–414.

Fixsen, D., Naoom, S. F., Blase, K. A., Friedman, R. M., & Wallace, F. (2005). *Implementation research: A synthesis of the literature* (FMHI Publication No. 231). Tampa, FL: National Implementation Research Network.

Flouri, E., & Buchanan, A. (2003). The role of mother involvement and father involvement in adolescent bullying behavior. *Journal of Interpersonal Violence, 18*(6), 634–644.

Fontaine, R. G., & Dodge, K. A. (2006). Real-time decision making and aggressive behavior in youth: A heuristic model of response evaluation and decision (RED). *Aggressive Behavior, 32*(6), 604–624.

Forero, R., McLellan, L., Rissel, C., & Bauman, A. (1999). Bullying behaviour and psychosocial health among school students in New South Wales, Australia: Cross sectional survey. *British Medical Journal, 319*(7206), 344–348.

Fox, C. L., & Boulton, M. J. (2005). The social skills problems of victims of bullying: Self, peer and teacher perceptions. *British Journal of Educational Psychology, 75*(2), 313–328.

Frank Porter Graham Child Development Institute. (2011). *State Implementation & Scaling-Up of Evidence-Based Practices Center.* Accessed at http://sisep.fpg.unc.edu on January 15, 2014.

Frisén, A., & Bjarnelind, S. (2010). Health-related quality of life and bullying in adolescence. *Acta Paediatrica, 99*(4), 597–603.

Fullan, M. (2007). *The new meaning of educational change* (4th ed.). New York: Teachers College Press.

Galen, B. R., & Underwood, M. K. (1997). A developmental investigation of social aggression among children. *Developmental Psychology, 33*(4), 589–600.

Gingiss, P. M., Roberts-Gray, C., & Boerm, M. (2006). Bridge-it: A system for predicting implementation fidelity for school-based tobacco prevention programs. *Prevention Science, 7*(2), 197–207.

Gini, G. (2006). Bullying as a social process: The role of group membership in students' perception of inter-group aggression at school. *Journal of School Psychology, 44*(1), 51–65.

Gini, G., Albiero, P., Benelli, B., & Altoè, G. (2007). Does empathy predict adolescents' bullying and defending behavior? *Aggressive Behavior, 33*(5), 467–476.

Gini, G., Pozzoli, T., Borghi, F., & Franzoni, L. (2008). The role of bystanders in students' perception of bullying and sense of safety. *Journal of School Psychology, 46*(6), 617–638.

Glew, G., Fan, M., Katon, W., Rivara, F. P., & Kernic, M. A. (2005). Bullying, psychosocial adjustment, and academic performance in elementary school. *Archives of Pediatric and Adolescent Medicine, 159*(11), 1026–1031.

Goossens, F. A., Olthof, T., & Dekker, P. H. (2006). New Participant Role Scales: Comparison between various criteria for assigning roles and indications for their validity. *Aggressive Behavior, 32*(4), 343–357.

Gottfredson, D. C., & Gottfredson, G. D. (2002). Quality of school-based prevention programs: Results from a national survey. *Journal of Research in Crime and Delinquency, 39*(1), 3–35.

Gould League. (2005). *Schoolgrounds for living and learning—2005 case studies: Arthurs Creek Primary School.* Accessed at www.gould.org.au/html/documents/2005CaseStudies_000.pdf on May 31, 2010.

Griffiths, C., & Weatherilt, T. (2011). *Shared concern method training manual.* Perth, Australia: Department of Education.

Halas, J. (2002). Engaging alienated youth in physical education: An alternative program with lessons for the traditional class. *Journal of Teaching in Physical Education, 21*(3), 267–286.

Hall, J. A., Herzberger, S. D., & Skowronski, K. J. (1998). Outcome expectancies and outcome values as predictors of children's aggression. *Aggressive Behavior, 24*(6), 439–454.

Hall, M., Waters, S., & Shaw, T. (2009). *Child centred environments to limit early aggression intervention trial 2009: Final Report.* Perth, Australia: Child Health Promotion Research Centre, Edith Cowan University.

Hamilton, G., Cross, D., Hall, M., Resnicow, K., & Young, D. (2003). *The role of extra-curricular activities in reducing smoking among adolescents: Final report.* Perth, Australia: Western Australian Centre for Health Promotion Research, School of Public Health, Curtin University of Technology.

Hanewald, R. (2008). Confronting the pedagogical challenge of cyber safety. *Australian Journal of Teacher Education, 33*(3), 1–16.

Happé, F., Malhi, G. S., & Checkley, S. (2001). Acquired mind-blindness following frontal lobe surgery? A single case study of impaired 'theory of mind' in a patient treated with stereotactic anterior capsulotomy. *Neuropsychologia, 39*(1), 83–90.

Havet-Thomassin, V., Allain, P., Etcharry-Bouyx, F., & Le Gail, D. (2006). What about theory of mind after severe brain injury? *Brain Injury, 20*(1), 83–91.

Hawkins, D. L., Pepler, D. J., & Craig, W. M. (2001). Naturalistic observations of peer interventions in bullying. *Social Development, 10*(4), 512–527.

Hawley, P. H. (2003). Prosocial and coercive configurations of resource control in early adolescence: A case for the well-adapted Machiavellian. *Merrill-Palmer Quarterly, 49*(3), 279–309.

Hazler, R. J. (1996). Bystanders: An overlooked factor in peer on peer abuse. *The Journal for the Professional Counselor, 11*(2), 11–21.

Hazler, R. J., Miller, D. L., Carney, J. V., & Green, S. (2001). Adult recognition of school bullying situations. *Educational Research, 43*(2), 133–146.

Hemphill, S. A., Kotevski, A., Herrenkohl, T. I., Bond, L., Kim, M. J., Toumbourou, J. W., et al. (2011). Longitudinal consequences of adolescent bullying perpetration and victimisation: A study of students in Victoria, Australia. *Criminal Behaviour and Mental Health, 21*(2), 107–116.

Hoelscher, D. M., Feldman, H. A., Johnson, C. C., Lytle, L. A., Osganian, S. K., Parcel, G. S., et al. (2004). School-based health education programs can be maintained over time: Results from the CATCH Institutionalization study. *Preventive Medicine, 38*(5), 594–606.

Hoffman, M. L. (1960). Power assertion by the parent and its impact on the child. *Child Development, 31*(1), 129–143.

Holroyd, R. A., & Armour, K. M. (2003). *Re-engaging disaffected youth through physical activity programs.* Presented at the British Educational Research Association Annual Conference, Heriot-Watt University, Edinburgh, Scotland.

Hurst, T. (2001). An evaluation of an anti-bullying peer support programme in a (British) secondary school. *Pastoral Care in Education: An International Journal of Personal, Social and Emotional Development, 19*(2), 10–14.

International Union for Health Promotion and Education. (n.d.). *Achieving health promoting schools: Guidelines for promoting health in schools, version 2.* Saint-Denis, France: Author.

James, D., Lawlor, M., Courtney, P., Flynn, A., Henry, B., & Murphy, N. (2008). Bullying behaviour in secondary schools: What roles do teachers play? *Child Abuse Review, 17*(3), 160–173.

Jankauskiene, R., Kardelis, K., Sukys, S., & Kardeliene, L. (2008). Associations between school bullying and psychosocial factors. *Social Behavior and Personality, 36*(2), 145–162.

Janson, G. R., & Hazler, R. J. (2004). Trauma reactions of bystanders and victims to repetitive abuse experiences. *Violence and Victims, 19*(2), 239–255.

Juvonen, J., & Gross, E. F. (2008). Extending the school grounds?—Bullying experiences in cyberspace. *Journal of School Health, 78*(9), 496–505.

Kajs, L. T. (2006). Reforming the discipline management process in schools: An alternative approach to zero tolerance. *Educational Research Quarterly, 29*(4), 16–28.

Kallestad, J. H., & Olweus, D. (2003). Predicting teachers' and schools' implementation of the Olweus Bullying Prevention Program: A multilevel study. *Prevention and Treatment, 6*(1), 3–21.

Kaltiala-Heino, R., Rimpelä, M., Marttunen, M., Rimpelä, A., & Rantanen, P. (1999). Bullying, depression, and suicidal ideation in Finnish adolescents: School survey. *British Medical Journal, 319*(7206), 348–351.

Kaltiala-Heino, R., Rimpelä, M., Rantanen, P., & Rimpelä, A. (2000). Bullying at school—An indicator of adolescents at risk for mental disorders. *Journal of Adolescence, 23*(6), 661–674.

Kaukiainen, A., Björkqvist, K., Lagerspetz, K., Österman, K., Salmivalli, C., Rothberg, S., et al. (1999). The relationships between social intelligence, empathy, and three types of aggression. *Aggressive Behavior, 25*(2), 81–89.

Kim, M. B. J., Catalano, R. F., Haggerty, K. P., & Abbott, R. D. (2011). Bullying at elementary school and problem behaviour in young adulthood: A study of bullying, violence and substance use from age 11 to age 21. *Criminal Behaviour and Mental Health, 21*(2), 136–144.

Kochenderfer, B. J., & Ladd, G. W. (1996). Peer victimization: Cause or consequence of school maladjustment? *Child Development, 67*(4), 1305–1317.

Kumpulainen, K. (2008). Psychiatric conditions associated with bullying. *International Journal of Adolescent Medicine and Health, 20*(2), 121–132.

Kumpulainen, K., Räsänen, E., Henttonen, I., Hämäläinen, M., & Roine S. (2000). The persistence of psychiatric deviance from the age of 8 to the age of 15 years. *Social Psychiatry and Psychiatric Epidemiology, 35*(1), 5–11.

Lagerspetz, K., Björkqvist, K., & Peltonen, T. (1988). Is indirect aggression typical of females? Gender differences in aggressiveness in 11- to 12-year old children. *Aggressive Behavior, 14*(6), 403–414.

Landstedt, E., & Gådin, K. G. (2011). Deliberate self-harm and associated factors in 17-year-old Swedish students. *Scandinavian Journal of Public Health, 39*(1), 17–25.

Larson, R.W., Wilson, S., Brown, B. B., Furstenberg, F. F., Jr., & Verma, S. (2002). Changes in adolescents' interpersonal experience: Are they being prepared for adult relationships in the twenty-first century? *Journal of Research on Adolescence, 12*(1), 31–68.

Laukkanen, E., Shemeikka, S., Notkola, I. L., Koivumaa-Honkanen, H., & Nissinen, A. (2002). Externalising and internalising problems at school as signs of health-damaging behaviour and incipient marginalisation. *Health Promotion International, 17*(2), 139–146.

Learning through Landscapes. (2003). *National School Grounds survey 2003*. Accessed at www.ltl.org.uk/pdf/LTL -Survey-20031288585139.pdf on May 31, 2010.

Lee, C. (2010). An ecological systems approach to bullying behaviors among middle school students in the United States. *Journal of Interpersonal Violence, 26*(8), 1664–1693.

Li, Q. (2007). New bottle but old wine: A research of cyberbullying in schools. *Computers in Human Behavior, 23*(4), 1777–1791.

Li, Q. (2008). Cyberbullying in schools: An examination of preservice teachers' perception. *Canadian Journal of Learning and Technology, 34*(2), 75–90.

Li, Q., Cross, D., & Smith, P. K. (Eds.). (2011). *Cyberbullying in the global playground: Research from international perspectives*. Chichester, United Kingdom: Wiley-Blackwell.

Life Education Committee of Kankakee and Iroquois. (2008a). *Snapshots of your child's social and emotional well-being: Grades 4 to 6 (middle childhood)*. Accessed at http://casel.org/publications/snapshots-of-your-childs-social-and -emotional-well-being- 4–6-years on January 13, 2014.

Life Education Committee of Kankakee and Iroquois. (2008b). *Snapshots of your child's social and emotional well-being: Grades 7 and 8 (early adolescence)*. Accessed at http://casel.org/publications/snapshots-of-your-childs-social -and-emotional-well-being-7–8 on January 13, 2014.

Life Education Committee of Kankakee and Iroquois. (2008c). *Snapshots of your child's social and emotional well-being: Grades 9 to 12 (early to late adolescence)*. Accessed at http://casel.org/publications/snapshots-of-your-childs-social -and-emotional-well-being-9–12 on January 13, 2014.

Life Education Committee of Kankakee and Iroquois. (2008d). *Snapshots of your child's social and emotional well-being: Kindergarten to grade 3 (early to middle childhood)*. Accessed at http://casel.org/publications/snapshots-of -your-childs-social-and-emotional-well-being-k-3 on January 13, 2014.

Life Education Committee of Kankakee and Iroquois. (Ed.). (2008e). *Snapshots of your child's social and emotional well-being: Stairsteps to adulthood*. Accessed at http://casel.org/publications/snapshots-of-your-childs-social-and -emotional-well-being on January 13, 2014.

Lodge, J., & Frydenberg, E. (2005). The role of peer bystanders in school bullying: Positive steps towards promoting peaceful schools. *Theory into Practice, 44*(4), 329–336.

Luiselli, J. K., Putnam, R. F., Handler, M. W., & Feinberg, A. B. (2005). Whole-school positive behaviour support: Effects on student discipline problems and academic performance. *Educational Psychology, 25*(2–3), 183–198.

MacNeil, G., & Newell, F. (2004). School bullying: Why, how, and what to do. *The Prevention Researcher, 11*(3), 15–17.

Malone, K., & Tranter, P. (2003). Children's environmental learning and the use, design and management of schoolgrounds. *Children, Youth and Environments, 13*(2). Accessed at www.colorado.edu/journals/cye/13_2 /Malone_Tranter/ChildrensEnvLearning.htm on April 14, 2014.

McBride, N., Midford, R., & Cameron, I. (1999). An empirical model for school health promotion: The Western Australian school health project model. *Health Promotion International, 14*(1), 17–25.

McBride, N., Midford, R., & James, R. (1995). Structural and management changes that encourage schools to adopt comprehensive health promotion programs. *Health Promotion Journal of Australia, 5*(1), 17–23.

McNeely, C. A., Nonnemaker, J. M., & Blum, R. W. (2002). Promoting school connectedness: Evidence from the National Longitudinal Study of Adolescent Health. *Journal of School Health, 72*(4), 138–146.

Midthassel, U., & Roland, E. (2008). The Norwegian manifesto against bullying: Opportunities, challenges and results on a national and school level. In D. Pepler & W. Craig (Eds.), *Understanding and addressing bullying: An international perspective* (pp. 215–229). Bloomington, IN: AuthorHouse.

Ministerial Council on Education, Employment, Training and Youth Affairs. (2011). *National Safe Schools Framework*. Carlton South, Australia: Author.

Mishna, F., Cook, C., Saini, M., Wu, M.-J., & MacFadden, R. (2010). Interventions to prevent and reduce cyber abuse of youth: A systematic review. *Research on Social Work Practice*, 1–10. Accessed at http://icbtt.arizona .edu/sites/default/files/Mishna,_Cook,_Saini,_Wu,_&_MacFadden_RSWP_online.pdf on January 13, 2014.

Mussen, P. H. (Ed.). (1983). *Handbook of child psychology: Formerly Carmichael's Manual of child psychology* (4th ed.). New York: Wiley.

Nansel, T., Overpeck, M., Pilla, R. S., Ruan, J., Simons-Morton, B., & Scheidt, P. (2001). Bullying behaviors among US youth: Prevalence and association with psychosocial adjustment. *Journal of the American Medical Association, 285*(16), 2094–2100.

National Children's Home. (2002). *1 in 4 children are the victims of "on-line bullying."* Accessed at www.nch.org.uk /information/index.php?i=237 on January 13, 2014.

Naylor, P., & Cowie, H. (1999). The effectiveness of peer support systems in challenging school bullying: The perspectives and experiences of teachers and pupils. *Journal of Adolescence, 22*(4), 467–479.

O'Connell, P., Pepler, D., & Craig, W. (1999). Peer involvement in bullying: Insights and challenges for intervention. *Journal of Adolescence, 22*(4), 437–452.

Oliver, R., & Oaks, I. (1994). Family issues and interventions in bully and victim relationships. *School Counselor, 41*(3), 199–202.

Olweus, D. (1993). *Bullying at school: What we know and what we can do.* Cambridge, MA: Blackwell.

Olweus, D. (1994). Bullying at school: Long-term outcomes for the victims and an effective school-based intervention program. In L. R. Huesmann (Ed.), *Aggressive behavior: Current perspectives* (pp. 97–130). New York: Plenum Press.

Olweus, D. (1996). *The revised Olweus bully/victim questionnaire.* Bergen, Norway: Research Centre for Health Promotion, University of Bergen.

Owens, L. D. (1996). Sticks and stones and sugar and spice: Girls' and boys' aggression in schools. *Australian Journal of Guidance and Counselling, 6,* 45–55.

Owens, L., Daly, A., & Slee, P. (2005). Sex and age differences in victimisation and conflict resolution among adolescents in a South Australian school. *Aggressive Behavior, 31*(1), 1–12.

Owens, L., Shute, R., & Slee, P. (2000). "Guess what I just heard!": Indirect aggression among teenage girls in Australia. *Aggressive Behavior, 26*(1), 67–83.

Palfrey, J., & Gasser, U. (2008). *Born digital: Understanding the first generation of digital natives.* New York: Basic Books.

Patchin, J. W., & Hinduja, S. (2006). Bullies move beyond the schoolyard: A preliminary look at cyberbullying. *Youth Violence and Juvenile Justice, 4*(2), 148–169.

Patterson, G. R. (1982). *Coercive family process.* Eugene, OR: Castalia Press.

Patterson, G. R., & Dishion, T. J. (1985). Contributions of families and peers to delinquency. *Criminology, 23*(1), 63–79.

Payton, J. W., Weissberg, R. P., Durlak, J. A., Dymnicki, A. B., Taylor, R. D., Schellinger, K. B., et al. (2008). *The positive impact of social and emotional learning for kindergarten to eighth-grade students.* Chicago: Collaborative for Academic, Social, and Emotional Learning.

Pearce, N. (2010). *Critical success factors for building school capacity to engage parents in school-based bullying prevention interventions.* Unpublished thesis, Edith Cowan University, Perth, Australia.

Pearce, N., Cross, D., Monks, H., Waters, S., & Falconer, S. (2011). Current evidence of best practice in whole-school bullying intervention and its potential to inform cyberbullying interventions. *Australian Journal of Guidance and Counselling, 21*(1), 1–21.

Perren, S., Dooley, J., Cross, D., & Shaw, T. (2010). Bullying in school and cyberspace: Associations with depressive symptoms in Swiss and Australian adolescents. *Child and Adolescent Mental Health Journal, 4*(28).

Pikas, A. (1989). A pure concept of mobbing gives the best results for treatment. *School Psychology International, 10*(2), 95–104.

Pikas, A. (2002). New developments of the shared concern method. *School Psychology International, 23*(3), 307–326.

Plog, A., Epstein, L., Ines, K., & Porter, W. (2010). Sustainability of bullying interventions and prevention programs. In S. Jimerson, S. Swearer, & D. Espelage (Eds.), *Handbook of bullying in schools: An international perspective* (pp. 559–570). New York: Routledge.

Poulin, F., & Boivin, M. (1999). Proactive and reactive aggression and boys' friendship quality in mainstream classrooms. *Journal of Emotional and Behavioral Disorders, 7*(3), 168–177.

Price, J. M., & Dodge, K. A. (1989). Reactive and proactive aggression in childhood: Relations to peer status and social context dimensions. *Journal of Abnormal Child Psychology, 17*(4), 455–471.

Prinstein, M. J., & Cillessen, A. H. (2003). Forms and functions of adolescent peer aggression associated with high levels of peer status. *Merrill-Palmer Quarterly, 49*(3), 310–342.

Pulkkinen, L. (1996). Proactive and reactive aggression in early adolescence as precursors to anti- and prosocial behavior in young adults. *Aggressive Behavior, 22*(4), 241–257.

Raskauskas, J., & Stoltz, A. D. (2007). Involvement in traditional and electronic bullying among adolescents. *Developmental Psychology, 43*(3), 564–575.

Resnick, M. D., Bearman, P. S., Blum, R. W., Bauman, K. E., Harris, K. M., Jones J., et al. (1997). Protecting adolescents from harm: Findings from the National Longitudinal Study of Adolescent Health. *Journal of the American Medical Association, 278*(10), 823–832.

Rigby, K. (1994). Psychosocial functioning in families of Australian adolescent schoolchildren involved in bully/victim problems. *Journal of Family Therapy, 16*(2), 173–187.

Rigby, K. (1996). *Bullying in schools and what to do about it.* Melbourne, Australia: ACER Press.

Rigby, K. (1997). What children tell us about bullying in schools. *Children Australia, 22*(2), 28–34.

Rigby, K. (2005). The method of shared concern as an intervention technique to address bullying in schools: An overview and appraisal. *Australian Journal of Guidance and Counselling, 15*(1), 27–34.

Rigby, K. (2011). *The method of shared concern: A positive approach to bullying in schools.* Melbourne, Australia: ACER Press.

Rigby, K. & Barnes, A. (2002).The victimized student's dilemma: To tell or not to tell. *Youth Studies Australia, 21*(3), 33–36.

Rigby, K., & Bauman, S. (2009). How school personnel tackle cases of bullying: A critical examination. In S. Jimerson, S. Swearer, & D. Espelage (Eds.), *Handbook of bullying in schools: An international perspective* (pp. 455–468). New York: Routledge.

Rigby, K., & Griffiths, C. (2011a). Addressing cases of bullying through the method of shared concern. *School Psychology International, 32*(3), 345–357.

Rigby, K., & Griffiths, C. (2011b). *Applying the method of shared concern in Australian schools: An evaluative study DEEWR.* Accessed at www.ncab.org.au/Assets/Files/Report%20on%20the%20Method%20of%20Shared %20Concern%20DEEWR%20%20R%20and%20G.pdf on January 13, 2014.

Rigby, K., & Johnson, B. (2006). Expressed readiness of Australian schoolchildren to act as bystanders in support of children who are being bullied. *Educational Psychology, 26*(3), 425–440.

Rigby, K., & Smith, P. K. (2011). Is school bullying really on the rise? *Social Psychology of Education, 14*(4), 441–455.

Rivers, I., Poteat, V. P., Noret, N., & Ashurst, N. (2009). Observing bullying at school: The mental health implications of witness status. *School Psychology Quarterly, 24*(4), 211–223.

Roberts-Gray, C., Gingiss, P. M., & Boerm, M. (2007). Evaluating school capacity to implement new programs. *Evaluation and Program Planning, 30*(3), 247–257.

Robinson, G., & Maines, B. (2008). *Bullying: A complete guide to the support group method.* Thousand Oaks, CA: SAGE.

Roland, E. (2002). Bullying, depressive symptoms and suicidal thoughts. *Educational Research, 44*(1), 55–67.

Roland, E., & Galloway, D. (2002). Classroom influences on bullying. *Educational Research, 44*(3), 299–312.

Rowe, F., Stewart, D., & Patterson, C. (2007). Promoting school connectedness through whole school approaches. *Health Education Research, 107*(6), 524–542.

Sainio, M., Veenstra, R., Huitsing, G., & Salmivalli, C. (2009, April). *The role of defending relations for victimized children: Does it matter who the defender is?* Poster presented at the Biennial Meeting for the Society for Research in Child Development, Denver, CO.

Salmivalli, C. (1999). Participant role approach to school bullying: Implications for interventions. *Journal of Adolescence, 22*(4), 453–459.

Salmivalli, C., Kaukiainen, A., Kaistaniemi, L., & Lagerspetz, K. M. J. (1999). Self-evaluated self-esteem, peer-evaluated self-esteem, and defensive egotism as predictors of adolescents' participation in bullying situations. *Personality and Social Psychology Bulletin, 25*(10), 1268–1278.

Salmivalli, C., Kaukiainen, A., & Voeten, M. (2005). Anti-bullying intervention: Implementation and outcome. *British Journal of Educational Psychology, 75*(3), 465–487.

Salmivalli, C., Lagerspetz, K., Björkqvist, K., Österman, K., & Kaukiainen, A. (1996). Bullying as a group process: Participant roles and their relations to social status within the group. *Aggressive Behavior, 22*(1), 1–15.

Salmivalli, C., Lappalainen, M., & Lagerspetz, K. M. J. (1998). Stability and change of behavior in connection with bullying in schools: A two-year follow up. *Aggressive Behavior, 24*(3), 205–218.

Salmivalli, C., & Voeten, M. (2004). Connections between attitudes, group norms, and behaviour in bullying situations. *International Journal of Behavioral Development, 28*(3), 246–258.

Schwartz, D., McFadyen-Ketchum, S. A., Dodge, K. A., Pettit, G. S., & Bates, J. E. (1998). Peer group victimization as a predictor of children's behavior problems at home and in school. *Development and Psychopathology, 10*(1), 87–99.

Singer, M. I., Miller, D. B., Guo, S., Flannery, D. J., Frierson, T., & Slovak, K. (1999). Contributors to violence behavior among elementary and middle school children. *Paediatrics, 104*(4), 878–884.

Skapinakis, P., Bellos, S., Gkatsa, T., Magklara, K., Lewis, G., Araya, G., et al. (2011). The association between bullying and early stages of suicidal ideation in late adolescents in Greece. *BMC Psychiatry, 11*(22).

Skiba, R. J., & Peterson, R. L. (2000). School discipline at a crossroads: From zero tolerance to early response. *Exceptional Children, 66*(3), 335–347.

Slee, P. T. (1994). Situational and interpersonal correlates of anxiety associated with peer victimisation. *Child Psychiatry and Human Development, 25*(2), 97–107.

Slonje, R., & Smith, P. K. (2008). Cyberbullying: Another main type of bullying? *Scandinavian Journal of Psychology, 49*(2), 147–154.

Smith, J. D., Schneider, B. H., Smith, P. K., & Ananiadou, K. (2004). The effectiveness of whole-school antibullying programs: A synthesis of evaluation research. *School Psychology Review, 33*(4), 547–560.

Smith, P. K. (2004). Bullying: Recent developments. *Child and Adolescent Mental Health, 9*(3), 98–103.

Smith, P. K., Howard, S., & Thompson, F. (2007). Use of the support group method to tackle bullying and evaluation from schools and local authorities in England. *Pastoral Care in Education: An International Journal of Personal, Social and Emotional Development, 25*(2), 4–13.

Smith, P. K., Mahdavi, J., Carvalho, M., Fisher, S., Russell, S., & Tippett, N. (2008). Cyberbullying: Its nature and impact in secondary school pupils. *Journal of Child Psychology and Psychiatry, 49*(4), 376–385.

Smith, P. K., & Sharp, S. (Eds.). (1994). *School bullying: Insights and perspectives.* London: Routledge.

Smith, P. K., & Shu, S. (2000). What good schools can do about bullying: Findings from a survey in English schools after a decade of research and action. *Childhood, 7*(2), 193–212.

Smith, P. K., & Slonje, R. (2010). Cyberbullying: The nature and extent of a new kind of bullying, in and out of school. In S. R. Jimerson, S. M. Swearer, & D. L. Espelage (Eds.), *Handbook of bullying in schools: An international perspective* (pp. 249–262). New York: Routledge.

Smith, P. K., Talamelli, L., Cowie, H., Naylor, P., & Chauhan, P. (2004). Profiles of non-victims, escaped victims, continuing victims and new victims of school bullying. *British Journal of Educational Psychology, 74*(4), 565–581.

Smokowski, P. R., & Holland, K. (2005). Bullying in school: Correlates, consequences, and intervention strategies for school social workers. *Children and Schools, 27*(2), 101–110.

Snider, M., & Borel, K. (2004). *Stalked by a cyberbully: Cellphones and the Net are kids' social lifelines—They can also be their social death.* Accessed at http://data.edupax.org/precede/public/Assets/divers/documentation/7b3_internet /7b3_003_Stalked_by_a_Cyberbully.pdf on January 20, 2014.

Solberg, M. E., & Olweus, D. (2003). Prevalence estimation of school bullying with the Olweus Bully/Victim Questionnaire. *Aggressive Behaviour, 29*(3), 239–268.

Sourander, A., Helstelä, L., Helenius, H., & Piha, J. (2000). Persistence of bullying from childhood to adolescence—A longitudinal 8 year follow-up study. *Child Abuse and Neglect, 24*(7), 873–881.

Sourander, A., Klomek, A. B., Ikonen, M., Lindroos, J., Luntamo, T., Koskelainen, M., et al. (2010). Psychosocial risk factors associated with cyberbullying among adolescents: A population-based study. *Archives of General Psychiatry, 67*(7), 720–728.

Srabstein, J., & Piazza, T. (2008). Public health, safety and educational risks associated with bullying behaviors in American adolescents. *International Journal of Adolescent Medicine and Health, 20*(2), 223–233.

Stevens, V., De Bourdeaudhuij, I., &Van Oost, P. (2001). Anti-bullying interventions at school: Aspects of programme adaptation and critical issues for further programme development. *Health Promotion International, 16*(2), 155–167.

Stockdale, M. S., Hangaduambo, S., Duys, D., Larson, K., & Sarvela, P. D. (2002). Rural elementary students,' parents,' and teachers' perceptions of bullying. *American Journal of Health Behavior, 26*(4), 266–277.

Stuss, D., & Anderson, V. (2004). The frontal lobes and theory of mind: Developmental concepts from adult focal lesion research. *Brain and Cognition, 55*(1), 69–83.

Tapscott, D. (1998). *Growing up digital: The rise of the net generation.* New York: McGraw-Hill.

Taylor, H. E., & Larson, S. (1999). Social and emotional learning in middle school. *The Clearing House: A Journal of Educational Strategies, 72*(6), 331–336.

Taylor, R. D., & Dymnicki, A. B. (2007). Empirical evidence of social and emotional learning's influence on school success: A commentary on "Building academic success on social and emotional learning: What does the research say?," a book edited by Joseph E. Zins, Roger P. Weissberg, Margaret C. Wang, and Herbert J. Walberg. *Journal of Educational and Psychological Consultation, 17*(2–3), 225–231.

Thaker, S., Steckler, A., Sánchez, V., Khatapoush, S., Rose, J., & Hallfors, D. D. (2008). Program characteristics and organizational factors affecting the implementation of a school-based indicated prevention program. *Health Education Research, 23*(2), 238–248.

Trach, J., Hymel, S., Waterhouse, T., & Neale, K. (2010). Bystander responses to school bullying: A cross-sectional investigation of grade and sex differences. *Canadian Journal of School Psychology, 25*(1), 114–130.

Tunnecliffe, M. (2000). *Critical incidents and debriefing.* Palmyra, Australia: Emergency Support Network.

United Nations. (1991). *Convention on the rights of the child.* Florence, Italy: Author.

Vaillancourt, T., Brittain, H., Bennett, L., Arnocky, S., McDougall, P., Hymel, S., et al. (2010). Places to avoid: Population-based study of student reports of unsafe and high bullying areas at school. *Canadian Journal of School Psychology, 25*(1), 40–54.

van der Wal, M. F., de Wit, C. A. M., & Hirasing, R. A. (2003). Psychosocial health among young victims and offenders of direct and indirect bullying. *Pediatrics, 111*(6), 1312–1317.

Vandebosch, H., & Van Cleemput, K. (2008). Defining cyberbullying: A qualitative research into the perceptions of respondents. *Cyberpsychology and Behaviour, 11*(4), 499–503.

Vandebosch, H., & Van Cleemput, K. (2009). Cyberbullying among youngsters: Profiles of bullies and victims. *New Media and Society, 11*, 1349–1371.

Vitaro, F., Brendgen, M., & Tremblay, R. E. (2002). Reactively and proactively aggressive children: Antecedent and subsequent characteristics. *Journal of Child Psychology and Psychiatry*, *43*(4), 495–505.

Vitaro, F., Gendreau, P. L., Tremblay, R. E., & Oligny, P. (1998). Reactive and proactive aggression differentially predict later conduct problems. *Journal of Child Psychology and Psychiatry*, *39*(3), 377–385.

Vitiello, B., & Stoff, D. M. (1997). Subtypes of aggression and their relevance to child psychiatry. *Journal of the American Academy of Child and Adolescent Psychiatry*, *36*(3), 307–315.

Vreeman, R. C., & Carroll, A. E. (2007). A systematic review of school-based interventions to prevent bullying. *Archives of Pediatric and Adolescent Medicine*, *161*(1), 78–88.

Wang, J., Iannotti, R. J., & Nansel, T. R. (2009). School bullying among adolescents in the United States: Physical, verbal, relational, and cyber. *Journal of Adolescent Health*, *45*(4), 368–375.

Waters, S., Cross, D., & Runions, K. (2009). Social and ecological structures supporting adolescent connectedness to school: A theoretical model. *Journal of School Health*, *79*(11), 516–524.

Waters, S., Cross, D., & Shaw, T. (2010). Does the nature of schools matter? An exploration of selected school ecology factors on adolescent perceptions of school connectedness. *British Journal of Educational Psychology*, *80*(3), 381–402.

Weissberg, R. P., & O'Brien, M. U. (2004). What works in school-based social and emotional learning programs for positive youth development. *The ANNALS of the American Academy of Political and Social Science*, *591*(1), 86–97.

Whitney, I., & Smith, P. K. (1993). A survey of the nature and extent of bullying in junior/middle and secondary schools. *Educational Research*, *35*(1), 3–25.

Williams, K. R., & Guerra, N. G. (2007). Prevalence and predictors of Internet bullying. *Journal of Adolescent Health*, *41*(6), S14-S21.

Wilson, S. J., Lipsey, M. W., & Derzon, J. H. (2003). The effects of school-based intervention programs on aggressive behavior: A meta-analysis. *Journal of Consulting and Clinical Psychology*, *71*(1), 136–149.

Wolke, D., Woods, S., Bloomfield, L., & Karstadt, L. (2001). Bullying involvement in primary school and common health problems. *Archives of Disease in Childhood*, *85*(3), 197–201.

World Health Organization. (1996). *Promoting health through schools: The World Health Organization's global school health initiative*. Geneva, Switzerland: Author.

Ybarra, M., & Mitchell, K. (2004). Youth engaging in online harassment: Associations with caregiver-child relationships, Internet use, and personal characteristics. *Journal of Adolescence*, *27*(3), 319–336.

Yoon, J. S., & Kerber, K. (2003). Bullying: Elementary teachers' attitudes and intervention strategies. *Research in Education*, *69*, 27–35.

Young, S. (1998). The support group approach to bullying in schools. *Educational Psychology in Practice*, *14*(1), 32–39.

Zins, J. E., & Elias, M. J. (2006). *Social and emotional learning*. In G. G. Bear & K. M. Minke (Eds.), *Children's needs III: Development, prevention, and intervention* (pp. 1–13). Bethesda, MD: National Association of School Psychologists.

Zubrick, S. R., Silburn, S. R., Gurrin, L., Teoh, H., Shepherd, C., Carlton, J., et al. (1997). *Western Australian child health survey: Education, health and competence*. Perth: Australian Bureau of Statistics.

Friendly Schools Plus Series Set
The *Friendly Schools Plus* series by Donna Cross, Shane Thompson, and Erin Erceg uses an evidence-based, whole-school approach to reduce bullying and to foster a supportive school culture. This approach recognizes that all aspects of students' school life influence their academic performance and health. The seven *Friendly Schools Plus* resources provide educators with tools to create effective programs that support students academically and socially, help students practice healthy interpersonal behaviors in school and online, and encourage parental and stakeholder school involvement.
KTB001

The seven books in the *Friendly Schools Plus* series
by Donna Cross, Shane Thompson, and Erin Erceg

Friendly Schools Plus Teacher Resource: Early Childhood (Ages 4–6)
BKB001

Friendly Schools Plus Teacher Resource: Early & Middle Adolescence (Ages 11–14)
BKB005

Friendly Schools Plus Teacher Resource: Early Childhood (Ages 6–8)
BKB002

Friendly Schools Plus Evidence for Practice: Whole-School Strategies to Enhance Students' Social Skills and Reduce Bullying in Schools
BKB006

Friendly Schools Plus Teacher Resource: Middle Childhood (Ages 8–10)
BKB003

Friendly Schools Plus Friendly Families
BKB007

Friendly Schools Plus Teacher Resource: Middle Childhood (Ages 10–11)
BKB004